LANDMARK

A History of Britain in 50 Buildings

LANDMARK

A History of Britain in 50 Buildings

Anna Keay & Caroline Stanford
Foreword by Griff Rhys Jones

FRANCES LINCOLN LIMITED
PUBLISHERS

A Quintessence Book

First published in the UK in 2015
by Frances Lincoln Limited
www.franceslincoln.com

A catalogue record for this book is available from the British Library.

ISBN: 978-0-7112-3645-5

This book was designed and produced by
Quintessence Editions Ltd
The Old Brewery, 6 Blundell Street, London, N7 9BH

Project Editor	Ruth Patrick
Editor	Frank Ritter
Editorial Assistant	Hannah Phillips
Designer	Damian Jaques
Production Manager	Anna Pauletti
Editorial Director	Ruth Patrick
Publisher	Mark Fletcher

This edition is printed on text paper from sustainable sources.

Colour reproduction in the UK by Portland Media Print Services Ltd.
Printed in China by 1010 Printing International Ltd.

1 2 3 4 5 6 7 8 9

CONTENTS

FOREWORD
GRIFF RHYS JONES

Well, what sort of book is this, then? *Britain in Fifty Buildings*? *A Guide to Our Vernacular Architecture*? *Romantic Holiday Opportunities Made Easy*? Happily, it's all of these and more. Here are the stories of fifty properties – from water tower to manor, and from castle to bungalow – and the historical context that created or defined them.

People used these buildings. They opened the doors and stood by the windows. They swept the floors. They organized their affairs in these rooms. They quarrelled, romanced, slept and, perhaps, most of all, they got on with their lives, just as we do, even in the midst of 'interesting times'.

These houses make history human. You don't have to be an incurable romantic to warm to the settled, long-running saga of domesticity in these places. It helps if you are, of course, because it makes the experience even better. And experience is actually on offer here, because each of the fifty is a Landmark Trust house available to rent. You can take your friends or your family or your dog or your neighbours and hire the place. You can immerse yourself in the reality of an historic artefact. There can't be many books where you can read all about it so winningly, and then go and live it.

I first found out about the Landmark Trust from new friends at university, forty years ago. Back then, somehow, they seemed to know all about gunpowder tea, Kettle's Yard, William Morris wallpapers and the Landmark Trust – things my family didn't. This was in the early 1970s, and I was as green as the tea. I don't drink green tea very often these days, but I still visit Landmark Trust houses. My first was the Martello Tower in Aldeburgh. My girlfriend packed her Laura Ashley dresses and her stout walking stilettos and led me away to a building I had actually known well for years. I had sailed past it, on my dad's old wooden boat – you see, I did have something to bring to the romancer's table – but I had no idea that you could stay there.

I still bump into people who were there on that 'study' weekend. We walked down the roaring shingle beaches, played charades and visited the Cross Keys. It was a self-indulgent love-in, like a photo-shoot for a linen catalogue mentored by E. M. Forster. But I remember the round walls, the furniture that had trouble fitting them and the simple, white elegance of the interior. I remember the dramatic setting and, of course, the sense of history: the clangour of association that goes with thick redoubts and heavy doors.

Do you detect a terrible whiff of privilege about all this? Well, don't. With a bit of effort it is accessible to anyone with the catalogue and a computer or phone.

We seemed to warm to Napoleonic sea defences, because soon we were off, during another holiday, to explore Fort Clonque on Alderney, this time guided by Emma Smith, the daughter of the founder himself, John Smith. Landmark seemed then like a well-established, long-running show, though in fact we were young and so was the Trust. It was created in 1965, and the fifteen years that it had then been running were nothing – at least nothing to me now, looking back on thirty-five years of further growth and expansion.

We set off one morning to buy a lobster. We rented bicycles from somewhere and I rode across the island and back along the causeway to the cluster of fortifications on the seaweedy rocks, with the feelers of the huge, still-lively crustacean poking up through a cardboard box strapped to the front basket. In the great room we even found a wash-pot massive enough to cook it, and in clouds of steam boiled the thing to a scrabbling end.

Since then I have tried to sample as many Landmarks as I can. Each cast-iron latch lifted takes me into a new experience and a place to explore. It is usually a prelude to an overall sensation of peace. Uncluttered, simple and appropriately furnished with proper stoves or fires, the spaces talk to you. I have never been to a Landmark property that hasn't earnt its place in that ever-expanding catalogue. Each of them has something to offer the visitor beyond a bunk down. The buildings themselves are the holiday.

After possession, I settle in and read the visitor books. Why aren't we having as much active fun as this family? My goodness, they not only climbed the nearby tor in the middle of the night, they also managed to wade across the river and visit an obscure village potter before coming back to make wild damson jam – with two dogs and six children!

Personally, I prefer to relax, as I did at Wortham Manor or St Winifred's Well or the Egyptian House. As I did at Calverley Old Hall, where I lived for a few weeks during the run of a Feydeau farce in Leeds. I used to rent Landmarks when I was on tour with a play. Before the panic started and I had to head off to Leeds in the gathering dusk, it was the very epitome of downtime and lazy, self-satisfied bliss to be able to wake late, come down rickety stairs and make breakfast with nothing but the loud ticking of a clock and a view across a churchyard to an empty moor. I was lucky. Not many people hire Landmarks just to sit in them. Mostly we take them in order to busy ourselves with exploration. But I recommend it. You can get close to the breathing soul of an historic location, particularly if you absorb it with a book in hand.

Take this book with you, in fact. And contemplate your predecessors. We now need another four volumes to cover the rest of the properties. No Landmark house is anything but special, but the fifty here are very special indeed. I defy you to sit and read this volume without instantly making plans, romancing a bit and reaching for your diary.

LANDMARK
INTRODUCTION

The Landmark Trust was fundamentally the creation of an individual, Sir John Lindsay Eric Smith, working together with his wife Christian. For its first twenty-five years, from its inception in 1965, John and Christian were the Landmark Trust, determining its purpose and philosophy, overseeing its projects and, from their charitable trust, providing the considerable sums of money that enabled it to achieve so much.

It was growing up on the Smith estate at Ashfold, near Crawley in Sussex, that John Smith developed a precocious interest in historic buildings and landscapes, and in naval and industrial history. The Smiths were a banking dynasty, and while John Smith's application to the family business, as a director of Coutts Bank among other things, precluded the professional career in architecture he might otherwise have chosen, he soon found other ways to channel his enthusiasm and interest in historic buildings. His sister, Fortune, married Hugh Fitzroy, Earl of Euston (later the eleventh Duke of Grafton), who was already active in building conservation and vice chairman of the Society for the Protection of Ancient Buildings. When John Smith was put up for the National Trust Historic Buildings Committee in the summer of 1952, Lord Esher said, 'Well, it's a good thing to have a proletarian name on the committee – anybody know the man?', to which Lord Euston, already a member, replied, 'Yes, he's my brother-in-law.'

Smith brought his energies and interests to the business of running, rather than advising, the National Trust as a member of the Executive Committee of the Council from 1959 and then as chairman of the General Purposes Committee. Among his considerable achievements were persuading the Trust to interest itself in more varied sorts of heritage. A personal interest in industrial architecture – a passion he shared with his friend, the industrial heritage pioneer Tom Rolt – saw Smith almost single-handedly persuading the National Trust to lease, and then purchase in 1965, the endangered Stratford Canal.

The Landmark Trust had its genesis in Smith's dismay at the rate at which places were being damaged or destroyed in the early 1960s, a time when some 400 listed buildings a year were being demolished. Smaller buildings of character and interest were being lost everywhere, and he knew from experience that the National Trust was not the answer. Being necessarily a 'sort of middle of the road national institution', it could not be expected to take on small buildings, 'or anything too way out', and 'which often needed perseverance and money just as much as love'.

The 'money' point was crucial. It was in his career in finance that John Smith came up with the brilliant notion that would provide the money to fund the creation of the Landmark Trust. In the early 1960s, many commercial properties in London and elsewhere were held on long leases, which, with infrequent rent reviews, were occupied at well below the market rate. Smith realized that many firms would gladly part with their favourable rent arrangements in return for a capital sum – capital being hard to raise at the time – but did not want the inconvenience of moving premises. Smith's scheme was to use the access to capital he enjoyed through the family banks to buy tenants out of their remaining leases, and then continue to rent them their premises for a new market rate which the tenants could set against tax. If the entity that was making the purchases was not an individual or company but a charity, and so not subject to tax on income, then the profits to be made were substantial.

Having been unable to persuade the National Trust to exploit this opportunity, Smith decided to go it alone, and set up his own charity, the Manifold Trust, in August 1962. The Manifold Trust was designed from the first to receive and then distribute funds to charitable causes, and it soon became clear that it would be a great success. Smith resigned as chair of the National Trust General Purposes Committee in 1964, feeling the frustrations of a large and complex organization, and started to think in earnest about creating a historic buildings charity that he might personally direct and which could be nimbler and more inventive. He cited the demolition of a Thomas Telford junction house at Hurleston on the Shropshire Union Canal as the single incident that finally 'maddened us into starting the Landmark Trust'.

By deed dated 24 May 1965, a new charitable trust was created, with a sum of five pounds sterling being provided by the Earl of Euston to the two trustees, John and Christian Smith. The trust was to have two goals: 'the preservation of small buildings or structures of historic interest, architectural merit or amenity value, and where possible finding suitable uses for them,' and 'protecting and promoting the enjoyment of places of historic interest or natural beauty.' While the objects of the new Landmark Trust could have been realized in any number of ways, Smith had already formulated the very specific model that he had in mind: historic buildings would be acquired and repaired, and then let to the public for holidays. The intention from the first was that the preservation of the buildings and using them were to have parity of importance. Smith knew that this approach was unorthodox, and remarked in his notes that, 'Many individuals and bodies – e.g. the Georgian Group, are only interested in preservation, and would sooner see a good building fall down rather than filled with holidaymakers!' As well as taking great care of exceptional buildings, the Landmark Trust's plan was to ensure that that 'the holidays we provide must be absolutely the very best'.

Hurleston Junction house on the Ellesmere Canal in 1959; its demolition 'maddened' John and Christian Smith into establishing the Landmark Trust.

Paxton's Tower Lodge (below) and Church Cottage were the first 'Landmarks' to open in the spring of 1967.

Four of the six buildings available in the first Landmark Handbook for 1968 were in the Devon hamlet of Coombe.

While the word 'Landmark' spoke of the conspicuous, the intention was not simply to seek out the spectacular, but also to retrieve from neglect more modest places 'of merit', 'handsome small buildings which add greatly to the scene'. This interest in and concern for places of character was something that John Smith took with him into a new arena later in 1965 when he was elected Conservative MP for the Cities of London and Westminster. While this meant he had less time than he had expected for the fledging Landmark Trust, it gave him the opportunity to influence national policy.

Within a year of his election, Smith was a sponsor of one of the most important pieces of post-war legislation for historic places, the 1966 Civic Amenities Act, which obliged local authorities to designate places of particular character and beauty as conservation areas. John Smith spoke eloquently in its favour in July 1966, arguing that 'preservation and amenity',

far from being reactionary, 'are part of the object and true aim of all politics and one of the true end-products of all industry – the making of England a more agreeable place to be in'. Talking of historic towns and villages, he explained: 'We do not wish to embalm such places, to make no changes, but to control and slow down the rate of change. To care for them in this way means not that the present is dead, but that the past is alive. If we can give our children the benefit of such places, they will advance into the future not alone, but accompanied and supported by the friendly hosts of the past.' That the legislation was introduced as a Private Member's Bill also appealed to him. 'I am also pleased that this is not a Government Bill, but a Private Member's Bill,' he said. 'The first steps in public amenity were taken by private citizens in the great age of self-help, when people banded together and did it for themselves, instead of waiting for the State to do it for them.'

John Smith during a family visit
to Fort Clonque, Alderney, in 1967.

The Landmark Trust was from the first a highly personal enterprise and many of the people involved were, and would continue to be, connected to the Smiths in some direct way. The Trust's long-serving first Secretary (a post that would in the late 1980s become Director), Group Captain W.R. (Bill) Williams, was appointed in 1965 after the Smiths met him walking his bull terriers in the woods at their Berkshire estate of Shottesbrooke. Similarly, Church Cottage at Llandygwydd in Cardiganshire, the first endangered building that the Landmark would restore, was suggested by Leonard Beddall Smith, whom the Smiths met in his capacity as diocesan architect for Shottesbrooke church. Church Cottage and Paxton's Tower Lodge in Carmarthenshire opened their doors to the first Landmark Trust holiday makers in 1967.

John Smith was keen that the Landmark Trust should take time to consider what buildings it might acquire, and not rush into anything but, before the charity was technically constituted he already had a number of buildings in mind, among them Fort Clonque, the spectacular Victorian coastal fort on Alderney, of which he wrote in February 1965, 'If you can secure that ... then success is assured'. Knowing that at first they would need to seek out buildings, the Smiths drew up a list of bodies that might have suitable places on their books – among them the Forestry Commission and Trinity House – and together the couple toured the endless small roads of Great Britain looking for possible 'Landmarks'. The breadth of their taste is shown by notes of a trip they made to St David's via Ross-on-Wye from 18 to 21 May 1965, with Bill Williams driving. John Smith jotted down details of a forge, an octagonal lodge, a Swiss Cottage (which Christian Smith remembers as little more than a pile of bamboo), some toll-bridge cottages, a ruined stone warehouse and a brick windmill tower.

While Landmark was a self-contained operation, Smith's list of the organizations it would be useful to 'make friends with' shows that it was far from isolationist. Of the six buildings available for rent in the first handbook for 1968, five had been taken on in collaborations with the National Trust.

Four buildings in the Devon hamlet of Coombe were acquired by Landmark in tandem with the National Trust, with the two organizations working together to save this unspoiled settlement and its exceptional setting; a comparable partnership had been behind the acquisition of Paxton's Tower Lodge. These were small beer, however, compared to the ambitious partnership of Landmark and the National Trust that was about to unfold for the rescue of the island of Lundy.

On 23 June 1968, Albion Harman was taken ill on the small island of Lundy, 18 kilometres/11 miles off the coast of north Devon, and died in hospital shortly afterwards. The death of the only son of Martin Coles Harman, Lundy's colourful and charismatic former owner, brought the family to the reluctant decision that the extraordinary inhabited island that they had owned for four decades must be sold. The notion that the National Trust might acquire it occurred to many but there were apparently insuperable difficulties; after visiting and considering the purchase price and the running costs, the National Trust declined in April 1969. A month later, following alarming reports that Lundy might be bought by a casino operator or a group of Scientologists, the Bahamas-based businessman Jack Hayward pledged £150,000 to fund a purchase. Just as important as Hayward's well-publicized donation was an arrangement that had been struck behind the scenes between the Landmark Trust and the National Trust.

Lundy Island, which was taken
on in 1969 when Landmark had
only a handful of buildings.

While the acquisition cost was an initial hurdle, the potential financial drain that the island might represent to the National Trust was a massive deterrent. In 1968–9, while Lundy's future remained undecided, John Smith accompanied a trio of fellow MPs – Jeremy Thorpe, David Owen and Peter Mills – on a visit. Being a member of the National Trust's executive committee as well as proprietor of the Landmark Trust, Smith had good reason to be interested. Albion Harman's sister, Diana, met the party at the landing bay, and remembers him being transfixed by 'the granite, the rocks, the barn, the linhay, the pathetic buildings crying out for attention and the lack of modern stuff'. It seemed, she recalls, to be love at first sight. Smith proposed that Landmark should take Lundy on a long repairing lease. When this was taken together with Hayward's offer of the purchase price, the National Trust no longer objected and the sale went ahead.

There is no doubt that the biggest contribution to the 'saving' of Lundy was that of Smith and Landmark. The liability that Lundy represented was daunting indeed. Not only had the island suffered from serious under-investment since the Second World War, but the one road from the beach to the village had been washed away by a storm in February 1969. Its financial demands had defeated the Harmans, and it was clear that the purchase price would need to be spent many times over to keep the island running. Conscious of this, Smith established a limited company under the auspices of Landmark to contain the Lundy operation should it go seriously awry. The Harmans had begun to operate some of the island's buildings as holiday cottages, but these required investment, while Smith was keen to rationalize and reform the hotel that formed the heart of Lundy's tiny village. Philip Jebb, one of Smith's most trusted architects, would make seventy visits to Lundy between 1969

Wortham Manor, an early, large and complex project for Landmark, was completed in 1975.

The Pigsty, where the painstaking retention of parts of the decayed pillars embodied Landmark's conservation style.

and 1985, reforming the hotel into a series of lettable houses around a small square, restoring the ruinous cottages within the medieval keep and building a new house for the agent (known as Government House), among much else. The works were done with care and forethought that made them appear timeless. When Felix Gade, resident agent on Lundy from 1925, reflected on his life he wrote that 'praise be to the National Trust and the Landmark Trust [that Lundy] is almost exactly as it was fifty years ago.'

While the acquisition of Lundy dominated much of the rest of the 1960s, the 1970s saw the Landmark Trust get into its stride on the British mainland with five or six restored buildings being opened for bookings each year. Soon there was little need actively to seek sites, as 'people began to tell us of all too many buildings in trouble'. The restorations at Purton Green and the New Inn in Suffolk were completed in 1971, the Egyptian House in Penzance and the Aldeburgh Martello Tower in 1973, Alton Station, Wortham Manor and the Grammar School in 1975. For buildings to be taken on at this pace without the charity ballooning in personnel and bureaucracy – both of which the Smiths were determined to avoid – required great industry among a small group of people.

John Smith himself took the lead in viewing buildings, deciding on whether to proceed and working out the overall approach to their repair and restoration. That he was able to put so much of his own time into Landmark was as important to its success as the funds that came through the Manifold Trust. An exceptionally wide range of building types interested and appealed to Smith, with the result that the Landmark would soon acquire a startlingly original and eclectic collection: castles, gatehouses and ornamental landscape buildings but also the world's first industrial housing at Cromford in Derbyshire, a prison in Lincolnshire, an Italianate railway station in Staffordshire, coastal artillery forts, an ornamental

pigsty, a West Highland watermill and the engine house of a Cornish copper mine. From the late 1960s Smith had a crucial lieutenant on the building projects in Tom Dulake, a young former employee of the Society for the Protection of Ancient Buildings who became the Landmark Trust's 'Building Advisor'. With the Manifold Trust generating considerable income, Landmark was able to acquire buildings in competitive commercial sales, as well as taking on and repairing many that had little or no market value.

Soon a small collection of favoured Landmark architects was assembled, among them Paul Pearn in Plymouth, Philip Jebb in London, Martin Stancliffe in York and Stewart Tod in Edinburgh. For these architects, the experience of working for the Landmark Trust, compared to cathedral authorities or the National Trust, was striking: Landmark involved no committees of taste or complex hierarchies. Once an architect had won

The retained machinery of the
oat mill at Tangy in Kintyre.

Smith's trust, they were given a largely free hand to propose and implement their schemes. Martin Stancliffe recalls the almost daunting scope he was given, and the faith that Smith placed in him: 'If that's what you think will work, we must do it,' was a common refrain. As a client, Smith had some clear overarching principles: the buildings should not be sacrificed to their use, and visitors could tolerate – indeed might enjoy – idiosyncrasies in arrangement for a short stay that would be frustrating in a permanent residence. At Tangy Mill in Kintyre, all the machinery for grinding the oats remained in situ, with beds placed in the gaps between, while at Swarkestone Pavilion the bathroom was located in a turret, accessible only by a dash across the lead roof.

Philip Jebb, already a friend of the Smiths before the advent of the Landmark, had worked on many high-quality London commissions, including the creation of the Clermont Club in

William Kent's 44 Berkeley Square. Even so, he shared Smith's feeling for the preciousness of vernacular buildings and the handsome 'unselfconscious' buildings of the Industrial Age, and at Fort Clonque and on Lundy he gave free rein to these instincts. His genius for managing small or awkward spaces satisfactorily was perfectly suited to Landmark, and is evident in the ingenious adaptations of the tiny Chateau at Gate Burton in Lincolnshire and the Library at Stevenstone.

Many of the Landmark Trust building rescue projects involved substantial demolition or removal of secondary extensions, just as the Smiths had demolished large eighteenth-century additions to their own house at Shottesbrooke in the 1960s. At Ascog House on Bute, for instance, a Victorian extension as big as the seventeenth-century house was knocked down to retrieve the latter. Smith was also fanatical about the need to reinstate historic ground levels to ensure a building had

Top and above: The tiny Chateau
in Gate Burton, Lincolnshire

its proper proportions in elevation. But perhaps more remarkably, for the time, was the Smiths' determination that every scrap of the primary or more significant historic fabric should be preserved and reused if at all possible. At Culloden Tower, where vandals had torn down the carved wooden overmantels and then tried to burn the trampled remnants, Martin Stancliffe was astonished to be presented with two carrier bags containing scores of charred fragments and instructions to use every piece. That the restored interiors incorporate so much of the historic fabric was not thanks to conservation convention but to John Smith's perfectionism: 'good enough is not good enough' was one of the mottoes he and his teams lived by.

If the work of the architect was largely John Smith's domain, the interiors were the province of his wife, Christian, co-trustee and partner with her husband in the Landmark Trust enterprise

from the beginning. The task of furnishing the first Landmark Trust building, Church Cottage, was given to Leonard Beddall Smith's wife, Corynne, Countess de Lukacs Lessner, but the results were felt to be fussy, and Christian sought something simpler and less ornate. Sonia Rolt, wife of the Smiths' friend Tom Rolt, was asked whether she would help. She was in many ways an unlikely choice, her adult life having been spent largely on canal boats and as a pioneering campaigner for the canal movement. But a traineeship in the theatre and an instinctive feel for timeless, unpretentious English interiors – as were to be found at the Rolts' medieval home of Stanley Pontlarge in Gloucestershire – were qualifications enough. The old laundry at nearby Sudeley Castle was taken on as a furniture store and here Sonia Rolt accumulated her 'chair mountain', a large collection of chairs and tables, chests and bed ends – things that, in Christian Smith's words, Sonia was 'brilliant at buying for five shillings that would be just the job'. Tom Rolt would recall the pleasure of helping Sonia furnish a building. The couple would hire a van, into which would be loaded 'what struck my untutored eye as a depressing load of assorted junk', but which would become cheerful and characterful when installed in one of the Landmark Trust's gently restored buildings.

While Sonia Rolt found the furniture and pictures, Christian Smith determined the paint colours and interior finishes, and took a particular personal interest in the textiles. Choosing a classic design for the buildings' crockery was solved by a visit to Peter Jones and the choice of 'Old Chelsea', but other aspects of the buildings' interiors were trickier. The problem of finding suitable curtains for Chapel Cottage at Coombe would be solved by the Smiths' near neighbour Jennifer Maskell-Packer and her potter husband Bob. Jennifer would create a design based on a photograph of a device or feature in the building in question, and they would then screen-print fabric in the stables at Shottesbrooke. These hand-printed textiles would become one of the defining characteristics of the Landmark Trust's interiors.

The Landmark properties were from the first self-catering buildings, to which visitors, who Smith enjoyed calling 'campers' in tribute to Billy Butlin, originally brought their own linen and towels. As televisions and music systems became increasingly common in holiday cottages across Britain, the Landmark Trust resisted the trend, adding to its buildings' otherworldly feel.

With his exacting and enquiring mind, Smith was determined that the best possible understanding of each

Introduction

Top and above: Peake's House in
Colchester, with printed textiles
designed by Jennifer Maskell-Packer.

building should inform the treatment of its fabric, and indeed inspire the character of the furnishing. For two decades from 1978, research was the responsibility of the architectural historian Charlotte Haslam (née Dorrien-Smith), a cousin of John Smith who had worked on the Pevsner 'Buildings of Wales' guides. The wide-ranging and original primary research undertaken on each building would guide the approach to the treatment of the fabric itself – in the configuration of the rooms in Kingswear Castle or at Fox Hall, for example – and would be represented for visitors in a detailed 'history album' in each completed building.

Each Landmark Trust property was also provided with a collection of books – fiction, poetry, history, geography and natural history – that illuminated some aspect of that particular place. Choosing these was the task of Sonia Rolt, who was succeeded in her furnishing role from the late 1970s by John Evetts, and of Clayre Percy, an Oxford friend of Christian, who was also involved in furnishing and writing the history albums

for a number of Landmark properties in the north of England and her native Scotland.

The visitors to the Landmark Trust's buildings were struck from the first by their combination of old and new and their very particular atmosphere. Smith's desire that the restorations should be conceived with reverence for the original fabric, and 'that everything at each property should be perfectly done, but unaffected, indeed unnoticeable', rejected the contemporary vogue for starkly contrasting modern with historic work, and led to the creation of places of unusual beauty and harmony.

A visitor to the Bath Tower, Caernarfon in 1974 wrote in appreciation of the 'romantic atmosphere' and another of the feeling of 'coming home'. At first the buildings were let by the week from April to November only, but this soon expanded to year-round letting. Come 1974, a decade after the charity's foundation, 10,000 people a year were staying in the buildings. The operation was at first run by Bill Williams and his

A bedroom on the principal floor of Auchinleck.

Christian Smith printing fabric for Wortham Manor.

Martin Drury (centre) and Peter Pearce (right), Chairman and Director of Landmark, inspect works at Silverton Park Stables in 2007.

colleagues in the Landmark office at Shottesbrooke, and by a growing band of housekeepers and local 'secretaries' (later regional property managers) who looked after the individual buildings. An exceptional *esprit de corps* was fostered by the Smiths across the widespread Landmark estate, not least through memorable gatherings – one year, the whole Landmark office went on an outing to the Mull of Kintyre, travelling from Berkshire in a tiny aeroplane – and the parties thrown for all the craftsmen and staff involved in projects at their completion.

In 1979, Landmark, which until then had been operating in the British Isles, acquired its first overseas building. This was not the result of a deliberate expansion in operations, but a response to a specific request. When the Keats–Shelley Memorial Association approached John Smith, asking whether the Manifold Trust could contribute to the endowment they sought for 26 Piazza de Spagna in Rome, where John Keats died in 1821, Smith proposed an alternative: Landmark would take on the similar apartment on the second floor and fund the

The Villa Saraceno, designed by Andrea Palladio, was opened by Landmark in 1994 after a complex restoration.

Association's outstanding repair costs. This foray into Italy was successful and, in 1989, alarmed by reports of the swift degradation of the few remaining farm villas built by Andrea Palladio, Landmark bought the Villa Saraceno. Finally opened in 1994, this would be the charity's most ambitious project to date.

Following the retirement of Bill Williams in 1982, the role of Secretary became that of Director, to which position Robin Evans was appointed in 1986, coming to Landmark, like his successor Peter Pearce a decade later, from the National Trust. The charity's first marketing employee, the Information Officer, was taken on in 1987; she was known by Smith with wry humour as 'Miss Information'. By this time John Smith was beginning to contemplate his retirement. While his enthusiasm for rescuing buildings had never waned, he had become frustrated by an increasingly hard-line conservation establishment. In particular, following the creation of English Heritage in 1985, he sensed that the freedom he had once enjoyed to adapt buildings as he and his architects thought proper, was diminishing. He complained that 'English Heritage has developed too much

of a documentary approach. I feel it doesn't always have a clear view of what ought or ought not to be done to a building and so it is often easier to say "don't do it".'

In 1988 it was decided that the Landmark Trust should be continued on a different footing. To allow more people to participate a new structure was needed, and in 1989 the Landmark Trustee Company was formed to act as sole trustee of the Landmark Trust, of which both Smiths became directors (in effect trustees of Landmark). In May 1988 Smith had written to Martin Drury, whom he knew in Drury's capacity as the Historic Buildings Secretary of the National Trust, and asked him to join them. This began the process of Smith's gradual withdrawal from the Landmark and in 1992 he retired and Drury became Chairman in his place. When Martin Drury was made Director General of the National Trust in 1996 he in turn stood down and Barty Smith – John and Christian Smith's son – took over until Drury's return on his retirement from the National Trust in 2001. A more conventional board of trustees was built up, which included the Trust's long-running quantity surveyor,

The Gothic Temple, Stowe, was taken on by Landmark in 1970.

The library at Auchinleck, home of James Boswell.

The Old Campden banqueting houses and landscape at Chipping Camden were acquired by Landmark between 1987 and 1998.

Theo Williams, Director of the Avoncroft Museum Michael Thomas and Hugh Cookson, who brought financial expertise.

Shortly before his resignation Smith had visited Vermont on the initiative of David Tansey, an American Landmark enthusiast who had worked for the charity on and off for a decade, to view Rudyard Kipling's house, Naulakha. The property was bought in 1992 and, after the demolition of additions and extensive repairs, opened in December 1993; a series of buildings in Vermont would follow. In 1999 the owners became an independent charity as Landmark Trust (USA) with start-up funds from the Manifold Trust.

The change that the Landmark Trust was to undergo after John Smith's resignation was enormous, for as well as losing its charismatic founder the charity had to become financially self-supporting. Smith felt that the Landmark Trust was now sufficiently well established to stand on its own feet. In the early

1990s, the charity was still receiving £3 million a year from the Manifold Trust, but by the end of 1995 the financial support had ceased entirely. These would be challenging years. After more than twenty-five years, in which, in Smith's words, Landmark 'did not have to think about money at all', it now had to revise its financial arrangements. It was realized that, with discipline, the day-to-day operation of the charity, including the maintenance of its buildings, might be met from bookings income, but there would never be enough to fund expensive new building rescue projects. At this point Landmark could have ceased to undertake building rescue projects altogether, but the Trustees were determined that this should not happen. Now that Landmark had been operating for three decades, it was beginning to receive bequests from supporters that could help fund such projects. Also, fortuitously, 1994 was the foundation year of the Heritage Lottery Fund, to which Landmark was able to apply for

Clavell Tower, Dorset, was moved
and restored during 2002 and 2003.

funds for capital works. The rate of acquisition and restoration
of buildings necessarily slowed. But, while an average of two
buildings opened each year in the late 1990s and early 2000s,
the complexity and ambition of the projects did not diminish.

Theo Williams had connections with the Bath Preservation
Trust, and Landmark took on the ground floor of Beckford's
Tower in 1999. Here, the presentation of the rooms involved
re-creating an important and well-documented historic interior,
to an extent that Landmark had not attempted before. In 1997,
Beckford's Tower was surpassed in this respect when Landmark
took on A.W.N. Pugin's family house, the Grange in Ramsgate,
in a purchase funded by the Heritage Lottery Fund. Here
Landmark reinstated a series of historic interiors to their form
in Pugin's day, with a host of missing features and decorative
finishes being identified and recreated by John Evetts and
Christian Smith.

A series of highly ambitious building projects was also
undertaken. At Dolbelydr in Denbighshire, a sixteenth-century
building more spectacularly derelict that any in Landmark's
history was acquired, opening in 2003, and at Kimmeridge in
Dorset the Landmark Trust took down the imperilled Clavell
Tower before it was claimed by coastal erosion, and rebuilt the
tower stone by stone some yards further back from the cliff
edge. This period also saw a fresh concern with the gardens
and landscapes of existing and new Landmark properties –
a particular interest of Martin Drury – and the Trust's
acquisition from 1987 of the Old Campden banqueting houses
at Chipping Camden in Oxfordshire, along with the large and
important historic landscape in which they stand. In these cases,
and indeed with almost all of the building rescue projects
undertaken by Landmark since the mid-1990s, public and other
donations were the means by which the work was achieved.

Landmark's buildings were always available for people to book, but from the late 1980s it began to hold regular public open days in response to demand, from local people in particular, to see inside the buildings. One of the first open days, run by Charlotte Haslam and Julia Abel Smith, was held at the Culloden Tower in Richmond in 1989; almost 400 people came to view the ornamental eye-catcher. Such initiatives would grow, so that in 2014 more than 15,000 people would visit Landmark Trust sites on free open days. Public access and institutional ambition combined spectacularly in the project, completed in 2012, to rescue Astley Castle in Warwickshire. A derelict medieval fortified house on a moated site, Astley Castle had been a Landmark 'candidate' for over a decade but potential cost and the sheer dilapidation of the building had prevented a solution being found. In a new departure, the decision was taken in 2007 to invite a shortlist of architects to propose a solution that involved providing accommodation within a contemporary building on the site. The scheme of the winning architects, Witherford Watson Mann, spliced new brickwork into the

shattered walls. A groundbreaking approach to the rescue of a historic building, it won the 2013 RIBA Stirling Prize for the best building of the year by a British architect.

Over its fifty years the Landmark Trust has been original and influential in many respects. The founding premise, formulated in 1965, that significant historic buildings not only should be saved, nor only saved and used, but saved, used and made available to everyone and anyone to inhabit, was itself innovative and enduring. This fundamentally egalitarian model for exceptional buildings would strike a chord, and the fact that the constituency of Landmark visitors has grown with its ever-expanding estate is testament to its success. The range of John Smith's interests and the single-mindedness with which a small and initially well-funded charity was able to act were also crucial. The range of buildings thereby rescued and fitted up for domestic use also would be influential. The eighteenth-century cotton mill at Edale, for instance, was brought to John Smith's attention by Peter Jackson, Labour MP for the High Peak, and

Edale Mill, acquired by Landmark in 1970, was converted into flats.

Astley Castle, an ambitious contemporary scheme that opened in 2012.

Landmark's conversion of the building into seven flats in 1973 was a very early example of what would later be a mass movement of making apartments in industrial mills. The clarity and confidence of the small charity in what it did, and the way it worked, also mattered. Its resistance to fads in interior design, materials and technology gave the experience of staying in a Landmark building a timeless appeal, and visitors had the confidence to book buildings, however unusual or unfashionable, just because Landmark had taken them on.

That Landmark was able to weather the transition from being a highly personal charity, handsomely financed and run by its pioneering founders, to one funded almost entirely through its own income and donations confirmed John Smith's confidence in its independence in the longer term. It also demonstrated what could be achieved when, as Smith expressed it in 1965, 'people banded together and did it for themselves'.

The work of the Landmark Trust over half a century has ensured that some two hundred extraordinary places created by our ancestors remain with us still, and its work stretches on into the future. Over 50,000 people now stay every year in the Landmark Trust's buildings and experience the pleasure of carrying the key of the door in their pocket, 'a stimulus more powerful than a mere ticket of admission', and the possibility, for which Landmark was founded, that they 'might go back home with an interest awakened that would grow, and perhaps last them all their lives'. **AK**

ACKNOWLEDGEMENTS

Thanks are due to the following people for providing personal insights into the history of the Landmark Trust: Lady Smith, Barty Smith, Sonia Rolt, Diana Keast, Robin Evans, John Ewers, Tom Dulake, Louis Jebb, Martin Drury, Julia Abel Smith, John Evetts, Martin Stancliffe, David Tansey and Richard Haslam. A number of others, as well as many current and former members of the Landmark staff, shared their knowledge and experience, in particular Donald Amlot, solicitor to the Landmark Trust for half a century.

In 2014, Landmark staff and trustees visit a major new project: Llwyn Celyn, a derelict hall house in Monmouthshire.

LANDSCAPE & LORDSHIP
1250–1534

The Middle Ages were turbulent centuries, without settled government and marked by frequent civil strife and external warfare as unruly barons challenged monarchs and each other. Scotland and Wales were separate kingdoms, and rich men built castles not mansions. Ruled from Rome, the Catholic Church amassed ever more land and built great cathedrals and monasteries. Society was feudal, a complicated web of rights and duties between lord and villain, in a landscape that was essentially agrarian and where existence was often precarious. By the end of period, these feudal ties were weakening, as Henry VIII declared himself head of the new Church of England. The Landmark Trust's properties of this period testify to passionate conflict, both political and religious.

Woodsford Castle in Dorset is a fortified manor house, built at a time when the nobility always had to be on their guard against armed attack.

The exterior of Purton Green today, with wattle and daub panels beneath traditional long-straw thatch.

Decorative details carved on the timber framing of the highly ornamental arcade.

PURTON GREEN
SUFFOLK

1250

REDISCOVERED MEDIEVAL HALL

'The past is a foreign country. They do things differently there.'
L.P. Hartley, *The Go Between* (1953)

In the year 1250 or thereabouts, a small thatched house stood in a cluster of smaller buildings known as Purton Green, deep in the countryside of Suffolk.

England was still settling down after the upheaval of the Norman conquest: there had been two centuries of jostling for power between tough, opportunistic, quarrelsome Norman and Angevin monarchs, wrestling with their own family members and powerful barons, with the distractions of their lands and power relationships on the Continent, and with the glamour of crusades to the Holy Land. In 1215, King John, pushing his barons' patience too far and taxing their pockets too deeply, was forced to confirm the grant of the Magna Carta, the first stirrings of movement toward a balanced constitution, at Bury St Edmunds. This was one of the most important centres in medieval England, just 16 kilometres/10 miles or so north-east of Purton Green.

John's son, Henry III, counted first of the House of Plantagenet, inherited the throne in 1216, aged nine. After a decade of more balanced regency by the barons under Louis of France, Henry began to revert to type, taxing heavily and favouring his French relatives. In the 1250s, opposition started to coalesce around his brother-in-law Simon de Montfort, who in 1264 took the audacious step of imprisoning his monarch as instability returned. Three years later, Henry was forced to summon a 'parlement', or conference, of the barons in Bury.

So what of this particular corner of Suffolk in 1250? According to the Domesday Book, in 1086 Suffolk was one of the most populated and prosperous counties in England, accounting for well over half of the freemen in the entire country. Its gentle countryside and good communication routes allowed its agriculture and its wool and hemp cottage industries to flourish. Monastic building expanded under East Anglia's wealthy earls, who established major foundations at Clare (1248), Kersey (1218), Ipswich and Flixton (1248). Beneath the high events of court and castle, the peasant's life (for in these distant times such archetypes can only prevail, as in ancient folk tales) was 'monumentally stable' as W.G. Hoskins pithily summarized their condition in his seminal work on a medieval Midlands village.

The manor house now called Purton Green was far above a peasant's house, but it and others like it were the glue that held together the humbler hovels and outbuildings that clustered around such houses, perhaps enclosed by a fence or even a moat. There was no church – the name 'Green' implies an outlying settlement – and the hamlet was served by All Saints Church, at nearby Stansfield.

Early vernacular buildings are notoriously difficult to date, constructed of the materials to hand and resistant, though not immune, to the vagaries of fashion. However, the timber framing at Purton Green contains two distinctive features that were used from about 1150 but almost universally superseded soon after 1300. The first is that the two cross-frames that support its roof are constructed as scissor-braces, so-called for their diagonal criss-cross form. The second feature is that further width was given to the hall by the addition of side aisles. The presence of both these features allows the house to be dated to the second half of the thirteenth century. Key developments in construction after 1300 rendered scissor-braces and side aisles largely obsolete, and they rarely survive. Where they do, their remnants

Thirteenth-century revolutionary Simon de Montfort demands reform from his brother-in-law, King Henry III.

Timbers ancient and new frame the solid tread oak staircase heading to the upper chamber.

are found, as at Purton Green, embedded inside later accretions and adaptations that enabled the survival of these early structures.

The concept of the open hall lay at the heart of domestic housing design from the very earliest times. In the thirteenth century, this house at Purton Green was perhaps 1.5 metres/ 5 feet wider than today, and the shaggy thatched roof swept down to 1.5–1.8 metres/5–6 feet above ground level. At the centre of the house, both physically and socially, was the hall, a large space open to the rafters. When its side aisles were intact, the Purton Green hall was some 10 metres/30 feet square: an imposing and dignified space.

Like all halls, Purton Green was arranged according to strict hierarchical conventions. Smoke from a central hearth set in the floor towards one end of the hall filtered its way up through light slanting from small mullioned windows with sliding wooden shutters and no glass, to escape through a slatted opening or gablet. At the 'low end' of the hall was a cross passage with service and storage rooms beyond; the 'pantry' for dry goods, the 'buttery' for wet and further rooms were above, probably accessed by a ladder. At Purton Green, the cross passage has a decorative arcade with six Gothic arches running along it, its posts supporting the side aisles for extra width. At the high end of the hall, to which the fire is closer, the master of the household and his family would sit at a long cross table on benches looking down the hall. The family's private chambers led off behind the high end.

Under the same hierarchy, each visible roof truss in the building had its upper and lower face, the upper face more highly finished and set towards the master. The decorative value of the scissor-trusses was used to the full for soaring patterns of chevrons and saltires. The octagonal arcade posts have carved capitals, in a sophisticated decorative scheme designed to impress, and to be viewed at their best from the high table.

Such halls held the kernel of medieval domestic life. Each was a communal space for the wider household (servants and workers as well as family) to live, eat, work and sleep. It was the arena for social, ceremonial, judicial and business life. Purton Green is an example of some status, probably built by one Walter de Priditon (or Purton), steward to the Earl Marshall, who was a senior member of the king's household. This basic format for existence, however, was played out in all but the very humblest medieval dwellings, right up to the palace of the king himself.

Every researcher of vernacular buildings dreams of discovering the heavy, soot-encrusted roof timbers of an open hall hidden in the attic of a much-altered farmhouse. Leaping

England's agricultural economy grew during the twelfth and thirteenth centuries. During July and August most of the local population helped with the hay making.

The modified and derelict farmhouse before restoration work began in 1965.

There would have been no glass in the windows in the thirteenth century, just sliding wooden shutters.

New wood has been carefully pieced into this arcade pillar to save as much original fabric as possible.

forward some 800 years to 1965, the year the Landmark Trust was founded, this was exactly what happened to George and Sylvia Colman in this Suffolk field. They published their findings, and then wrote to John Smith to ask if his new charity might consider taking this building on.

John Smith used the resources of the Manifold Trust to buy and then restore the house to present as far as possible its original medieval form. Even for someone with his vision, this was a courageous move. Conservation in 1965 was not the passionate activity it has become today; the painstaking and expensive retrieval of such a building must have seemed at best eccentric, demanding the skills of an archaeologist as much as an architect. Luckily, John Warren combined both. The eventual Landmark reveals more of the thirteenth century than had been visible through its later accretions but still allows the later development of the house to speak. Purton Green is a lone

survivor of the long-deserted medieval villages that lie beneath today's landscape, subsumed after being abandoned or deliberately cleared by landowners in later centuries. Purton Green's cluster of associated buildings has long since disappeared, but here we can still catch the medieval tang of wood smoke in open fields and try to imagine the lives of the villagers long ago.

In John Smith's own words for the 1971 edition of *The Landmark Trust Handbook*: 'The people of the Middle Ages have vanished in every way; we do not think or act in the least as they did, which is in some respects a pity. The atmosphere of their world is elusive indeed, but compelling and binding for those who find it. It is present in full measure here and we hope that through the hall at Purton Green, blackened by smoke and time, many will enter a world for which they have been looking.' **CS**

The open hall with scissor-braced roof trusses dates Purton Green to the late thirteenth century.

William de Marisco of Lundy dragged through London to his execution in 1242, in an illustration by chronicler Matthew Paris.

Traḥꝛur Willꝭ de ꝗꝛꝛꝼco ꝗꝺef ꝺ parꝛbulum.

Lundy was famous in the Middle Ages for the rabbits cultivated on the island. The cost of the new castle was partly met by the sale of rabbit pelts.

The castle was built by Henry III in 1243 to prevent Lundy from becoming a haven for pirates.

THE CASTLE
LUNDY

ROYAL STRONGHOLD AGAINST PIRACY

In the middle of the night on 9 September 1238, an assassin crept through the window of King Henry III's bedchamber at the palace of Woodstock in Oxfordshire. He barred the door before stealing towards the royal bed with a naked blade in his hand. But when he struck it was in vain, as by serendipity alone the king was spending the night with his wife in her apartments. When a terrified maid raised the alarm, the would-be assassin was captured and confessed under torture that he had been sent to kill the king by William de Marisco of Lundy. For the next three years a manhunt would be pursued across the country, one that would end on this tiny island 14.5 kilometres/ 9 miles north of the Devon coast.

William de Marisco was a notorious pirate. Operating in the western seas between south-west England and Ireland, he and his associates preyed on the shipping in those busy waters, capturing and ransoming men and merchandise and terrorizing the coastal settlements. That they could do so was thanks to the Marisco family's property of Lundy. A narrow island 5 kilometres/3 miles long and 0.8 kilometres/½ mile wide, it rises from the sea on soaring, jagged cliffs, and was considered impregnable. A place where ships wrecked easily and only the initiated could land, it was the perfect pirate's lair.

Despite his nefarious ways, William de Marisco's family had been a respectable and influential lot. In 1190 his uncle had been granted the island of Lundy by King Richard I. Despite its size and intimidating aspect, the island was in fact productive and domesticated. It had rich pastures supporting horses, cows and sheep, various fortifications, ponds and mills, and here the prized foreign species of the rabbit had been successfully introduced in the previous century. Marisco's father, Geoffrey, served the king in Ireland where he rose to be head of the legal system as justiciar. But the bloody and bitter politics of Ireland took their toll, and after William was implicated in the murder of a royal agent, he began a swift slide into banditry and revenge killing that soon reached the highest levels.

After eluding capture for three years, holed up on Lundy with a band of outlaws and fellow plunderers, Marisco was finally hunted down. On a foggy February day in 1242, the king's agents scaled the rocky cliffs, overwhelmed the guards and made a surprise attack. Marisco was captured and taken to the Tower of London. Five months later he and his associates were tried and condemned to death. After being dragged through the streets from Westminster to the tower he was hanged, drawn and quartered. The gruesome 'quarters' of his mutilated corpse were then displayed in the market places of four major towns as

warnings to those who crossed the king. The experience left Henry III determined that never again should Lundy serve as a haven for his enemies. Marisco's execution for treason brought Lundy into royal ownership and on 17 July, three days after his trial, the Sheriff of Devon and Henry de Tracy were ordered to go there to organize the building of a royal castle.

The first step in the enterprise was to establish a supply of lime and stone for the masonry walls but, as the instructions acknowledged, the speed of progress would depend entirely on the weather. To build an effective fortification on Lundy's challenging island terrain required real expertise and, in the spring of 1243, the sheriff visited the island with a 'man skilful, faithful and discreet in mason's work' to choose the precise location for the new structure. Marisco's own castle had probably been an inland spot near today's village, but the mason agreed on a commanding site at the south-eastern tip of the island overlooking its one landing beach. Here work soon began on 'a good tower with a bailey wall'.

The costs of building would reach a substantial £200, but the island covered much of this, for the works were to be paid for from the sale of the rabbits that then ran plentifully over its surface. With rabbit fur prized as a luxurious edging for the collars and cuffs of royal and aristocratic clothing, and the mammal not native to Britain, Lundy's rabbit colony was a gold mine. Later in the century it was reckoned that 2,000 rabbits could be culled a year, making it by a long way the most lucrative of the island's produce. By 1322, rabbit pelts provided four times as much income each year as both the arable and pasture farming combined.

The castle that was erected that summer is a squat, squarish structure built of rough dressed granite probably quarried on the island, while the lime for its mortar was brought over from Devon by boat. Austere and undecorated, with simple battlements on the roof and staggered towards the cliff on its eastern front, its visibility to passing vessels was a statement in itself. A curtain wall encircled the castle on the landward sides

The commanding position chosen for the castle, and the staggered facade on its seaward face, made it visible to passing shipping.

The interior of the castle was fitted out as cottages for the families of workers at the island's granite quarry.

and extended part of the way along the elongated triangle that forms the tip of the headland. This would be reinforced with new defensive features during the English Civil War in the 1640s, but the northern section remains intact, punctuated by mural towers and providing excellent fields of fire over the shallow waters below. Outside the walls a ditch was dug as an additional line of defence. The narrow path up from the landing bay 'in the which two men together can scarce go in the front' was now firmly in the castle's lee.

When first built, the keep, which measures 15.5 x 11.5 metres/ 51 x 38 feet, probably had two large chambers on two floors. The entrance was on the south-eastern face and can still just be seen in the masonry. As soon as it was complete it was in use. A sizeable garrison had already been established, consisting of a constable, forty sergeants of two ranks, four mariners with two ploughmen and a shepherd to tend to the land. The task of the garrison was to keep Lundy in royal hands, but this was an expensive business, and in time the crown would again grant the island to a loyal lord to manage instead.

While Lundy periodically changed hands over the centuries, the castle would remain the principal building on the island for more than five hundred years, housing a series of occupants, some distinguished, some disreputable. Despite the castle's presence, piracy remained a menace in the seas around the island. Shortly before the Civil War, the island was owned by the charismatic Cornish royalist Sir Bevil Grenville, whose personal affection for Lundy was such that he swore, 'I have so many reasons to be in love with it, as I shall never call or woo any man to buy it.' But despite his improvements to Lundy, which included the erection of two houses adjacent to the castle, the pirates preyed. A particularly nasty raid took place in July 1633, when eighty Spaniards landed on the island, imprisoned and tied up the inhabitants – killing one man in the process – and proceeded to ransack the island and sail away with everything of any value.

The construction of the elegant Millcombe House by William Heaven after his purchase of Lundy in 1836 marked a new chapter in the island's history. Heaven went on to erect accommodation for the workers of his granite quarries within the shell of the keep a decade or so later. In 1968, Lundy was put up for sale once again and the island was bought by the National Trust in an arrangement that saw the Landmark Trust immediately take on responsibility for managing it. The castle had by then become derelict again, but between 1979 and 1988 the Landmark Trust repaired and restored the quarry workers' cottages that now once more nestle securely within the enduring walls of Henry III's keep. **AK**

It was after his failure to assassinate Henry III (above) that Lundy's owner, William de Marisco, was hunted down and finally executed.

William Heaven converted the castle for the workers in his Lundy granite quarry, and created a new principal residence at Millcombe House.

Caernarfon's historic town walls shimmer in the River Seiont. Bath Tower is the second one from the left.

BATH TOWER
GWYNEDD

1283

ARCHITECTURE AS MIGHT

'To Caernarfon, where I thought to have seen a Town and a Castle, or a Castle and a Town; but I saw both to be one, and one to be both,' wrote John Taylor in 1652. 'I have seen many gallant fabrics and fortifications, [but] for compactness and completeness of Caernarfon, I never yet saw a parallel.' The Bath Tower is one of eight defensive towers that stud the town walls of Caernarfon, a fortified town overlooking the Menai Straits in north-west Wales.

Caernarfon Castle was planned and built by the great warrior king, Edward I (1239–1307). It was part of his strategic plan for an 'iron ring' of castles and fortified towns throughout north and mid-Wales as he sought a definitive solution to centuries of jockeying for power by Welsh princes and the English, the force of Norman systems of government and land tenure crashing against ancient Welsh custom and jurisdiction.

The Bath Tower is one element of the architectural representation of this monarchical campaign. Edward did not seek out trouble in Wales in the 1280s; he had plenty elsewhere (his tomb in Westminster Abbey bears the simple epithet *malleus Scotorum*, or 'Hammer of the Scots') – but he did expect orderly acquiescence from a still fragmented land. Wales was divided into princedoms in the early thirteenth century, their princes owing nominal homage to the English throne. The Welsh royal families vied with each other for influence. Henry III, Edward's father, was beset by his own assertive barons, some of the most troublesome ruling the Marches and south Wales. Civil war broke out in 1255 between the powerful Llywelyn ap Gruffudd of Gwynedd and his brothers. By 1267, Llywelyn was acknowledged Prince of all Wales. However, resentment at continually abrasive English administration and the treachery of Llywelyn's brother Dafydd led to defiance and simmering rebellion. In 1282, Edward entered Wales in a decisive military campaign, in which Llywelyn was killed.

Edward now instigated his monumental project for ten new castles to establish his supremacy in the principality once and for all. Caernarfon was one, and Builth, Aberystwyth, Flint, Rhuddlan, Ruthin, Hope, Conwy, Harlech and Beaumaris completed the formidable chain. Five sites, including Caernarfon, also had planned and fortified towns. The ten castles represent the culmination of the English castle-building tradition; manifestation of a powerful monarch's focused will and fully mobilized national resources, the needs of defence finding expression in masterly architectural effect.

The Caernarfon site was a well-chosen peninsula overlooking the straits to Anglesey, protected to the east and

north by the mountains of Snowdonia. It also had a mythical reputation. A Roman fort built nearby in AD 75 features in *The Dream of Macsen Wledig*, later included in the canon of *The Mabinogion*, a collection of early Celtic legends. The story was first written down by Geoffrey of Monmouth in 1136 but sprang from a much earlier Welsh oral tradition. Macsen Wledig (the Welsh name for Magnus Maximus, Roman Emperor AD 383–8) dreams of a beautiful maiden in a wondrous castle across the ocean. In due course, his dream meets reality when he travels to Britain and finds and marries his princess, Helen Luyddawc, and builds three castles for her, the biggest of them at Arfon.

When the presumed body of Magnus Maximus was discovered during the construction of Caernarfon Castle, Edward reinterred it with honour, and abruptly changed his plans to make Caernarfon his seat of Welsh government, astutely magnifying both Caernarfon's continuity as an imperial stronghold as well as Welsh tradition.

The building programme at Caernarfon began in 1283, supervised by Master James of St George (*c.* 1235–1308) a mason and military engineer of international renown. Master James had overseen the building of fortifications in the Alpine region of Savoy for many years before he came to Wales, and is counted one of the greatest military architects in history.

The project was not an entirely French affair, however. The masons of the newly instituted King's Works were already experienced castle designers, and men like Master Richard the 'Engineer' of Chester and Master Walter of Hereford also played essential roles, especially after 1295 when work resumed following a fierce attack by the Welsh the previous year. Such men combined the skills of architect and engineer: when the constraints of medieval population levels, transport and communication – boat, horse or messenger – are taken into account, appreciation rapidly turns into awe.

Caernarfon Castle is unmistakably Roman in design. Its distinctive bands of coloured stone and its polygonal towers, uncommon in English castle architecture, are often cited as deliberate references to the renowned fortifications of Constantinople, founded by Constantine I. His mother, at least according to Geoffrey on Monmouth, was no other than Empress Helen of Gwynedd.

The accounts of the Chamberlains of North Wales survive for 1284. From these, we learn that enormous shiploads of stone

This aerial view reveals how carefully Edward I's engineers planned both the castle and the fortified town at Caernarfon.

and timber were docked at a new quay, in ships from northern France and Ireland as well as southern England. Lead, coal, lime, sand, iron, nails and glass came by barge and cart. Legions of quarrymen, diggers, specialist ditchers known as *fossatores*, stone-layers, masons, carpenters, joiners, glaziers, tilers, smiths, plumbers and painters were employed as contract labour. Each trade might be subdivided: medieval masons specialized in carving, new-build or restoration work. Hundreds of diggers levelled platforms in the rock base of the castle to cut enormous foundation trenches some 6 metres/20 feet deep.
It was harsh and extremely dangerous work.

The castles were constructed with wooden scaffolding, cranes, pulleys and hoists. Wooden handcarts, sledges and even hods brought materials over wet and muddy ground. Small details resonate across the centuries; for example, Matthew of Silkstone, a carpenter, was paid twenty shillings for making a crane to hoist timbers, and needed 3.6 kilograms/8 pounds of grease to lubricate it. The work required tenacity and strength.

The massive workforce was mostly skilled and highly mobile. The surnames of labourers John de Cotyngwk, Hugh de Crauene and Henry de Elreton identify them as hailing from Yorkshire. Other craftsmen came from France: Philip of Ewyas from Sète was principal carpenter at Caernarfon, Master Mannasser de Vaucouleurs from Champagne was 'master and director of the diggers' at Caernarfon and later a town bailiff.

Building work continued at Caernarfon for more than half a century, although the town walls were given priority, and the castle itself was never finished. By the nineteenth century, the town had become a notable tourist destination, famed for its sea bathing, and the Bath Tower gets its name from the public baths built behind it in Church Street in 1823. Later, it became a dwelling and as such was bought, derelict, by the Landmark Trust in 1967. The tower was suffering severe subsidence, with one wall some 45 cm/18 inches out of true; consequently, new cement foundations were laid to a depth of 6 metres/20 feet. The tower was re-roofed and the services carefully restricted to the Victorian additions to the rear.

The cumulative importance of such small interventions was underlined in 1986, when Caernarfon was designated part of the UNESCO World Heritage Site known as 'The Castles and Town Walls of Edward I in Gwynedd'.

Only his castles now bear witness to Edward I's imperial ambitions for England over Wales. The Welsh are now governed by their own separate assembly. As an old Welshman said to Henry III in 1163, 'No other race than this and no other tongue than this of Wales, happen what may, will answer in the great day of judgment for this little corner of the earth.' **CS**

The estuary glimpsed through an arrow slit in Bath Tower, named after the public baths built to the rear in 1823.

The stained glass of unknown date in the bathroom was already installed when Landmark took on Bath Tower.

A fifteenth-century illustration showing the king and knights of the Order of the Garter – of which Sir Guy de Bryan was one – worshipping St George.

A fifteenth-century manuscript of the Prologue of *The Canterbury Tales* by Geoffrey Chaucer, which describes a knight such as Sir Guy de Bryan.

Today's thatched roof at Woodsford Castle gives the building the appearance of a large farmhouse and belies its earlier function as a fortified manor.

WOODSFORD CASTLE
DORSET

CHIVALRY AND NATIONAL IDENTITY

'A knyght ther was,' wrote Geoffrey Chaucer in the Prologue to *The Canterbury Tales* (1475) 'and that a worthy man,/That fro the tyme that he first bigan To riden out, he loved chivalrie,/Trouthe and honour, fredom and curteisie./Ful worthy was he in his lordes werre,/And therto hadde he riden.'[1] Chaucer was writing in the late fourteenth century, and his words well describe Sir Guy de Bryan, from 1350 the first Lord Bryan, and responsible for the construction of Woodsford Castle.

With its enormous thatched roof, Woodsford is a far cry from the architecturally orchestrated castles built by Edward I. Complex though it is, much has been lost: originally, it enclosed a ward on all four sides, with corner towers from which we can imagine pennants fluttering. More fortified manor than instrument of warfare, Woodsford is the residence of a lord made imposing through the trappings of fortification, representing a more vernacular tradition of castle building. Baronial castles like these formed the framework

of medieval Britain; hubs of administration and justice sustained by vast estates.

Licence to crenellate the earlier manor of Woodsford was issued to William de Whitfield in 1335 by the young Edward III, whose long reign stretched from 1327–77. Nothing is left of this earliest building phase, although it seems likely that Lord Bryan adapted and added to it when he bought the manor in 1367. Bryan typifies his century. Writing first in 1586, antiquarian William Camden described him as a renowned warrior, who *suum habuit castellum* ('built himself a little castle') and there is perhaps something in that diminutive that suggests a conscious chivalric display as much as a seriously intimidating and impregnable structure in his building campaign.

Edward III's reign was a time of knights and tournaments, as another alpha monarch wrested back the reins of power by leading his barons from the front. Edward enjoyed warfare, which the chivalric code embellished and codified. He led an abundance of military adventures against the Scots and the French, and held splendid tournaments that honed the skills of knightly passion as well as providing a lavish spectacle. Edward was still a Plantagenet, and French still the language of the court, but he was also the first monarch explicitly to champion Englishness as a means to rally opposition to external threat. The 1352 Statute of Pleading, for example, made English the language of the law courts. Lower down the social scale,

---

[1] Translation from the Middle English: 'A knight there was, and he a worthy man, Who, from the moment that he first began To ride about the world, loved chivalry, Truth, honour, freedom and all courtesy. Full worthy was he in his liege-lord's war, And therein had he ridden.'

Top: Woodsford Castle originally enclosed a full garth or courtyard; today only a portion survives.
Above: The Black Death swept across Europe in the mid-fourteenth century. Death was swift, nasty and almost inevitable for those infected.

Sir Guy de Bryan's fine Gothic memorial in Tewkesbury Abbey. He was buried at Slipton church in Devon.

yeomen and villeins were also starting to find their voice, and to struggle under the feudal yoke.

There certainly were external threats, and places like Woodsford still needed to be fortified. It stands in Dorset near a relatively minor crossing of the River Frome, a few miles inland. The threat of French invasion or attack was a real one, and the English harassed the French in a similar way in northern France. The French had attempted an invasion at seventeen-year-old Edward's accession to the throne in 1327; Edward in turn claimed the French throne as his own in 1337. Predictably, Edward's claim was rejected by the French, ushering in the so-called Hundred Years War, a series of conflicts unresolved until the 1450s. Sir Guy de Bryan was part of the king's inner circle throughout, a fitting representative of his time.

Bryan was the same age as Edward and grew up with him. Described as Edward's 'beloved groom', he received payments and was 'continually at the King's side'. The fifth of his name, he was born into a family of minor Marcher gentry at Walwyn's Castle in Pembrokeshire, sometimes known as 'Little England Beyond Wales' and a reminder that Anglo-Welsh relations were not universally strained. Fortified houses in west Wales were often built with their main rooms above a vaulted undercroft, and de Bryan built the same at Woodsford. These boyhood roots may explain the very unusual form of the original castle – not quite castle, tower house or fortified manor, but encompassing something of each.

By the time Lord Bryan acquired Woodsford in 1367, however, he had risen far above his origins. He had become, William Dugdale recorded, 'a person of very great note in his time', entrusted with martial and diplomatic affairs of the highest importance. He held lands in Gloucestershire, Kent and Somerset, as well as Dorset. He was Warden of the Forest of Dean (1341–90), he fought in Scotland in 1327 and 1337 and in Flanders in 1339, he bore the king's standard in defence of Calais in 1349, and fought at the Battle of Crécy in 1346. Edward rewarded Bryan's service with lucrative wardships and a second marriage to a very rich second wife, Elizabeth Montacute. None of the other lands Bryan amassed had a castle, so building one was a natural expression of his great wealth and status.

The timing of Bryan's elevation to the barony in 1350 was probably not a chance one. The Black Death arrived in England in 1348, appearing first in Dorset. 'The seventh year after it began, it came to England and first began in the towns and ports joining on the seacoasts, in Dorsetshire, where, as in other counties, it made the country quite void of inhabitants so that there were almost none left alive,' wrote contemporary chronicler Geoffrey the Baker. Modern estimates believe that up

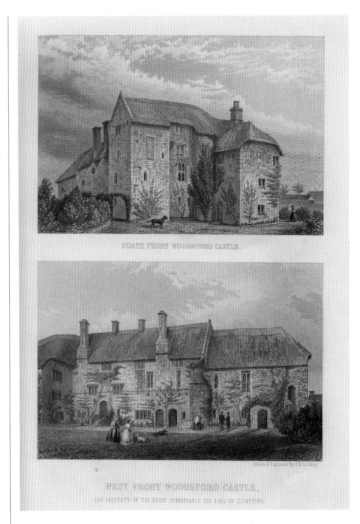

Woodsford Castle in the 1880s. It was well known to author Thomas Hardy, whose father repaired it.

By the 1950s, the castle had become a rambling farmhouse.

During restoration, branches that had been used as simple rafters were found beneath the decaying thatch.

The form and function of an ancient latch are reproduced in this modern replacement.

to a third of the total population perished, and it was no respecter of rank. The plague (and there was more than one outbreak) had wide-ranging economic and social consequences: labour became scarce and land was left untenanted. The laws of supply and demand sat awkwardly with the feudal system, as the reduced labour force was able to demand higher wages, which in turn encouraged greater geographic mobility. This was the age of the building of many of England's great cathedrals and churches, and skilled craftsmen were already in much demand when the plague hit.

The country recovered remarkably quickly. Edward's competent royal administration and the stabilizing influence of local lords like Bryan helped, but one modern interpretation is that the rupture of the Black Death was the catalyst that reordered English society and revitalized the economy. In 1351, the Statute of Labourers fixed wages at the pre-plague level and attempted to check peasant mobility by giving their lords first claim on their labour. However, the genie of economic individualism was not so easy to put back into the bottle. While generalization is always hazardous, overall the second half of the fourteenth century saw a gradual weakening of feudal land tenure, especially in the open country or 'champaign' that stretched from Oxford to Dorset. Commutation of feudal service into wage labour weakened the lords' interest in preserving uniformity. Land holdings that reverted to the lords during the Black Death were absorbed by surviving tenants into enlarged holdings, blurring the rigid social strata of feudalism. Such changes can be traced through the transgression of traditional behaviour patterns in the courts: hay left uncarted and spoilt by a defaulting villein; haymaking and reaping weather missed because tenants chose to harvest their own crops instead. Land was starting to become a commodity rather than a means of social control, knights, gentry, free peasants and ambitious villeins all eagerly buying or leasing, rather than holding it through homage to their lord.

Guy de Bryan weathered all these changes and more. In 1369, he was made Admiral of the Fleet, and there was indeed need for crenellation in these years, as the French continually harassed the south coast from 1360–90. Bryan must have played a significant role in 1377, when the French plundered the Dorset coast from Poole to Lyme Regis. Perhaps as a consequence of his elevation, in 1370 he was made the fiftieth member of the Order of the Garter, that most lasting symbol of the chivalric era awarded to only twenty-six of the monarch's closest companions at one time. Edward had founded the order in 1348, in self-conscious evocation of King Arthur's mythical Knights of the Round Table. According to Polydore Vergil 150 years later, the garter of Edward's favourite, Joan of Kent, slipped down her leg at a ball in Calais. To defuse the general hilarity, the king gallantly tied the blue garter around his own thigh, declaring *Honi soit qui mal y pense* ('Shame on he who thinks evil.') The order continues today with the same motto.

Guy de Bryan died aged seventy-nine in 1390, and is buried in a magnificent tomb in Tewkesbury Abbey. In truth, he can have spent relatively little time at Woodsford. He was constantly campaigning, attending court at Westminster and serving as an ambassador as far afield as Rome. In many ways, far more representative of life at Woodsford would have been the community around the castle: the yeomen who worked the fields, survived the plague and grappled with French marauders. For all the glamour and glitter of the chivalric court, the English voices that began to create their own literary legacy for the first time in the fourteenth century – William Langland in his *Vision of Piers Plowman (c.* 1380), Chaucer in his *Canterbury Tales* (1475) – give us just as true a flavour of this colourful era.

Guy de Bryan did not found the dynasty he hoped for. His name died out in a generation, and Woodsford passed by inheritance to the Staffords and then the Strangways, later Earls of Ilchester. By 1630 the castle was 'almost ruinated', but around 1660, the main range was transformed into a very large farmhouse, its circulation improved, smaller rooms inserted and the whole tamed by the addition of a thatched roof. Woodsford had entered another phase, as a house of some status at the heart of a large tenant farm. In the 1850s, a careful restoration was carried out by John Hicks of Dorchester, assisted by builder Mr Hardy, whose son, Thomas, later joined Hicks' office to train as an architect before finding fame as an author and poet.

In 1977, the castle was sold, for the first time in its long history, to the Landmark Trust, for ruination again threatened and the huge roof was near collapse. Emergency repairs were carried out, although tenant farmers lived out their years there until 1987. Local craftsman Leonard Hardy then worked almost single-handedly on the castle for three years, under architect Peter Bird's supervision and with ongoing scrutiny of the complicated fabric by specialists like Nicholas Cooper, Laurence Keen and John Smith himself. Woodsford finally opened as a Landmark in 1992, a mighty fragment of the chivalric age. **CS**

Somewhat altered since, the so-called King's Room was once Sir Guy de Bryan's great hall.

Landmark's selected furniture carefully echoes original motifs.

A view from the north of Rosslyn Castle as rebuilt in the mid-fifteenth century by William Sinclair, third Earl of Orkney.

Robert the Bruce, among whose powerful supporters were the Sinclairs of Roslin.

The only remaining roofed remnant of the once-great medieval castle of Rosslyn is this range, created in the 1590s.

ROSSLYN CASTLE
MIDLOTHIAN

C. 1400

SCOTTISH HISTORY PLAYS OUT IN THE EARL OF ORKNEY'S SEAT

As the River North Esk curls its way towards the Firth of Forth, it makes a sharp loop south and then north again at Roslin (the settlement spelt differently from the castle and earldom), encircling a high stone outcrop on three sides. From its position atop this rocky escarpment, Rosslyn Castle enjoys a prospect with as much drama and romance as the story of the Sinclair family who owned it from the twelfth century – tangled always in the bloody fortunes of the rulers of Scotland.

Topography had already given this place its name a millennium ago ('ross' is a rocky promontory, and 'lynn' a waterfall), and on 14 September 1280 it was granted to the powerful William Sinclair (or St Clair), a descendant of the Norman William de Santo Claro. A close friend and advisor of Scotland's King Alexander III, William was guardian to the king's youngest son, but could do nothing as death claimed each of the king's three children in turn and a reign of peace and plenty rapidly came to an end. In 1290 his seven-year-old granddaughter, Queen Margaret the 'Maid of Norway', the last of the Canmore line, was crossing the North Sea when illness ended her short life. The crisis that followed gave the voracious

King Edward I of England the opening he needed, and he launched a brutal campaign to conquer Scotland. In the decades that followed, the Sinclairs would become important members of the Scottish resistance under the pennant of its brilliant leader Robert the Bruce. The battle of Roslin was fought only 0.6 kilometre/1 mile away in 1303, and saw some 8,000 Scots defeat a mounted English army of more than 20,000. In 1330, it was William Sinclair's grandson and namesake who set off from Rosslyn for Palestine to bury the casket containing Robert the Bruce's heart in the dusty soil of the Holy Land.

The Wars of Independence lasted well into the fourteenth century and saw the Scots finally see off the English invaders. But a price was paid, as the noble leaders in those wars gained power and land holdings such that the kings who followed the Bruce often struggled to assert their authority over such mighty subjects. Among those who benefitted were the Sinclairs of Roslin, whose own position was greatly enhanced when in 1379 the King of Norway recognized them as Earls of Orkney, which brought what was virtually independent sovereignty over Shetland and Orkney.

The most powerful family in Scotland at the beginning of the fifteenth century was that of Douglas, into which two generations of Sinclairs, the second and third Earls of Orkney, advantageously married. Henry Sinclair, second Earl of Orkney, was travelling with the twelve-year-old King of Scotland, James I

in 1406, when their ship was seized by English pirates. James was delivered to King Henry IV of England and would spend the next eighteen years as his prisoner, while Orkney bought his own release. Going home with his Douglas kinsmen, Orkney was then to enjoy unfettered power in Scotland.

The apogee of Rosslyn and the Sinclair dynasty came in the mid-fifteenth century. When King James I, now aged thirty, finally returned to Scotland in 1424 – after the payment of a colossal ransom – among those waiting to greet him at Berwick was the teenage William Sinclair, son of the second Earl of Orkney. Having finally gained his throne, James I was determined to reassert royal authority and the international standing of Scotland. Among his coups was a treaty with King Charles VII of France, which brought with it a sensational marriage for his daughter Margaret, to the French Dauphin. William Sinclair, now Admiral of the Fleet, had command of the vessels accompanying Princess Margaret to France and travelled on to attend her wedding in the great castle of Tours. It was on Orkney's arm that Princess Margaret entered the royal palace there. As an expedition on which the reputation of James I's vision of Scotland depended, it demanded enormous expenditure. Sinclair took with him an entourage of over 100 retainers, dressed in gold and velvet finery, and was personally honoured by the King of France. At the wedding feast

Sinclair stood as the King of Scotland's proxy, and took second place only to the Archbishop of Reims at the French king's table.

Over the following decades Sinclair would hold a glittering array of high offices; as well as Admiral of Scotland, he was Lord Chief Justice and one of the regents for James III. After a dispute he was confirmed as Earl of Orkney and was given the Earldom of Caithness (hence the prevalence of the name Sinclair in the north of Scotland) and lived in enormous state, dining on gold and silver plates 'in the most princely manner'.

One of the ways James I had expressed his view of the stature and dignity of the Scottish monarchy was in buildings, on which he had spent lavishly through the 1420s and 1430s. Wresting back control of the great royal castles at Edinburgh and Stirling from their aristocratic keepers, he built elegant new royal apartments in each. At Linlithgow in a dazzling waterfront position between Edinburgh and Stirling he started work on an ambitious new palace; in no way defensive, this was a European pleasure palace, adorned with elaborate sculpture and decorative stonework.

It is not surprising, therefore, that William Sinclair, third Earl of Orkney, also set about aggrandizing his seat at Rosslyn. Whatever had stood on the rocky promontory over the Esk was taken down and Orkney raised new buildings in its place. Across the dry chasm hewn out of the rock, he erected a

Rosslyn Castle by Hugh William Williams, c. 1800. The castle was a favoured subject with romantic artists and poets.

Below the surviving west range are three monumental storeys containing kitchens and service rooms; a great staircase led down to the gardens.

handsome bridge that sailed into the castle borne on soaring arches from the gorge bottom. Facing this approach, and like Linlithgow more domestic than defensive, stood a substantial range of buildings, five storeys tall and some 21 metres/70 feet long. Beyond this, within the walled enclosure on the crown of the rock, he erected a large residential tower, curved on one face and reminiscent of the great thirteenth-century tower of the royal palace at Tours he had so recently seen.

Having rebuilt his castle and undertaken works to the landscape around it, Orkney turned in the late 1440s to his most famous architectural project, the erection of a magnificent church, a college for a small body of priests, at the top of the hill behind Roslin. After a stellar career his star waned, and when he died an old man in 1484 he had traded his Orcadian title for a lucrative Scottish substitute, watched his children begin to squabble over their vast inheritance, and managed to build only the chancel of his magnificent church of St Matthew.

It was William Sinclair, son of another Lord Chief Justice, who rebuilt the western range of Rosslyn Castle in the 1590s. Here, on the precipitous edge of the rock, he created an enormous five-storey range in which the principal rooms were entered from the castle courtyard on the fourth storey, raised on three great lower storeys built against the rock itself. The arrangement was ingenious. On the high entrance level were a substantial great hall and withdrawing chamber, while a massive vaulted kitchen, bakehouse and storerooms were conveniently located below. A tremendous stair that plunged through the centre of the whole building allowed the lords of the castle to walk down from the castle into gardens on the riverside below without passing outside. The main rooms were redecorated by William Sinclair in the 1630s, and the fine Jacobean plaster ceiling in the drawing room was installed.

National politics, which played such a part in the making of Rosslyn Castle, would also be its downfall. In the autumn of 1650, after the execution of Charles I, Oliver Cromwell and the English Republican Army invaded Scotland. In early November Cromwell's protégé, the brilliant Scottish soldier Colonel George Monck, besieged Rosslyn. Six hundred men pounded the castle walls with cannon and grenades, bringing the Earl of Orkney's buildings and walls crashing down. John Sinclair, who only weeks before had buried his father in the Rosslyn Chapel, held the castle with a garrison of just twenty-five but was soon forced to surrender. The siege of 1650 reduced much of Rosslyn Castle to a ruin, but the western range of the 1590s largely survived.

The whole site still belongs to a branch of the Sinclair family, Earls of Rosslyn since 1801. Following repairs, the castle has been managed by the Landmark Trust since 1984. **AK**

The drawing room of Rosslyn Castle with its elaborate, fully restored Jacobean plaster ceiling.

Colonel George Monck, later Duke of Albermarle, whose siege of Rosslyn Castle in 1650 destroyed much of the medieval fabric of the building.

This much grander shrine to St Winifred at Holywell in Flintshire is still visited by pilgrims today.

Visitors to St Winifred's Well find the building hidden in a leafy hollow.

The cusped roof trusses clearly suggest that this little building was constructed for religious purposes.

ST WINIFRED'S WELL
SHROPSHIRE

1485

LATE MEDIEVAL RELIGION: THE CULT OF THE SAINTS

'More fair than all the vernal flowers/Embosom'd in the dales St Winifride in beauty bloom'd,/The rose of ancient Wales.' Hymn to St Winifred, *Westminster Hymnal* (1912).

Landmark's association with St Winifred comes through its rescue of a tiny timber-framed building in south Shropshire, dated by tree-ring analysis to 1485 and built above a holy spring that fills a plunge bath in front of it. It was described in 1602 as Woolston Chapel, after the village in which it stands. Details in the timber framing also reveal a building of both religious use and high status. A written record of the name of St Winifred's Well appears only in 1837, but almost certainly refers to a much older oral tradition.

This cult of the saints sheds its poetic enchantment across all the centuries of the Middle Ages, but the saints were never so well loved as during the fifteenth and early sixteenth centuries. The cult of St Winifred is a Petri dish that peculiarly captures all the colour, complexity and jeopardy of late medieval life. Life then for most, to borrow Thomas Hobbes' pithy phrase 200 years later, was 'nasty, brutish and short'. Almost 80 per cent

of people lived in villages and hamlets, up to half of them at subsistence level and chronically underemployed. Diets were unbalanced, and the food supply was precarious and dependent on the annual harvest. People of all classes were very vulnerable to pain, sickness and early death: the few trained physicians were generally avoided for doing more harm than good in their treatments. Most chose to rely instead on home remedies, wise women – and faith in miracles.

Religion was a channel through which supernatural power might relieve the human condition, and the saints occupied a position of 'neighbourliness and homeliness' between humankind and heaven. People hoped that veneration of these honoured friends would empower their intercession with God himself. This 'magical' role had pagan roots. Christian missionaries stressed the superior efficacy of their saints compared to pagan gods, and actively absorbed pagan practice and the worship of wells, trees and stones, simply modified to prompt association with a Christian saint rather than a pagan deity. Hundreds of 'magical' springs became 'holy wells', still employed for miraculous healing and decorated with flowers and offerings.

Such places offered hope, and there was much scope for embellishment. Pedlars and pilgrims spread tales of miraculous cures, and the laity travelled to give thanks or seek the intercession of their favourite saints, this earliest tourist

industry expressing and engaging a lay public eager for pious entertainment and wonder.

Winifred, Wenefrydde or, in Welsh, Gwenffrewi lived in the mid-sixth century in north Wales. Her cult united Welsh and English devotees, notwithstanding the continual growl of Welsh resentment at English rule. Her story was first recorded in John Mirk's *Festial* (*c.* 1403), a collection of sixty-four sermons for the major feasts of the church calendar written in English in the 1380s. Mirk was a canon of Lilleshall Abbey, which lies some 48 kilometres/30 miles west of Woolston.

In the *Festial*, a priest could find for 'alle the principale festis of the yere a schort sermon needful for hym to techyn and othur for to lerne'. The *Festial* ran to countless written copies and several printed editions until the very eve of the Reformation,

serving as the main source of sermon material for both religious and lay consumption.

Mirk records that Winifred was the daughter of Theuith, a mighty man in Wales and patron of a monk called Benouw, also later canonized. Under Benouw's teaching, Winifred wished to become a nun. One Sunday, her parents went to church to hear Benouw preach, but Winifred was ill and stayed at home, where she received a visit from Prince Caradoc, who tried to seduce her. Winifred fled, running towards the church, at which Caradoc tried to rape her, threatening to smite off her head if she would not yield. Winifred knelt down, saying, 'I would rather you killed me than defile my body, that I have vowed to keep in maidenhead to my Lord Jesus Christ as long as I live.' With a single stroke, Caradoc cut off her head, which tumbled downhill

St Winifred's Well today, the spring still bubbling up from beneath its walls.

Pilgrims bathing in St Winifred's Well would have seen these water outlet holes at upper and lower levels.

to the church to the consternation of all inside. Benouw saw Caradoc and prayed that God avenge his wickedness, whereupon Caradoc fell down dead and his body 'melted and vanished away and sank into the earth and his soul drowned in hell'. Benouw asked the congregation to pray with him that Winifred's promise to God might be fulfilled. He then set her head upon her body, and Winifred sat up, wiping the dust from her face and spoke, as whole and sound as she had been before. Where Winifred's head fell, 'anon sprang a fair well there, where none was seen before'.

Winifred became a nun under St Benouw's teaching, and in time abbess of her own convent in Gwtheryn, Conwy. She died in AD 636 and was buried at Basingwerk Abbey, Flintshire.

St Winifred was therefore always associated with holy springs. Today, she is chiefly remembered at the shrine in Holywell in north Wales. This shrine attracted pilgrims from 1115 but needed a papal indulgence in 1427 to rescue it from ruin. Around 1500, a very fine Late Perpendicular chapel with an open bath before it was built there. Royal sanction uniquely protected this shrine during the Dissolution, and it came to overshadow the little well chapel at Woolston. However, in earlier centuries, the cult was most closely associated with Shrewsbury Abbey, and this gives the Woolston St Winifred's Well a closer affinity with the story of the saint.

Shrewsbury Abbey was founded in 1083 without a patron saint to bear the monks' prayers to God, and the monks 'made of [this] grete mone'. In 1138, Prior Robert was sent to abduct Winifred's bones from their resting place in Basingwerk and bring them to Shrewsbury Abbey, an act not without controversy, although the abbey was allowed to keep the bones.

The future Henry V invoked St Winifred at the Battle of Shrewsbury in July 1403 and credited her with healing his head wound. He made a barefoot pilgrimage from Shrewsbury to her well, traditionally the Holywell one but more plausibly at Wooslton. Such royal endorsement was invaluable.

By 1485, the year the timber to build the Woolston shrine was felled, other strands come together. Firstly, in 1484, William Caxton, the first English printer, published *The Lyf of the Holy Blessid Vyrgyn Saynt Wenefryde*. Caxton had included an entry on Winifred in his *Golden Legend or Lives of the Saints* (1483), but the *Lyf* is his only known life of an individual saint. The version Caxton 'reduced into English' from Latin is thought to be an abridged version of Winifred's life by Prior Robert written in about 1140 – very shortly after the translation of her bones to Shrewsbury – and it provides new details of the St Winifred cult.

In particular, it records that it was decided to rest and wash the bones about 16 kilometres/10 miles from Shrewsbury, where a well gushed forth and where water 'yet runneth in a great course . . . and ever after the stones that lie and rest in that water been besprint as it were with drops of blood'. This probably records the origins of the Woolston St Winifred's Well.

Both Richard III, on the throne from 1483, and his queen, Anne Neville, were supporters of St Winifred, as was Sir William Stanley, who owned land in Woolston and whose arms also appear on the Holywell chapel. Consequently, money was forthcoming to construct a well-built chapel on this site, ancillary to Shrewsbury Abbey and a pilgrimage stop.

The private bath later became a public bathing place much frequented by local people. Ale houses grew up nearby, and there were rumours of promiscuous behaviour. Around 1755, use of the well was suppressed and the chapel became a courthouse. In the 1820s, this was converted to domestic use, and a chimney and bread oven inserted.

By the time Landmark bought St Winifred's Well in 1987, its timber frame was rickety and the brick panels that had replaced earlier wattle and daub were unstable. Landmark re-roofed it and replaced the brick infill with traditional split laths and a daub of lime and sand, cow hair and a few handfuls of dung.

St Winifred's Well embodies the complexity of the political, social and religious roles of such shrines, as well as the beliefs that underpinned them: 'Here miracles of might are wrought;/ Here all diseases fly;/Here see the blind, and speak the dumb,/ Who but in faith draw nigh.' **CS**

Many of the roof timbers had rotted badly and had to be replaced, but the main timber frame survived.

Breughel's *Peasant Dance* (1569) captures the enjoyment of all generations at parish celebrations.

The Priest's House is typical of church houses in standing near the south-west entrance of the parish church.

Church houses like the Priest's House were a source of pride to their parish, soundly built in the local style.

THE PRIEST'S HOUSE
DEVON

C. 1500

LATE MEDIEVAL RELIGION: CHURCH HOUSES

'There were no rates for the poor in my grandfather's day,' wrote Wiltshire antiquarian John Aubrey nostalgically in the late seventeenth century, '. . . the church ale at Whitsuntide did the business. In every parish is (or was) a church house to which belonged spits, crocks etc., utensils for dressing provisions. Here the housekeepers met, and were merry and gave their charity. The young people were there too, and had dancing, bowling, shooting at butts etc., the ancients sitting gravely by and looking on. All things were civil and without scandal.'

The Priest's House is one such church house, a well-built stone building on the west side of the churchyard of All Saints Church in Holcombe Rogus, on the Devon–Somerset border. Its name is misleading: rather than a priest's dwelling, it was built *c.* 1500 as a church house, and as such had a specific purpose.

Church houses (sometimes called parish or guild houses) sprang up in late medieval England between about 1450 and 1540, when the social influence and affluence of the parish church was at its height. They took a characteristic form and it is now generally accepted that there would have been a church house in most parishes across southern and central England.

Throughout the later Middle Ages, parishioners were responsible for the maintenance of the fabric and accoutrements of their parish church, and for this they had to raise money. Rather than relying on tithes or donations, this responsibility became the focus of communal entertainment. The biggest fundraisers were 'church ales', feasts to which the whole parish contributed. Originally, these ales were often held in the nave of the church itself (where there were as yet no pews) as the only building in the parish large enough to hold everyone. Through the fifteenth century, however, church authorities became opposed to such secular events being held in the church.

Church houses were built as an alternative venue. Most were purpose-built near the church, on manorial wasteland land or on a footprint given by a priest from his glebe (land entitlement), or by a monastery donating land to the secular parish. Most were built to the west, or south-west of the church.

Church houses were a source of pride to the parishes, who vied with each other to provide the best and most hospitable facilities. By their very nature, church houses are vernacular, traditional buildings, built according to local style and materials. However, they share various distinctive characteristics across the country. They were generally well constructed, and unusually large for an otherwise straightforward building. Some were built with a degree of embellishment. They have unexpectedly large rooms, two storeys, and large fireplaces

and chimneys for brewing and baking, at a period in which all of these were still far from typical of the average villager's dwelling. These large rooms were usually jettied in the case of timber-framed examples, and the upper room was generally open to the roof timbers. Often there was a separate external entrance for each storey.

Communal baking and brewing were done on the ground floor, while feasting took place on the floor above or an adjacent large room. For official church ales, malt, barley and wheat were collected by young men going from house to house and used to produce 'cakes' (bread) and ale. All were welcome, often bringing a small contribution to the feast, and paying a penny or two to get in. Funds could be further boosted by hiring out the brewing vessels, allowing local guilds to hold their feasts there, entertaining neighbouring parishes at Whitsuntide (the main celebration in the year) or providing lodging for visitors to the parish, whether for religious or craft purposes. The equipment for brewing and feasting can be traced through church inventories until well into the seventeenth century – trestles and benches, spits and cauldrons, trenchers and drinking bowls.

The function of church houses therefore became as much social as religious. Church ales took place for a wide variety of purposes, not just at Whitsuntide. They could also mark feast days of the parish saints, or the memory of a generous church donor. 'Bride ales' provided a wedding breakfast for poor couples, and other ales raised money for the poor and sick. 'Clerk ales' raised money to pay the wages of the parish clerk.

Church ales also provided a focus for folk traditions. Often, the costumes for May Games or Robin Hood plays were stored in the church house – at Bray in Berkshire were stored five garters with bells and four morris coats, a costume for Maid Marion, and a pair of breeches and a doublet for the fool. In Morebath, fees paid to the church by travelling players may well have gone for hire of the church house. At Dartington, also in Devon, there is even reference in 1566 to a 'tenyse courte' at the church house. A Whitsun ale in 1561 at Northill, Bedfordshire, invited ten parishes and laid on a minstrel, two fools, six morris men and some fireworks. Refreshments often went far beyond 'cakes and ale'. When St Mary's of Bungay in Suffolk held 'church ale games' for the district in the late 1560s, a typical

Today's cosy sitting room, with its large fireplace, panelling and moulded beams, was once used for parish gatherings.

A plate commemorating Landmark's twenty-fifth anniversary in 1990 stands on a window sill.

menu included eggs, butter, currants, pepper, saffron, veal, lamb, honey, cream, custards and pasties.

The ales, of course, were not always a model of decorum. A complaint lodged at Yeovil in 1607 describes how the parish had revived their Robin Hood play that year, with dancing and drinking around the church house going on into the small hours, the churchwardens allowing themselves to be carried on a cowlstaff (a pole used by two people to carry heavy vessels), to the great hilarity of all.

But this anticipates an era when church houses were under attack. In the 1530s, the English Reformation outlawed worship of images and candles lit before them. The purposes for which church houses existed were progressively undermined, even if their ales generally survived at first, by now the only means of raising money for church maintenance.

The still more radical Protestant reforms of the young Edward VI's advisors were a different matter. In November 1548, for example, the Commissioners for the West gave 'commandment unto the church wardens and other parishioners from henceforth to surcease from keeping any church ales, because it hath been declared unto us that many inconveniences hath come by them'. The churchwardens were still required to raise just as much money for the church's upkeep.

By the early seventeenth century, church ales risked being prosecuted. Church houses lay at the heart of the struggle for the soul of England's parishes that would eventually lead to civil war in the 1640s. As church ales died out, and as the parish church became less a communal institution than a tool to control behaviour, people had to gather elsewhere.

There are many examples of church houses becoming inns and alehouses; others remained in parish ownership and, as an extension of their original purpose in a different sense, became poorhouses or tenements. Others became schools. Rooms often continued to be used for parish meetings, though of a more serious kind than the ales.

The Priest's House became a private dwelling and, by Landmark's standards, was in relatively good condition when they took it on in 1984 – its Tudor builders had done their work well. Apart from rebuilding the north gable and two chimneys, the restoration was straightforward.

Church houses like the Priest's House (Landmark's Parish House is another) thus lay at the heart of the 'merrie England' of our collective folk memory. Sir Toby Belch's drunken outburst to puritanical killjoy Malvolio in Shakespeare's *Twelfth Night* – 'Dost thou think, because thou art virtuous, there shall be no more cakes and ale?' – is a phrase that evokes the centuries-old tradition embodied by church houses. **CS**

The church house in South Tawton, Devon, another fine example, is still in active parish use.

Long centuries of use can be read in the condition of the ancient fabric of the Priest's House.

A woodcut of 1502 depicting a medieval city under siege by an army of cavalry and foot soldiers. Cannon can be seen in the foreground.

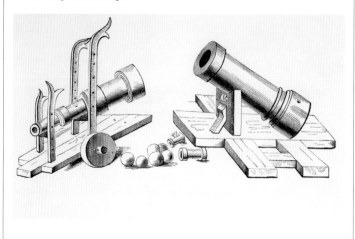

Two fifteenth-century cannon: one has a rolling carriage, the other is fixed. Kingswear Castle was built for cannon on flat, sledge-like carriages.

Kingswear Castle was positioned to protect the deep moorings of the Dart river. Two floors of cannon ports afforded a wide field of fire.

KINGSWEAR CASTLE
DEVON

1502

PROTECTING THE RIVER DART

Kingswear Castle is one of those rare buildings that actually changed English history; this and its sister fort, Dartmouth Castle, were the first castles in the country purpose-designed for cannon. The realization that if the correct combination of sulphur, charcoal and potassium nitrate (saltpetre) was ignited in a metal tube it could expel a heavy missile with devastating force sparked a revolution in warfare. The first image of a cannon in an English source dates to the 1320s, and over the fourteenth century they became important weapons of war. For the first century or two, cannon were a supplement to the traditional weapons of the longbow and crossbow. In the famous battles of the fifteenth century, among them Agincourt and Bosworth Field, large field cannon were used alongside archery and man-to-man fighting. The advent of this new technology spawned the infrastructure to support it. By 1461, the country's chief arsenal, the Tower of London, had a substantial gunpowder storehouse, and in the 1480s the Ordnance Office had been created, responsible for the supply of artillery and gunpowder.

The issue of what sort of buildings could best withstand gun attacks, while also discharging artillery fire themselves, became pressing. Before the rise of cannon, castles were built to repel arrows, staff weapons and the occasional siege engine, with high vertical walls pierced by thin arrow slits. At first these were simply adjusted to allow the new weapons to be used. Come the 1380s, keyhole slits – openings in walls that combined an arrow slit with a larger round hole through which a cannon could fire along fixed lines – were being created. But until the innovations at Dartmouth and Kingswear in the decade after 1480, the manoeuvrability of cannon was highly limited.

In the fifteenth century, there was still no permanent English army, just various royal guards and standing garrisons at potentially vulnerable places, among them Calais and Dover Castle. The Hundred Years' War was fought not by a centrally controlled royal force but by armed retainers raised by noblemen, and so towns or cities concerned about becoming targets of pirates or other attackers had to make their own arrangements. Particularly vulnerable were those on England's south coast, which was easily reached from France and Brittany.

The affluent towns on the River Dart, which flowed from its source high on Dartmoor into a sheltered estuary within a steep valley, were also concerned for their security from attack. They invested in their own protection and, from the 1460s, recognizing the importance of these works, the Crown also contributed.

In c. 1480, the mayor and burgesses of Dartmouth, Kingswear and the other settlements on the estuary began work on

A map of the Dart river and Torbay, Devon (1539–40) shows the cluster of fortifications established around this important deep-water harbour by the height of Henry VIII's reign.

Kingswear Castle before the Landmark Trust's restoration. The round tower had lost its windows and the building was in poor repair.

'a strong tower and bulwark of stone and lime' on the western bank of the river's mouth – that would become Dartmouth Castle. There had been buildings near the mouth of the river for some time but this new structure was to be right on the water's edge. On 1 August 1481, the towns made an agreement with the Crown that they would quickly complete the tower, 'keep it garnished with guns and artillery' and tie a great chain across the water to the eastern bank. For this service to national defence they received a lump sum of £30 added to their regular annual fee of £30. After Henry Tudor's invasion of 1485 the agreement was renewed, with the fee increased to £40. During the decade from 1491 a second tower or 'bulwerke', Kingswear Castle, was erected by the mayor and burgesses, also hard on the water's edge on the eastern side of the river. The positions were not new, but Dartmouth and Kingswear castles were remarkable for the novel way they accommodated cannon.

A square tower three storeys high, Kingswear is positioned obliquely to the river, so its southern and western sides command the water on the seaward and landward sides respectively. Built into the 1.5-metre/5-foot-thick walls on both storeys were large, splayed gun ports, in which a cannon could be placed and manoeuvred to aim. The ground floor of Kingswear was designed to accommodate cannon, and has nine gun ports on the three sides (west, south and east), allowing for a huge field of fire. Oak shutters sealed off the openings when not in use, while wooden uprights probably stood in the slots in the sills to prevent the cannon from recoiling. The gun ports at Kingswear and Dartmouth are almost level with the floor, built for cannon mounted on low, flat sledges rather than the wheeled carriages that would come later. The first floor served as both a second battery with further gun ports and as a guard room for a small garrison of gunners, containing both a fireplace and a latrine.

In 1522, Thomas Howard, second Earl of Surrey, visited the Dart estuary to see if the river might provide suitable winter mooring for royal ships. He wrote to Henry VIII from the royal warship, the *Mary Rose*, moored in the Dart that they 'never saw a goodlier haven after all our opinions. At the entry there is a blockhouse of stone with an old castle on the same side [Dartmouth] and another old castle on the other side besides another blockhouse [Kingswear]'. The harbour was ideal, and he was sending the Mayor of Dartmouth, 'a wise man', to London to tell the king about the virtues of the haven first-hand.

The early years of the sixteenth century saw a fundamental shift in the way coastal defence was managed, from being a local matter to one that was organized and funded centrally. This was brought about by a coincidence of circumstances: the annexation of Brittany to France, which created a single strong southern neighbour; Henry VIII's thirst for war, which made foreign attacks far more likely; and England's break with the Roman Catholic Church. As a consequence, Henry VIII embarked on a major campaign of building coastal forts, which adopted and adapted the innovations first seen on the Dart. In March 1539, a committee was appointed to supervise the building of forts and blockhouses all along the south coast from Poole to Penzance, part of a major programme of fortifying the whole south coast. Thirty artillery forts were built in under a decade.

By the 1570s, Dartmouth Castle was thought suitable for 'four pieces of ordnance royal' with brass recommended over iron because of the salty air. But by this time, technological advances meant that cannon could now fire far greater distances, making it unnecessary to have two forts on the Dart as the river could be defended from one. Kingswear's importance therefore fell, like that of many fortifications throughout Britain; but the outbreak of civil war in 1642 made it suddenly important again. Dartmouth declared for the king and its many defences, including Kingswear, were swiftly repaired. The following year, Charles I's nephew, Prince Maurice, successfully seized the town for the Royalists and during the course of the struggle Kingwear was severely damaged, the roof, 'togeather with ye Plattforme and all ye Tymber worke in ye Castle beeinge burnt ffire whch is alledged happonnd by accident'. Come the Restoration the castle had to be extensively repaired, at which time the roof, until then made of tarred timber, was replaced with lead and this then became the principal gun deck.

Kingswear was abandoned altogether in the following century and remained unloved until it was bought by Charles Seale Hayne in 1855. With funds to spare and a sense of romance, he set about restoring it as a summer residence. He added the small round tower with its heraldic corbels and replaced the flat leads of the castle itself with a conical roof. Inside he divided the ground floor into a kitchen and pantry, the second floor into bedrooms and dressing rooms and added the plaster ceiling decoration. After his death, a sequence of owners made further additions. In 1987, the Landmark Trust bought Kingswear, undertook extensive research on its original form, and, informed by this, reinstated much of the original arrangement, revealing the important gun ports, restoring correct floor levels and reinstating a lead roof that now provides a viewing deck over the deep waters of the River Dart. **AK**

Kingswear Castle on the east bank of the Dart estuary, with its sister fort, Dartmouth, on the far western bank.

A detached tower, added to Kingswear by Charles Seale Hayne in the late 1850s, now serves as a bedroom.

The ruins of Saddell Abbey; the Cistercian monastery was abandoned by the end of the fifteenth century.

King James IV of Scotland (1473–1513) whose determination to bring Kintyre to heel led to the construction of Saddell Castle.

SADDELL CASTLE
ARGYLL AND BUTE

1508

CRUSHING THE LORDS OF THE ISLES

In 1586, William Camden described the Mull of Kintyre as 'a promontory, which ... thrusteth itself forth with so great a desire toward Ireland (betwixt which and it there is a narrow sea scarce thirteene miles over) as if it would conjoin itself'. This pulling away from mainland Scotland was not just a cartographical curiosity but a political reality. The story of Saddell Castle is that of the violent struggle at the end of the Middle Ages between the Stuart kings and the fiercely independent lords of the Western Isles.

Saddell Castle stands on the breathtakingly beautiful eastern shore of Kintyre and was founded in 1508. The lovely coastal estate around it was formerly part of the lands of the Cistercian abbey founded here in 1160 by monks who sought just the remoteness that the position offered. By the early sixteenth century, however, all monastic life here had ceased and the lands lay fallow, presenting an opportunity that was seized upon by the agents of King James IV of Scotland.

Since the mid-1490s, James IV (1473–1513), still only in his early twenties, had been trying to bring the unruly people of the Western Isles to heel. The largely low-lying Kintyre peninsula,

some 48 kilometres/30 miles long, loomed large in his sights as both financially and tactically valuable. Its fertile soil was productive for arable crops and pasture, while it occupied a strategically crucial position in waters between the separate countries of Scotland, England and Ireland. In 1493, James IV took the title 'Lord of the Isles', which had long denoted almost separate sovereignty, from its holder, John MacDonald. As part of his crackdown he established new royal castles in Kintyre, among them one on the site of what later became Campbeltown, and ensured the remaining strongholds were in the hands of his people. The defiance of the clansmen of Kintyre was considerable, however, and when the king sailed from the peninsula in 1494 he witnessed from his departing ship John MacDonald attacking the castle and the royal governor being executed, strung up from the castle walls.

It was as part of the campaign of trying to entrench royal authority in Kintyre that the king negotiated with the Roman Catholic Church for the abandoned estate of Saddell Abbey to be granted to the Bishop of Argyll. Significantly the grant, which was made with the church's agreement on 1 January 1508, came with authority to build 'castles and towers' for the defence of the land. Within four years, Bishop David Hamilton had raised the handsome tower house of Saddell Castle.

The obvious position for the castle would have been that occupied by the abbey, 0.4 kilometres/¼ mile back from the

Saddell Castle was sited to assert the authority of the king and bishop of Argyll to those passing along the peninsula's south-eastern flank.

Archibald Campbell, first Marquis of Argyll and chief of the Campbell clan, took over control of Kintyre from his father, Archibald, seventh Earl of Argyll.

The original kitchen is now the dining room. The heraldic panels on the ceiling are late nineteeth-century additions.

shore. There the tumbledown abbey walls provided a convenient supply of cut stones, while the sheltered and verdant position was watered by a freshwater burn. Instead, the castle was placed prominently in an exposed new position almost on the water's edge. From the first, the bishop's building covered a generous six floors. The two lower storeys were not residential but contained a well, a small prison and unheated vaulted chambers for storing goods and arms. The middle floor housed a substantial kitchen and hall for the bishop to entertain, and the scale and quality of the bishop's work can be clearly seen in the huge surviving kitchen fireplace. The two upper floors were residential, each containing a comfortable apartment. At the top of the castle, garrets accommodated members of the bishop's extensive household. Around the base of the tower was a further wall, making the building both statuesque and defensive. Standing tall and proud with elaborate decorative detailing on its roof line, the new castle commanded the landscape for the main sea-borne traffic from mainland Scotland with strength and splendour.

But the story of Saddell would not stay peaceful for long. After the death of Bishop Hamilton in 1523 the castle changed hands and ended up in the ownership of the MacDonalds, and so its days of calm were numbered. The devastation came this time not from mainland Scotland, but from Thomas Radcliffe, third Earl of Sussex, the agent of Queen Elizabeth I of England as Lord Lieutenant of Ireland. With strict instructions to bring Ireland under full English control, Sussex targeted the MacDonalds who had long moved across the 21 kilometres/ 13 miles between Kintyre and Ireland and who had expanded into Antrim. On 14 September 1558 Radcliffe sailed to Kintyre and unleashed a ferocious and bloody attack; as he put it, 'I londed and burned the hole countrye.' Five days later he burned 13 kilometres/8 miles of southern Kintyre, including James MacDonald's 'chief howse', Saddell, which he found 'a fayre pyle and stronge' but left devastated.

In the end it was the Scottish king's use of the powerful Campbell family based in Inveraray at the northern tip of Kintyre that finally succeeded in bringing the peninsula under Edinburgh's control. In 1599, Archibald Campbell, seventh Earl of Argyll, was granted authority over Kintyre and, despite the bitter opposition of the MacDonalds, was determined to enforce it. In 1609, he started building a major new stronghold at Lochhead, 19 kilometres/12 miles south of Saddell, a settlement which would soon be renamed Campbeltown in recognition of its overlord. Campbell began the systematic process of the colonization, or 'plantation', of Kintyre, establishing his authority through the settling here of loyal tenants, a policy that would find real force in the time of his son, the steely Marquis of Argyll. As head of the fiercely Presbyterian Covenanting party in the 1650s, the marquis sought both to keep Kintyre in his control and to further his religious cause by settling a series of prominent Lowlanders on the peninsula.

First among the new Lowland settlers was the Ayrshire laird William Ralston, a friend of the Marquis of Argyll who held even more stringent religious views. In 1650 Ralston was granted the Saddell estate, with the old lands of Saddell Abbey still attached. Ralston set at once about repairing and refurbishing Saddell Castle, which still remained in a sad, perhaps ruinous, condition after the Earl of Sussex's raids. He ordered the masonry to be repaired, new timber floors to be laid and a new roof of 'firr and sklait'. The windows were to be glazed and given iron bars, and all was to be done and 'perfyted at the sight of craftsmen of skill' by 1 November 1652. The external appearance of the castle today, including the enlarged window openings, was much as it was when Ralston's work was complete.

While Ralston's line would run dry, Saddell Castle passed into the hands of a branch of the Campbell family, and remained in Campbell hands for the two centuries that followed. In the 1770s, the family abandoned the castle for the fashionable new Saddell House close by, and the castle became a historical curiosity. Despite a restoration in the late nineteenth century, the castle by the mid-twentieth century was badly decayed, and in 1971 was described 'derelict and rapidly becoming ruinous'.

The Landmark Trust bought Saddell Castle in 1975 and its future brightened. Following extensive repairs the castle was made habitable once again, with the arrangement of the accommodation not dissimilar to the sixteenth-century configuration. Since then the Landmark Trust has restored five further buildings on the Saddell estate, among them the Georgian Saddell House, three cottages along the shore and the gate lodge. The castle remains the heart of the estate and, ancient and imposing, its position and aspect are very much as they were 500 years ago. **AK**

The date-stone over the door to the castle, renewed in recent times, commemorates its foundation in 1508.

Saddell House, which also belongs to the Landmark Trust, was built to replace the sixteenth-century castle in the 1770s.

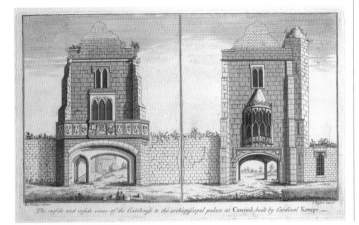

Cawood gatehouse in 1736, the earliest images of the entrance to the archiepiscopal palace.

Cardinal Thomas Wolsey by an unknown artist, *c.* 1520. Cawood was the scene of his arrest for high treason in November 1530.

The gate passage out through which Cardinal Wolsey rode on his mule after his arrest.

CAWOOD CASTLE
NORTH YORKSHIRE

1529

THE DOWNFALL OF CARDINAL WOLSEY

Approximately 16 kilometres/10 miles south of York, next to an ancient crossing over the River Ouse, stands the village of Cawood. Here, skirted by attractive streets, are the remaining buildings and grounds of Cawood Castle, palace of the Archbishops of York, princes of the medieval church. It was here on a cold November day in 1530 that the last and most powerful of all the medieval churchmen, Cardinal Wolsey, had his downfall, tumbling from royal grace, as one contemporary put it, 'like Lucifer'.

The Archbishops of York certainly already had a substantial house at Cawood in the thirteenth century, and probably had done so from the 1180s, if not earlier. On 1 March 1272, Archbishop Walter Gifford and his successors had been granted a licence to fortify their 'house of Cawode Co. York', and over the following 150 years, a series of wealthy and ambitious prelates added to and elaborated the palace. As part of this, new 'towers' were erected in the 1370s and a new hall in the early fifteenth century. The palace buildings were ranged around an enclosed courtyard on the south bank of the river. The main entrance was not on the river front, however, but looked south addressing the route from the Great North Road (the modern A1) towards the city of York.

Immediately south of the buildings was a large area of formal gardens with walks, avenues and ponds – it is now known as the Castle Garth.

Playing second fiddle in the English church only to his more senior episcopal colleague at Canterbury, the Archbishop of York exercised real power and influence, and the position was held by a series of dynamic and ambitious men in tandem with the highest political office. Among them was John Kempe, who became Archbishop of York in 1425 and was created Lord Chancellor of England by Henry VI the following year. His status within the wider Roman Catholic church was cemented when in 1438 he was made a cardinal. The eye-watering collection of offices he accumulated was given visual expression in the grand new entrance range he commissioned for Cawood Castle in around 1440. The centrepiece of this new work was a three-storey gatehouse built of high-quality magnesian limestone, together with a substantial and splendid brick range running east. On the ground floor of the gatehouse was a wide entrance for vehicles and a narrower pedestrian access, while large, comfortable chambers with highly ornate windows were created on the two floors above. Between the ground and first floors on the exterior of the building, broad bands of carved heraldry advertised Kempe's status. The royal arms took central position on the entrance facade, flanked by badges of the Kempe family and the see (episcopal territory) of York.

The restored windows above the gate reflect the high quality of the original palace, now demolished.

The crossed keys of the see of York and arms of Archbishop Kempe are visible above the gate of the interior courtyard.

On the inner front, a large cardinal's hat and the Kempe falcon dominate, with the royal insignia ancillary.

While Cawood witnessed occasions of great ceremony and consequence throughout the Middle Ages, none quite rival the events of 1529–30 for pathos and political significance. In the early years of the reign of King Henry VIII, another ambitious clergyman had combined the highest political and church offices. From very modest beginnings indeed, Thomas Wolsey, the son of a butcher and grazier of Ipswich, rose to spectacular wealth and power through an unstoppable combination of ambition and ability. Barely five years after the young king's accession to the throne Wolsey had, like Kempe before him, been made Archbishop of York, a Cardinal of the Roman Catholic Church, and Lord Chancellor of England. In his mid-forties, Wolsey became the single most powerful person in the kingdom after the king himself, and through his complete application to the king's wishes and monumental hard work,

he towered over English politics for almost twenty years. But his power, his reach and his appetites for material magnificence and grand enterprises made him many enemies. When Henry VIII finally lost faith in Wolsey, furious at his minister's inability to secure the divorce that would allow him to marry Anne Boleyn, Wolsey's enemies descended on their former task master. Dismissed from political office and disgraced in the winter of 1528, he narrowly avoided arrest or incarceration and in April 1529 withdrew to York, where a decade after being made archbishop, he finally took up residence in the palace at Cawood.

Wolsey passed under the stone gatehouse at Cawood at the end of September 1529, travelling by mule and accompanied as always by a great entourage. He set in train an extensive programme of repairs and improvements to the castle – which saw 300 'artificers and labourers' at work on the buildings – and began to see that life away from court had its attractions. His taste for lavish objects and occasions had not deserted him, and

he began planning a magnificent ceremony of installation as archbishop. But on 1 November 1530, as he sat down to dine in the great hall, he saw a glimmer of doom. His sumptuous silver cross was, as usual, placed on the dining table, but as a visitor bowed to his host it fell, striking the guest and drawing blood. Wolsey was greatly troubled by what he took as a terrible omen and quickly withdrew to his bedchamber. And well he might, for as the cross fell, William Walsh, one of Henry VIII's gentlemen of the privy chamber, was bringing catastrophic news.

A week later, dinner was once again under way at Cawood when a great clattering of hooves filled the courtyard. Walsh and the Earl of Northumberland entered the castle. Wolsey was dining privately in his first-floor chamber, and hearing of the earl's arrival assumed it was a social visit. Bustling down to greet the earl with effusive warmth, he took him into his own bedchamber to change his clothes and promised him a handsome dinner. The two were near a window by the fireplace when, in the words of Wolsey's gentleman usher, George Cavendish, 'the earl, trembling said with a very faint and soft voice unto my lord, laying his hand upon his arm "My lord", quoth he, "I arrest you of high treason."'

The cardinal, astonished and devastated, was to be taken to London for trial for intriguing against the king. When Cavendish came to him in his chamber, he found the great prelate a broken man. His words were ones of grief at leaving all those who had served him so faithfully for so long, and were spoken with such sincerity that, in Cavendish's own words, 'it would have caused the flintiest heart to have relented and burst for sorrow'. The following day, Wolsey asked to be allowed to say goodbye to his household. Northumberland reluctantly agreed, and in the Cawood great chamber each in turn of the cardinal's servants came forward and knelt at his master's feet to receive his blessing. With the winter light fading, the visibly enfeebled cardinal was helped onto his mule in the sharp air. As he approached the closed gates, the porter opened them for his master for the last time, and the party rode out through the crowd, bound for London.

The sorry cavalcade would never reach its destination. With Wolsey refusing to eat, and weak with misery and illness, he struggled to keep upright on his mule. When they arrived at Leicester Abbey, he told the abbot that he came to leave his bones among them, and so it would be. The cardinal, pale and

The east range of the castle, built from brick, butts up to the three-storey limestone gatehouse.

A view of Cawood Castle as it appeared in the nineteenth century.

spent, told his jailer that if only he had served God as diligently as he had the king, then he would not now be abandoned. As the morning light filled his chamber there he lost the power of speech and while the clock was striking eight, his troubled breath finally ceased. It was the end of an epoch. Within seven years, Henry VIII would have broken from the Catholic Church, begun the dissolution of the monasteries and have both married and executed the second wife he so sought.

Cawood Castle would remain an archiepiscopal palace until the 1640s. Of the palace buildings, the gatehouse and east range are now all that remains, almost all the other structures having been destroyed or dismantled at the end of the Civil War. The gatehouse stayed in use as an episcopal court for a time, for which purpose the attached staircase was built, but by the late twentieth century had fallen into very poor repair. Despite being Grade I listed and scheduled ancient monuments, the remaining buildings were in a dangerous condition, in divided ownership and had been obscured by a series of farm buildings. In 1985, the Landmark Trust bought the gatehouse and the east range, reunited them, undertook an extensive programme of repair, and three years later Cawood Castle was opened to visitors. **AK**

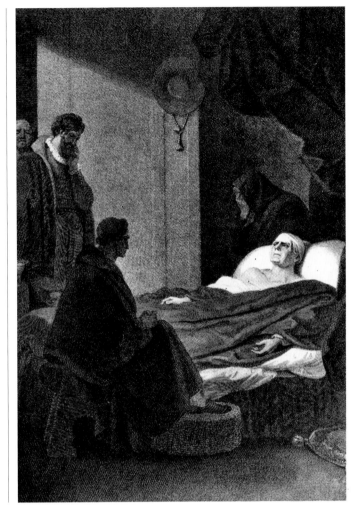

Cardinal Wolsey's death at Leicester Abbey, en route from Cawood to the Tower of London, was later much romanticized by artists.

The interior of the brick east range of Cawood Castle.

FORGING IDENTITIES

1534–1660

The Dissolution of the Monasteries opened up many new possibilities, not just of worship but also in the organization of the countryside. The personality of the monarch still set the tone, but increasingly assertive parliaments were bargaining for legislation in return for authorizing taxes. Learning flourished and elite architecture flowered into wondrous forms, while prosperous yeoman discovered chimneys and stairs. Union with Wales became a fact, and England and Scotland came to share a monarch. Religious fragmentation eventually brought the country to blows and saw a king beheaded and a republic declared; but this died with its architect, Oliver Cromwell. Landmark has preserved rare reminders of an assured aristocratic order that flourished, then disintegrated, in these years.

The Castle of Park in Dumfries and Galloway, built in 1590 and then improved in the eighteenth century, was the home of a Jacobean laird.

Laughton Place was once a sprawling manor house, of which only the Tudor tower now survives.

Laughton Place's tower, unstable and vandalized before the Landmark Trust effected its restoration.

The tower at Laughton Place was not built to be free-standing; great brick buttresses now support the building.

LAUGHTON PLACE
EAST SUSSEX

1535

SURVIVING VESTIGE OF A TUDOR MANOR

When the Landmark Trust acquired the Tudor tower at Laughton Place in 1978, every floor within the building had collapsed, all the windows had long since been smashed and the structure was dangerously subsiding on marshy ground. The fact that the building was standing at all was extraordinary. Everything else on the site had been demolished in 1938–9, with the tower itself only spared the same fate by the outbreak of the Second World War, when it served as an observation post.

The immediate setting of Laughton, which stands in an open landscape 10 kilometres/6 miles east of Lewes in East Sussex, is quite different from the site on which the tower was erected in the year 1535, at the very height of the reign of Henry VIII. Never intended to be a stand-alone structure, the tower was built onto a large existing house, the principal residence of the Pelham family, which dominated a rectangular moated enclosure, surrounded by gardens, barns and outbuildings.

The Pelham family's connection with Laughton began in the last years of the fourteenth century when the powerful John of Gaunt, uncle of the young King Richard II, gave his talented retainer John Pelham of nearby Warbleton the constableship of Pevensey Castle on the East Sussex coast. Pelham's devotion extended to Gaunt's son, Henry Bolingbroke, and when Bolingbroke invaded England and deposed Richard in 1399, he held Pevensey Castle against forces loyal to Richard. Writing from Pevensey during the siege, Pelham assured Bolingbroke, who he considered the 'dearest and best beloved of all earthly lords', of his loyalty. After Richard II's capture and before his tragic end at Pontefract Castle, Pelham acted for a while as his jailer. The rewards Bolingbroke, now King Henry IV, gave for such steadfastness were substantial: Pelham was knighted on the eve of Henry's coronation, made the king's sword-bearer and received grants of lands in Sussex such that he rivalled the powerful earls of Arundel.

Among these was Laughton Place which, when it was granted to Sir John Pelham in 1401, had already been a substantial property for centuries. Mentioned in the *Domesday Book*, Laughton had belonged to the Queen, Eleanor of Provence, in the 1260s, at which time the buildings comprised a stone hall and chamber, a chapel, queen's chamber and various other buildings – all reached by a gatehouse and drawbridge over the moat.

The builder of the surviving tower at Laughton Place was, however, a Tudor man: Sir William Pelham. Born here in the late 1480s, he rose from a position as a senior gentry figure in Sussex to more elevated circles through highly advantageous

marriages into the families of Henry VIII's close friends. His first wife, Mary Carew, was the niece of the king's favourite and jousting companion, Sir Nicholas Carew, who was a landholder and sheriff of Sussex. After her death, William married again, this time the daughter of Henry's trusted friend and Knight of the Garter, William, Lord Sandys. This illustrious new connection propelled Pelham further upwards. He was knighted in the mid-1520s and then in 1527 was made his father-in-law's deputy as Captain of the English town of Guînes in the Pas-de-Calais, which Sandys was unable to exercise in person as his own position of Lord Chamberlain kept him at court. It was probably in that capacity that Sandys secured Pelham a place at one of the most spectacular occasions of the reign – the coronation of the heavily pregnant Anne Boleyn. Sir William was one of the 'knights and gentlemen' who participated in the coronation banquet in Westminster Hall.

It was while moving in these fêted circles in the 1520s and early 1530s that Sir William Pelham encountered the new vogue for terracotta in architectural decoration that would become a defining feature of his work at Laughton Place. Terracotta was not in itself anything new; made from fine clay rich in iron that turned a deep red when kiln-fired at high temperatures, it had been widely used in the ancient world. However, partly due to this association with classical antiquity, it enjoyed a renaissance of its own in fifteenth-century Italy, which soon spread. In about 1507 the Florentine sculptor Pietro Torrigiano came to London to work for King Henry VII, going on to make the beautiful terracotta busts of which his effigy of the king himself is the best known. But it was the powerful prelate Thomas Wolsey who first introduced classically inspired terracotta as architectural embellishment in England. The long gallery that Wolsey built at Hampton Court in 1515–16 was richly ornamented externally with terracotta pilasters, egg-and-tongue mouldings and a riot of other loosely classical motifs. This quickly took off, and for the next twenty years many leading court figures, including the king's brother-in-law, the Duke of Suffolk, and Lord Sandys, commissioned terracotta embellishments on their own houses.

In the early 1530s, a man of consequence (able to provide fifty men to help put down the northern rebellion of 1536) but with court connections rather than offices, Pelham turned his

A painted terracotta bust of Henry VII by the Italian sculptor Pietro Torrigiani, made in 1509–11.

The decorative terracotta on the window sills and reveals of Laughton Place express a fleeting high fashion for the material that occurred just before the Reformation.

attention to his establishment at Laughton. In that year he built onto his house what now stands alone, a four-storey brick tower with a chamber on each floor. The first floor could be reached only from the body of the house and formed part of the suite of polite rooms there. The two upper chambers of the tower, each with a fireplace and windows on two sides, formed handsome prospect rooms overlooking Pelham's gardens and park, and were accessed by a spiral brick staircase from outside.

To build a residential tower onto an existing house was not in itself unusual, but what was remarkable about the work at Laughton was its use throughout the exterior detailing of terracotta. The window surrounds and mullions, the low plinth around the building's base, the decorative cusping below the parapet and the door into the main house are all dark red terracotta. These, like other instances of architectural terracotta, were made by pressing fine clay into plaster moulds bearing the 'negative' of the design, which were then fired in kilns at 800°C/1472°F. The moulding details at Laughton are a characteristic medley of conventional heraldic devices and personal cyphers, and more avant-garde renaissance elements, including urns, ribbon and pilasters.

The extent of Sir William Pelham's work was further revealed when in the summer of 1984 the Landmark Trust dredged the moat at Laughton Place. Stretches of sixteenth-century brick retaining wall were discovered, the remains of three brick bridges onto the site, and the footings of a series of octagonal brick turrets that punctuated the walls. In addition, an assortment of discarded objects – Bellarmine stoneware jars, clay pipes and shards of fourteenth-century pots – attested to life on the site in the Middle Ages.

Sir William died in 1538, his tower complete but the moat walls only part-built. By the end of the century, his heirs had built a new house within the park that Sir William had created at nearby Halland, and Laughton Place became a farm. It was still such when inherited by Henry Pelham, prime minister to George II from 1743. It was he who decided that the house must either be repaired or rebuilt, and his wishes were realized by his executors soon after 1760. The architect, one Mr White, made the tower the central element of a gently Gothick building with both battlements and pediment. The demolition of this work in the 1930s left the tower, which it had helped support, alone and in danger. The Landmark Trust undertook a major programme of repair and the re-floored, re-roofed and restored building opened for bookings in 1981. On its brick walls the pediment of the Georgian rebuilding remains, as do scars of the earlier houses, each, like the tower itself, ghosts of the buildings that once stood on this ancient site. **AK**

The curtains at Laughton Place, printed with the 'Pelham Buckle'.

The spectacular brick staircase leads to prospect rooms in the Tudor tower.

Henry VIII sits foursquare at the head of the Valor Ecclesiasticus. This decree set the Dissolution in train.

The irreverent humour of fifteenth-century masons is glimpsed in this waterspout on Woodspring's tower.

The fan vaulting in the former crossing evokes the splendour of the priory church before Thomas Cromwell's men arrived.

WOODSPRING PRIORY
SOMERSET

1537

THE DISSOLUTION OF THE MONASTERIES

'We are, by the sufferance of God, King of England; and the Kings of England in times past never had any superior but God.' Henry VIII's confident assurance as he seized Supremacy of the Church of England in 1534 was the prologue to the most wanton campaign of architectural destruction ever to occur in peacetime England. When Henry took the radical step of declaring himself head of the newly constituted Church of England, breaking with the Pope in Rome forever, England's monasteries became, at a stroke, an anomaly; irrelevant outposts of an alien religion. Woodspring Priory, near Worle in Somerset, was just one of hundreds of monastic sites left empty and desecrated.

Conflict between church and state was nothing new in the 1530s. Woodspring itself was a result of another such clash of wills. It was founded c. 1210 by William de Courtenay, grandson of Reginald Fitzurse. Fitzurse was one of the knights who acted upon Henry II's cry of frustration about his recalcitrant Archbishop of Canterbury and erstwhile friend, Thomas à Becket. 'Will no one rid me of this turbulent priest?' Henry is said to have cried out in 1170. Fitzurse and his companions took

him at his word and slew Becket in the nave of Canterbury Cathedral, to Henry's immediate regret. De Courtenay founded Woodspring Priory in penitence for his grandfather's part in the act. Becket, canonized in 1173, was patron saint of Woodspring Priory, his martyrdom depicted on its seal.

There was much about the medieval Roman Catholic Church to frustrate the state. It had its own parallel law courts. The cult of the chantries, under which souls might only be released from Purgatory to enter Heaven by the saying of masses for the deceased, encouraged ever-greater endowments by the wealthy. It is estimated that between 35 and 50 per cent of all English land was in the hands of the church by 1530, even if much of this wealth was used in a glorious flowering of ecclesiastical art and literature. Like so many, Woodspring Priory was at its zenith by 1500, enormous wealth embedded in its lofty church with fine tower, an infirmary, great barn, cloisters, refectory, prior's lodging and lands around, all in support of just ten Augustinian canons.

This ever-greater concentration of such resources in a parallel institution ruled from Rome arguably carried the inevitable seeds of its own destruction: the Crown, ever short of cash for warfare and its own extravagance, was bound to cast covetous eyes on such wealth. In 1414, Henry V had suppressed all 'alien' priories, outposts of parent houses on the Continent. Another Landmark, Wilmington Priory in East Sussex, was

one such, its very existence doubly suspect during Henry V's war with France.

What was new in the 1530s, however, was the gathering pace of the Protestant Reformation. This provided the intellectual underpinning and alternative religious conviction to justify sweeping away the older religion, increasingly seen as superstitious and obstructive in the individual's relationship with God. If a person stood in direct personal relationship with God as the reformers believed, there was no longer any need for priestly intercession with God, nor belief that the fate of a person's soul in the afterlife depended upon prayers said on Earth, nor efficacy in the worship of the saints and their relics. True, the Pope in Rome had also become an inconvenient obstacle to Henry VIII's desire to divorce Catherine of Aragon to marry Anne Boleyn, but Henry himself had long been a reformer, and so too were the men with whom he chose to surround himself.

Such were Thomas Cranmer, Archbishop of Canterbury, and Thomas Cromwell, administrator supreme who in January 1535 was appointed Vice-general and Vice-regent in Spirituals –

unprecedented power over the church for a layman under the king as Supreme Head. Cranmer and Cromwell had control over all ecclesiastical patronage, and they soon packed the bishops' bench with fellow reformers. In 1532, the Commons' Supplication declared that only laws made or formally received in England had any validity, further marginalizing institutions controlled from Rome. Moreover, the transfer of church taxes to the crown as new Head of the Church meant that a reliable assessment was needed of the assets upon which its new revenue would be based. In January 1535, Cromwell issued commissions for a great valuation of all ecclesiastical property, the *Valor Ecclesiasticus*.

In just six months, Cromwell's four ruthless inquisitors visited all the monasteries in the country. Visitations (or inspections) were nothing new to the monasteries, except that they were usually carried out by the bishops. This time there was a hidden agenda. Standards were ruthlessly applied: there was no great increase in the abuses uncovered, but unrealistically strict observance of the orders' own rules was required. The intention was to end not mend the monastic

The prior's lodgings became a farmhouse that extended even into the church itself, piercing its roof with incongruous chimneys.

houses, almost as much in sorrow as in anger, and to encourage their voluntary dissolution. Parliament was provided with plenty of evidence that much was amiss, and in January 1536, an act was passed to suppress all monastic houses with income of less than £200 a year. One of these was Woodspring Priory.

The process of dissolution was in fact executed everywhere with great efficiency, but also with unexpected humanity and regard for existing property rights and tenure within the monastic lands, most of which were already leased to yeomen or gentry. About a third of these 300 or so smaller houses gained a reprieve by paying for exemption. Of the rest, the monks were pensioned off or, for now, sent to larger houses of their order. Their personal goods were guaranteed them, and the state paid the monasteries' debts. Cromwell was experimenting in dissolution by agreement, 'seeing how horrible this kind of religion is, and how odious to the wiser sort of people'. The doctrinal underpinning resulted in far more violence to the architecture than to the people involved, still witnessed at Woodspring by the flat, defaced remnants of the saints' statues on the west front.

A false calm followed for eighteen months, in part due to the Pilgrimage of Grace, a show of resistance to the dismantling of the old religion in the North, but even this was dismissed by many as the protest of a backward and superstitious part of the country. It seems contemporaries had long ceased to care about the monasteries' spiritual values, and the monks had become too few to carry out the duties their rules involved. The monasteries behaved like any other landowner, efficiently exploiting their lands, and were therefore regarded as such by the populace. Full of worldliness and dulled by routine, the monasteries had lost all, or nearly all, of their meaning. Their fall was mourned by few – at least at the time. More traumatic to the populace was Cromwell's men's doctrinal wrecking progress through the country, defacing saints' images in stone and painted wood, destroying rood screens, locking up holy wells 'thatt none schall enter to washe [in] them'.

In December 1537 came a breakthrough, when the great priory at Lewes in East Sussex was persuaded to surrender. By 1540, all 800 religious houses had been dissolved and the crown was £90,000 a year better off. Some 9,000 monks and an unknown number of lay attendants and servants had been cast out. It must have been hateful and terrible for those involved, yet there was little or no resistance. Even Catholic historians like Eamon Duffy, who may regret the passing of the old religion, hold with regard to the monasteries that 'traditionalist outrage . . . was muted'.

The grandson of one of Becket's assassins founded Woodspring Priory in expiation of his grandfather's deed.

Thomas Cromwell (1485–1540), son of a blacksmith, rose to be Henry VIII's most trusted adviser and mastermind of the Dissolution.

The crown's redistribution of the monastic lands was swift, sold to the upwardly mobile of the Tudor period. Many an abbot or prior's lodging became the core of a great house, as at Warden Abbey in Bedfordshire, another building rescued by the Landmark Trust. The new order became firmly embedded in the self-interest of the landowning classes, who also had no compunction in raiding the monastic ruins for the building materials for their new great houses. Sometimes local communities intervened, as at Tewskesbury, where the town bought the great abbey to become its parish church. The former Abbey Gatehouse there is now also in Landmark's care, another remnant of this ancient upheaval left stranded by modern life.

Like most old buildings, monastic structures not plundered for stone proved ever-adaptable. Woodspring Priory is particularly remarkable in having had the body of the church itself adapted as a house in the 1570s. Its chancel was demolished as perhaps still too sacred to contemplate living in, but the crossing and north aisle were colonized for domestic spaces. Incongruous later chimneys still pierce the roof, proving that church conversions are nothing new.

By the time Landmark arrived at Woodspring in 1969, it was in a ruinous state. Six tons of bird droppings had to be removed from above the shell-like vaulting of the tower crossing, and it then took a single craftsman and his assistant eighteen months to repoint the tower. It would be another twenty years before restoration was completed, the process subject to delays and disputes with the Ministry of Works, to John Smith's chagrin.

The view of the Dissolution of today's society is probably still coloured by an attitude shift that occurred within a couple of generations of the act itself. The sight of these evocative and solitary ruins colonized by ivy and crows, and often in the most remote and beautiful parts of the countryside, was to generate feelings of deep regret and fears of sacrilege, of which there was no trace at the time. This shift prompted the development of English antiquarianism and has moulded our landscape aesthetics ever since. For us, if not for the people of that time, these are indeed Shakespeare's 'Bare ruin'd choirs, where late the sweet birds sang' (*Sonnet 73*, line 34, *c.* 1600).

As for Thomas Cromwell, architect of the monasteries' downfall, by 1540 he was beheaded at his king's command. **CS**

Landmark maintains the monks' infirmary at Woodspring, its wind-braced roof an exemplar of late medieval carpentry.

Only the moulded beams in the farmhouse kitchen reveal that it was once part of a powerful prior's lodgings.

The west front of the church shows signs of both defacement and later colonization for domestic use.

The later additions now co-exist comfortably alongside the monastic remnants at Woodspring – time healing the scars of past destruction.

Dolbeydr, built in 1578, was home to scholar Henry Salesbury, a founding father of the modern Welsh language.

DOLBELYDR
DENBIGHSHIRE

C. 1548

THE SURVIVAL OF THE WELSH LANGUAGE

'And take this advice from me, unless you save and correct and perfect the [Welsh] language before the extinction of the present generation, it will be too late afterwards.' This could have been written in the 1950s, but it was also the opinion of William Salesbury in 1547, one of the famous Welsh Bible translators of the sixteenth century. The survival of the Welsh language had been placed in serious doubt by Henry VIII's Act of Union in 1536, drafted by his great administrator Thomas Cromwell and followed by further measures in 1543, all designed to bring Wales firmly under the English Crown.

By 1530, the traditional model of seeking to control the unruly Welsh Marches (or borderlands) by traditional dynastic means of officers acting in the name of a royal Prince of Wales and a feudal Council of the Marches had once again failed. The English shires were still too often troubled by the zestful larceny and killings that characterized the power games of the Welsh gentry. The 1536 act expressed the problem like this:

'Because that the People of the same Dominion have and do daily use a speech nothing like, nor consonant to the natural Mother Tongue used within this Realm, some rude and ignorant

People have made Distinction and Diversity between the King's Subjects of this Realm, and his Subjects of the said Dominion and Principality of Wales, whereby great Discord Variance Debate Division Murmur and Sedition hath grown between his said Subjects.'

The Act wiped out any distinction between the administration and law of the principality and the Marches, extending English common law across the whole of Wales at the expense of Hywel Dda, local Welsh custom. The Welsh were guaranteed unified political and judicial status with the English, and Welsh shires and boroughs could elect their own representatives to Westminster for the first time. The means to enact this sweeping reform was captured in a short provision in the Act promoting English as the language of government.

Henceforth, all court hearings, law and oaths were to be in English. And to make things crystal clear, 'no Person or Persons that use the Welsh Speech or Language, shall have or enjoy any manner Office or Fees within this Realm of England, Wales, or other in the King's Dominion, upon Pain of forfeiting the same Offices or Fees, unless he or they use and exercise the English Speech or Language'. At a stroke, the value of the Welsh language was undermined and devalued, reverberations that still echo today. And almost immediately, a quiet campaign began to preserve this ancient Celtic language.

It was such concern to preserve and codify a largely oral language that, in 1593, led an Oxford-educated, minor Welsh gentleman and physician called Henry Salesbury (no known relation to William Salesbury) to publish the *Grammatica Britannica*. Anglo-Welsh dictionaries had preceded it, but this is generally accepted to be the first comprehensive Welsh grammar. It was written at Dolbelydr in Denbighshire. This high-status, stone-built gentry house with a fine first-floor solar open to the roof was built by Henry Salesbury's father *c.* 1548. It was a very modern house for its day, complete with a large chimney built into its end wall to heat both ground and first floors. Its quiet setting beside the River Elwy provided the perfect place for convalescence (Salesbury refers to an illness in his foreword) and study. Yet this was a book intended to go out into the world, published in London and dedicated to the Earl of Pembroke, Privy Councillor at the heart of the regime.

Not surprisingly, historians' interpretations of the effects of the Acts of Union vary. Some see them as a triumph of Tudor efficiency, bringing stability and a chance to share in England's prosperity. Others regard them as a tyrannical attack on Welsh

Untangling and reconstructing the fallen roof timbers was a giant jigsaw puzzle for the archaeologists and carpenters during restoration.

This many-light window with its diamond set mullions was a clear sign that Dolbelydr was once a house of high status.

identity, culture and economy, leaving the majority of the population adrift amid a legal and economic system whose language and focus were unfamiliar to them.

The Welsh gentry were already involved with the court and increasingly looked beyond Welsh culture and language. Commercially active, they travelled to Europe, where they bought books in English and Latin and absorbed ideas from the revived classical culture of the Renaissance. Robert Wynn, builder of Plas Mawr in Conwy, is typical of this interchange of ideas and culture, travelling with his patron Sir Philip Hoby to the Low Countries and perhaps also on Hoby's embassy to the Holy Roman Emperor Charles V in the late 1540s.

At a time when even English was newly emerging from under the Norman yoke, scholarly gentry saw the Welsh language as on a par with Latin and Greek. They studied ancient manuscripts and analyzed the grammatical structure of Welsh, even today a largely phonetic language. Henry Salesbury's *Grammatica*, written in Latin, falls squarely within this humanist movement. He was not alone in publishing a grammar; so too did Gruffudd Robert (1567), Sion Dafydd Rhys (1592) and John Davies (1621). Their objective was to show Welsh poets that they, too, could attain the standards of literary elegance seen on the Continent. The *Grammatica* was both a tool for learning a new language and a whetstone on which to hone it. It became the primer for generations of schoolchildren.

In the 1530s and 1540s, the English were liberated by the Protestant Reformation, which enabled them, thrillingly, to read the Bible in their own language and in print for the first time, after William Tyndale's translation. But for most Welsh people, English scriptures were as incomprehensible as the former Latin version. Personal Bible reading lay at the heart of the Protestant religion, and its availability in the vernacular was of crucial importance to its faith, as was widespread availability of copies through printing. Any imposition of the English language as the language of religion in Wales therefore posed a major doctrinal as well as political problem.

Alarmed at what he saw as the abasement of the Welsh tongue, William Salesbury campaigned for a Welsh translation of the Bible from 1547. In 1563, he and his associates achieved their aim in An Act for the translating of the Bible and the Divine Service into the Welsh Tongue. Here was a serious *quid pro quo* for the imposition of English in administration. True to Protestant principle, the act made Welsh the language of public religion in Wales. Welsh bishops were ordered to place a Welsh version of the Bible and Prayer Book alongside the English versions in every parish, to help the Welsh people to learn English as well as be godly.

The translation deadline of St David's Day, 1567 was met only for the New Testament, translated by William Salesbury in collaboration with Richard Davies, Bishop of St David's. William Salesbury made their purpose clear: 'If you do not wish to be worse than animals, obtain learning in your own language; if you do not wish to be more unnatural than any other nation under the sun, love your language and those who love it. If you do not wish utterly to depart from the faith of Christ . . . obtain the holy scripture in your own tongue, as your happy ancestors, the ancient British, had it.'

The Bible's universal distribution saved the Welsh language from becoming a collection of disparate dialects and it had far-reaching effects on all aspects of Welsh culture and nationhood, all prompted by this small group of North Welsh humanist scholars content to exist within the Tudor settlement but determined to champion the value and pedigree of their own language. Not until 1993 was Welsh reinstated as the official language of government in Wales.

Though long recognized as one of Wales' 'lost houses', Dolbelydr was a roofless ruin when Landmark first visited in 1982. It was not until 1999 that the farmer sold the building, and it took another two years to raise the money for its restoration. Landmark picked up the fallen roof beams from the ground, reconstructed the late sixteenth-century floorplan and carefully replaced the leaded lights in the mullioned window frames. Without men like Henry Salesbury, quietly writing away behind such leaded panes in the Meadow of Shining Spears, the Welsh language might have been lost forever. Without Landmark, so too would Dolbelydr. **CS**

Beside his inglenook fireplace, William Salesbury once worked on codifying the Welsh language in his *Grammatica Britannica*.

Freston Tower was built near the banks of the River Orwell in the year of Elizabeth I's visit to Ipswich in 1579.

FRESTON TOWER
SUFFOLK

1579

THE MERCHANT BUILDERS OF EAST ANGLIA

Standing solitary on rising ground on the south bank of the Orwell estuary, as the waters run from Ipswich to the sea, is the dramatic five-storey brick tower of Freston, a monument to the wealth and self-confidence of the merchants of Tudor England. Built in 1579, the year Queen Elizabeth I visited Ipswich, Freston Tower was the creation of the cloth merchant Thomas Gooding.

The late Middle Ages had seen the counties of East Anglia enjoy an economic boom fuelled by the textile trade. Woollen cloth was already being produced on a large scale in Suffolk and Essex by the thirteenth century, but during the fourteenth and fifteenth centuries the industry expanded massively. In the 1350s, the county of Suffolk was responsible for just over 3 per cent of English wool production. The Black Death of 1348, which claimed nearly half of the adult population, prompted a shift away from labour-intensive arable farming to sheep rearing. By the 1450s Suffolk was responsible for some 15 per cent of national wool production, making it England's pre-eminent textile manufacturing county.

Sheep farming occurred largely on the heaths and commons of the eastern counties, such as the Brecklands and the Broads, where the thin soil was thought to yield the richest wool. The real wealth, however, was not in the sheep themselves but in the production of cloth. The Stour valley, south of Freston, running from the coast inland to Sudbury, was the main manufacturing district, with the related activities – combing, spinning, dying, bleaching, weaving and fulling – spread around the county. The place names of Norfolk and Suffolk, the villages of Woolpit and Worsted among them, speak of the trade. The wealth generated by the textile industry can be seen in the numbers of fifteenth- and sixteenth-century houses in the area, and the numerous richly ornamented churches. Woven, but still undyed, cloth was exported from East Anglia to Flanders, the cloth production capital of Europe, for finishing; some of the cloth was then re-imported to England.

The great ports of East Anglia – Ipswich, King's Lynn, and Great Yarmouth – were the conduits through which the wool and the wealth flowed. At the time Freston was built, Ipswich was described as: 'a faire towne resembling a City, situate in a ground somewhat low, which is the eye (as it were) of this shire, as having an haven commodious enough, fensed in times past with a trench and rampire, of good trade and stored with wares, well peopled and full of inhabitants, adourned with fourteene Churches, and with goodly, large and stately aedifices'.

By this time Ipswich was the eleventh-largest town in England, famed for its luxury goods, with a special trade in cloth

'bought in the countryside and brought into the town by merchants, to export abroad via the quay'. In the main the ships passing down the Orwell to the Continent carried cloth, and those returning brought imported wine.

Thomas Gooding, builder of Freston, was brought up in the nearby village of Blaxhall. By 1553, when he was about fifty, he was wealthy enough to purchase the property of Freston Hall, which he did in April of that year. The house itself (of which parts remain in the privately owned buildings near the tower) stood a few miles south of the city, in a commanding position overlooking the Orwell estuary. With its outbuildings and pastures it cost a substantial £1,190. Freston became the principal element of Gooding's extensive property holdings, which included buildings in the centre of Ipswich and a number of parcels of land in the surrounding countryside, including the manor of Kesgrave, a short distance to the east of the town.

While Gooding now had an elegant country house, his business interests remained firmly in Ipswich where he was part of the mercantile elite. English towns were oligarchies in which those who were enfranchised as burgesses enjoyed trading advantages; they were exempt from various tolls and levies and entitled to various advantageous municipal rights. Membership of this group was either purchased or earned through lineage and prolonged apprenticeship. In some towns, more than half of the householders were burgesses, but in Ipswich fewer than a third ever were. Of these, a body of twelve 'portmen' controlled the business of the town; while notionally elected, they were effectively a self-perpetuating cabal.

Thomas Gooding became a portman of Ipswich in the 1550s, but in 1561, after being severely censured by his fellow burgesses for failing to pay his dues, he declared his intention to 'retire into the country'. Yet his good fortune continued, and when the heralds visited Suffolk in 1576 he was granted arms of six lions' heads on a golden background.

It was about now, more than twenty years after buying Freston Hall, that Gooding commissioned his striking six-storey brick tower. Its date of 1579, confirmed by dendrochronology, strongly suggests that the tower was built in time for Queen Elizabeth's visit to Ipswich in late August 1679. The visit was long anticipated and the merchants had paid out sums to

A gentleman of the Gooding family, the dynasty of Ipswich mercers for whom Freston Tower was built.

An Edwardian party of sightseers make their way into Freston Tower to avail themselves of the fine views from the top.

'beautify' the town; the men were also required to contribute to the cost of entertaining their sovereign. From Ipswich the Queen's travels took her to Harwich, giving her a spectacular view of Freston Tower as she passed down the river.

Freston was one of several tall brick towers built for Tudor merchants in the period. Another, erected for a wine merchant, survives in King's Lynn, one of at least three that once stood in the town. The buildings, giving splendid views of the merchants' vessels passing in and out of port, functioned as lavish prospect towers. The upper floors were the most important, as expressed at Freston by the sheer number of pedimented windows on the upper three storeys. The tower in King's Lynn was built adjoining the merchant's house and had fireplaces on each floor, and so could be used for entertaining all year round. Freston, standing in an orchard some yards from the house, had no fireplaces and was probably only used in summer, as a banqueting house for intimate gatherings. The rooms within were limewashed, but seem originally to have been adorned with rich textiles; the nails from which these were hung are mentioned in one early description of the building.

Successful merchants like Gooding used their wealth to accumulate objects of beauty, and Freston probably housed furniture of real quality. In his will, Gooding reserved 'all my armour as well for horsemen as footmen' for his eldest son, Robert. His collection of arms and armour, kept ready to be pressed into service should the town militia be called upon, included symbols of status and splendour. Among his other prized possessions were a great silver salt, two gilt bowls, valuable textiles including three tapestries, velvet- and needlework-covered chairs and silk-covered stools. Four paintings hung in his parlour at Freston Hall, and there were damask tablecloths and a bedstead decorated with 'imagework'.

Freston Tower was a spectacular undertaking, one of which the Gooding family were proud. When, in the early seventeenth century, Gooding's grandson let Freston Hall to one Christopher Hayward, he kept back the tower's lease for his own use.

Over the centuries Freston had a number of owners until the tower was bought as a holiday home by Claire Hunt and her husband in 1962. When Mrs Hunt gave the tower to the Landmark Trust on her death in 2001, a programme of research and repair began. The pinnacles, perhaps an eighteenth-century addition, were leaning alarmingly and had to be straightened; bricked-up windows were reopened; the window surrounds were re-rendered to resemble stone; leaded glass was reinstated; and the whole building was stabilized and made safe. After a year of being shrouded by scaffolding, Freston emerged, resplendent, from its chrysalis and was opened to visitors in 2004. **AK**

Freston Tower acted as a belvedere to the older house of Freston Hall; the lower storeys of the building on the hall side had no windows.

Tixall Old Hall, much as it was when
Mary Queen of Scots emerged
weeping from the gatehouse in 1586.

Today, Tixall Old Hall has gone;
only its extravagant gatehouse
hints at its past splendour.

TIXALL GATEHOUSE
STAFFORDSHIRE

1580

ELIZABETH I AND MARY QUEEN OF SCOTS

On 25 September 1586, Mary Stuart, Queen of Scots, emerged
weeping through Tixall Gatehouse. 'I have nothing for you',
she said to the hopeful local beggars who had assembled there.
'I am a beggar as well as you, all is taken from me.' The last act
of Mary's nineteen long years in English captivity had begun.

Exquisite Tixall Gatehouse was newly completed by Sir
Walter Aston, a staunch Protestant. It 'beautified or defaced
(I know not which) the fair house built by his father', according
to Sampson Erdswicke in 1598, a reminder of how architectural
innovation can be controversial in any age. The gatehouse
reflected but adapted the Italian Renaissance style, cheerfully
borrowing the ancient orders of columns but disregarding
the careful formality of ancient proportion as disseminated by
the translations of Sebastiano Serlio then reaching England.
Friendly, buxom angels watch from the spandrels above the
entrance on its inner side; knights try their best to look fierce
on the outer one.

On 11 August, Mary had ridden forth from her latest place of
incarceration at moated Chartley Castle, a few miles away. It was
a fine day and Mary dressed carefully, excited by the prospect of

a day's hunting, a rare concession from her dour jailer, Sir
Amyas Poulet. Instead, fast horsemen approached in a carefully
planned intervention. Elizabeth I's emissary, Sir Thomas
Gorges, informed Mary that Elizabeth had proof of Mary's
conspiracy against her own life and the state. She was to be
taken immediately to Tixall, then a walled estate, while her
apartments were searched.

The conspiracy uncovered was the so-called Babington
Plot. A young gentleman called Anthony Babington, in league
with John Ballard, a Catholic priest, had planned Elizabeth's
assassination to facilitate England's invasion by the Spanish.
At long last, the government agents had full proof of Mary's
complicity. During her grim meditative weeks at Tixall, Mary
must have realized that this time the game was finally up.

Mary and Elizabeth I never met face to face, but their fates
were entwined from the start of Elizabeth's reign in 1558. Mary
inherited the Scottish throne at six days old, but was brought
up as a Catholic at the French Court, where she married the
Dauphin, Francis. As the great granddaughter of Henry VII,
Mary was regarded by many Catholics, especially in Europe,
as the rightful Queen of England, and one who would restore
the true faith, in contrast to Elizabeth, offspring of an 'illicit'
marriage between Henry VIII and Anne Boleyn.

Hindsight lends the Tudor dynasty a stability and
inevitability that was far from evident to contemporaries.

From Henry VII's accession in 1485 until Elizabeth's death in 1603, this turbulent age was beset with plots and pretenders. Mary was one of the most persistent and dangerous threats, a focus for Catholic conspiracy both at home and in Europe. She presented Elizabeth with a conundrum: they were kinswomen and both sovereigns anointed by God, and female ones at that. To strike at Mary would undermine the divine right of rulers. Equally, Elizabeth herself had endured years of imprisonment and uncertainty under Mary I of England as second in line; she feared if she formally acknowledged Mary Stuart (or any other claimant) as her heir, she would similarly place her own position at risk from the plots of malcontents. There is plenty of evidence that she had due cause to be concerned.

In May 1568, Mary abandoned her exasperated nobles and her disastrous love life and fled from Scotland to England. Her arrival presented a dilemma for the English government that would preoccupy it for nineteen years. England was unwilling to go to war for Mary against her countrymen, but Mary's deposed condition nevertheless undermined the divine right of kings. There was no option but for Mary to remain in honourable custody in England as Elizabeth's guest. 'Our good Queen has the wolf by the ears,' commented Archbishop Parker wryly.

Mary was an inveterate intriguer, with foreign powers as well as disillusioned English Catholics. In 1570, Pope Pius V excommunicated Elizabeth, 'the pretended Queen of England, the serpent of wickedness'. This misguided papal bull effectively absolved all English Catholics from allegiance to Elizabeth, and was incitement to rebellion. It also hardened the hearts of the Protestant majority in zealous defence of their Queen, and transformed Catholic practice and intrigue from religious heresy to treason against the state. It is against such a background of insecurity that we arrive at Tixall Gatehouse in 1586.

The Babington Plot was a cleverly sprung trap, instigated by Sir Francis Walsingham, Elizabeth's Secretary of State and spymaster, 'a most subtle searcher of hidden secrets'. A confirmed Puritan, Walsingham was utterly loyal to the survival of Elizabeth's regime and, like most of her council, saw Mary for the ongoing threat she was. As external threats to England became increasingly real in the 1580s, it became ever clearer that a final solution for Mary had to be found. Walsingham's

Babington and his accomplices are arrested, and later hanged, drawn and quartered, as seen in this contemporary engraving.

The re-gilded weather vanes on each of the roof turrets of Tixall Gatehouse record the date of Landmark's restoration in 1977.

technique was to give conspirators enough rope to hang themselves. He managed an ever-increasing network of spies and 'projectors', initially at his own cost, a shifting cast of impecunious gentry and shady characters all seeking to make their way through 'service' in treacherous times. Codes and ciphers were used by all, and 'invisible inks' – orange or onion juice, milk, urine. Double agents were also common, despatched to seminaries training militant Jesuits on the Continent, or luring unsuspecting prisoners into implicating their accomplices.

When Mary was moved to the fortress at Chartley in 1585, Walsingham devised a scheme to intercept her plotting messages. A trainee priest, Gilbert Gifford, was coerced into playing double agent and Gifford paid a local brewer to carry Mary's messages in a waterproof packet slipped into the bunghole of his kegs. This enabled Walsingham to intercept and decode Mary's ciphered communications with the French.

By summer 1586, one of Walsingham's projectors, Robert Poley, was working to turn the Catholic Babington, a known plotter, to serve the state. Walsingham soon realized he might instead use the gullible twenty-four-year-old as unwitting bait for a bigger fish. In March, Philip II of Spain had sought the Pope's blessing for his Enterprise of England, a plan for invasion that would indeed come to fruition two years later with the Spanish Armada. A priest called John Ballard was to orchestrate simultaneous rebellion by the English Catholics (never as numerous or as militant as the Spanish believed). Ballard made contact with Babington, a rash youth already known to the authorities for having plotted to assassinate the entire Star Chamber Council the previous year. Poley, meanwhile, had found favour with Babington, who called him his 'sweet Robyn'. The plot coalesced under Poley's encouragement, all the time keeping Secretary Walsingham informed.

On 4 July, Babington wrote to Mary via the keg post, outlining the conspiracy. 'Six noble gentlemen, all my private friends' would 'despatch the usurper' (Elizabeth), Babington himself would rescue Mary, and the Spanish would invade. Mary took the bait and replied, in cipher, on 17 July. For such a seasoned plotter, she made the cardinal error of explicitly supporting in writing the death of Elizabeth and the overthrow of the regime. Thomas Phelippes, who intercepted the package and forwarded it to Walsingham, could not resist scratching the sign of the gallows on the back. Ballard was arrested on 4 August; Babington, panicking, tried to persuade one of the regicides, John Parry, to kill Elizabeth that very day. Parry was willing, but too shabbily dressed to enter the court. Babington gave him a ring to sell to buy a new suit of clothes, but the moment was lost. On 14 August, Babington was discovered

The gatehouse was a grimy, roofless shell before it was rescued by the Landmark Trust.

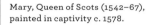

Mary, Queen of Scots (1542–67), painted in captivity c. 1578.

Stone-carved angels smile benignly from the spandrels above the arch on the inner elevation of the gatehouse.

hiding north of London, his face 'sullied with the rind of green walnuts'. London rejoiced with peals of bells and bonfires. Babington soon confessed all, in the naive hope that it might lead to a pardon.

Mary, meanwhile, riding out for Tixall with new hope on a sunny morning three days earlier, was oblivious to all of this. She had walked straight into Walsingham's trap. The execution of Babington, Ballard and five other conspirators on 20 September sends horrid echoes through history as one of the most savage in English judicial history, the men deliberately cut down early from the gallows for their disembowelling – so savage that Elizabeth sent instructions the next day for their fellow conspirators to be allowed to pass more mercifully into unconsciousness first.

There were now clear judicial reasons for Mary's own execution. She was returned briefly to Chartley and then taken to Fotheringhay Castle near Peterborough. In November, a commission led by Lord Burghley, Elizabeth's long-serving Lord Chancellor, tried Mary for treason. The tall, legendary beauty was now a plump, middle-aged woman with a limp. Mary gave a spirited defence, but was found guilty. The sentence was for queen and parliament to pronounce and this threw Elizabeth,

though not parliament, into an agony of indecision, still reluctant to execute a ruling monarch. Finally, on 1 February 1587, Elizabeth signed the death warrant and it was despatched north without delay. On 8 February, Mary was beheaded in the great hall at Fotheringhay.

The shadowy Robert Poley was imprisoned in the Tower of London for two years for his apparent part in the plot. But he was held 'at large', under lenient conditions. When he emerged, he was immediately given a mission to Denmark. A few years later, he was one of three men implicated in the death of playwright Christopher Marlowe in a tavern in Deptford, London – another who was caught up in Walsingham's web.

The angels and knights in Tixall Gatehouse's spandrels have therefore witnessed much. Perhaps ironically, within two generations, the Astons of Tixall had themselves converted to Catholicism. The gatehouse outlived the old hall, which was replaced in the eighteenth century by a pleasant house of unremarkable classical design. The gatehouse itself fell derelict; by the 1950s its roof had fallen in. It was one of the earliest buildings taken on by the Landmark Trust, acquired in 1968. Its amazing stonework encapsulates perfectly the spirit of the joyous, conflicted, querulous, creative years of Elizabeth's reign. **CS**

A stone staircase leads in a tight spiral
to fine rooms on the first and second
floors of Tixall Gatehouse.

The Castle of Park in the early twentieth century, before the demolition of the eighteenth-century wings.

Castle of Park was built on a natural plateau on the former lands of Glenluce Abbey in 1590.

CASTLE OF PARK
DUMFRIES AND GALLOWAY

1590

THE EFFECTS OF THE REFORMATION IN SCOTLAND

While it came a generation later, the Protestant Reformation in Scotland was quicker and more complete than its English equivalent, and it was nowhere more so than in the temperate and fertile lands of south-west Scotland. When the authority and assets of the monasteries that held such sway here were threatened and then overwhelmed, it would transform the

Bernard of Clairvaux, one of the leading figures of the Cistercian order, reads the Order of St Benedict.

political and physical landscape of Scotland. Castle of Park was a product of this revolution.

In the Middle Ages, the lowlands of Scotland were peppered with substantial monasteries – most were the northern outposts of the powerful European monastic orders. Glenluce Abbey in Galloway, on whose lands the Castle of Park would be built, was founded in c. 1192 by Roland, Lord of Galloway, the Constable of Scotland. The community there were Cistercians; this order of monks had arrived in Britain sixty years earlier, and had established, among others, Rievaulx Abbey in North Yorkshire, from which they forged north into Scotland. Glenluce was the seventh Cistercian house to be founded in Scotland, and the family who gave the lands and resources to establish it were a dynasty of benefactors. Roland of Galloway's granddaughter Dervorguilla would go on to found nearby Sweetheart Abbey and Balliol College, Oxford, which was named in memory of her husband, John de Balliol.

The Cisterians, who followed the letter of the highly ascetic order of St Benedict, deliberately sought sites that took them into the wilderness, 'far from the concourse of men'. The lands at Glenluce, a shallow valley on the banks of the Water of Luce, which gave it the name 'the valley of light', were an ideal location. The Cistercians would become hugely powerful in Britain and within a century had twenty-eight houses in Scotland alone.

1534–1660: Forging Identities

By the sixteenth century the original principles of an austere and communal life had in practice become widely debased. In 1553, the General Chapter at Citeaux attempted to restore discipline to the order, and sent a commissioner into Scotland who reported that many of the monks had special allowances for their own food and clothes, and some had private pleasure gardens. Glenluce was no exception: the gardens there were so splendid that King James IV and Queen Margaret tipped the gardener four shillings in admiration after a visit. Further accusations that the monastic ideal had been corrupted stemmed both from the many instances of clerical marriage, and from the system whereby abbeys could be headed by lay 'commendators' appointed by the sovereign. One or other of these certainly happened in May 1560 when Thomas Hay, who had both a wife (Katherine Kennedy, daughter of the powerful Earl of Cassillis) and children, was appointed as the last Abbot of Glenluce.

In 1560, the abuses of Scottish monks and priests combined with political unrest to help bring down the Roman Catholic Church. As the Scots reacted against their absentee sovereign, Mary Queen of Scots (who had lived in France since infancy and did not return to Scotland until 1561), the influence of Calvinist preachers in Scotland had blossomed. As a consequence in 1560, in a sensational move, the Scottish Parliament denied the authority of the papacy. While in England the process whereby monasteries and their lands were given to secular lords was often violent, in Scotland many monks were allowed to continue to live in their buildings and enjoy their revenues for life. At Glenluce, once in possession of the abbey, Thomas Hay began gradually, over a period of two decades, to dismantle the abbey lands and to oversee a slow process of secularization. As part of this, in 1572 he gave a parcel of the abbey lands, known as 'Park', to his son Thomas, on the occasion of Thomas's marriage.

Thomas Hay was quite young, perhaps even still a minor, at the time of his marriage to Janet Macdowell in 1572, which might account for the delay before he began building the imposing tower house known today as Castle of Park in March 1590. The date of the building's creation is recorded in an inscription, now damaged, over the door that read, 'Blissit be the name of the Lord/This verk vas begun the first day of March

The building's austere exterior belied the well-heated domestic spaces within.

The kitchen and service rooms
were on the vaulted ground
floor of the castle.

The castle's seventeenth-century
panelling had been removed,
leaving the stone walls unlined.

1590 be Thomas Hay of Park and Jonet Makdovel his spovs'. The house stands on a large plateau of ground south of Glenluce Abbey, on the other side of the river from the monastery, with views of the valley beyond. Four principal storeys high, the building is roughly rectangular, with a large stair contained in a projecting block, making it L-shaped. The building is tall and austere externally, its proud silhouette well suited to the raised plain on which it stands.

Here Thomas and Janet Hay created a comfortable and spacious house, which was clearly designed for show and comfort rather than defence. The entrance is on the ground floor into the spiral stair that runs the height of the building. Here, separate from the stair, were the kitchen and service rooms. The floor above was a large hall, perhaps with a screened-off passage at its entrance used as a servery. Above it are two further floors, each clearly designed to contain one set of apartments. The plan

is the same on each: an outer room at the southern end near the stair, and a more intimate inner room beyond, with a small pair of closets at its north end.

The Hay family would live at Park for the following two centuries, making modifications and improvements over the decades. The plain on which the castle stands was probably used for gardens from the beginning. A plan of the estate in the eighteenth century shows it divided into large compartments, one containing the castle, creating an elaborate formal garden. In the eighteenth century, the great hall was fitted out with elegant panelling (later removed), sash windows were inserted and two detached wings with large chimneys were added to increase the size of the accommodation.

In 1830, Sir James Dalrymple-Hay decided to move out of the Castle of Park and the house became tenant accommodation, which it remained until it was sold in 1894.

The first-floor hall of the castle was its principal entertaining space; it retains its sixteenth-century fireplace.

When the estate was bought by the Scottish Agricultural Department in the 1940s, the castle, now severely dilapidated and with the roof collapsing, was superfluous to their needs and transferred to the Ministry of Works. The poor state of repair of the Castle of Park prompted the Ministry of Works to demolish the wings, and set about repairing the roof, but work was set back when the building was struck by lightning in 1969. Further works followed in 1976–8, including re-flooring and the reinstatement of sash windows, and re-harling of the exterior, by coating it with lime and coarse sand. The works were critical, but when they were finished the interiors were incomplete and the building was unserviced and still without a use.

In 1990, the Landmark Trust took on the Castle of Park from Historic Scotland on a ninety-nine-year lease and set about making it habitable once more. The architects were Stewart Tod and Partners of Edinburgh, who by now had a long-standing relationship with the Landmark Trust, having worked on fourteen previous projects. Many long-lost or obscured historic features of the building were reinstated as part of this work, including a private spiral stair that once led from the hall to the upper floors and a rediscovered stair from the ground floor into the low end of the hall.

The hall itself was made into a new kitchen and dining room, with the former servery area given a half-height partition as an echo of the screen that may once have stood here. The bare stone walls of the hall and much of the building were plastered once again with lime-hair plaster, but in the sitting room something more ornate was needed in addition. Jennifer Maskell-Packer, who had designed the Landmark Trust's distinctive hand-printed curtain fabrics since the 1960s, decorated the ceiling and shutters with a pattern based on elements of the interiors of a Jacobean house near Edinburgh. **AK**

BEAMSLEY HOSPITAL
NORTH YORKSHIRE

1593

ALMSHOUSE BUILT BY TWO ELIZABETHAN ARISTOCRATIC WOMEN

This exceptional almshouse, round in plan, was the creation of two outstanding daughters of the Elizabethan age: Margaret, Countess of Cumberland and her child and heir Lady Anne Clifford. Educated, ambitious and devoted to one another, between them they created a foundation that would offer succour to poor women for the next four centuries.

Proverbs (19:17) states that 'he that hath pity upon the poor lendeth unto the Lord; and that which he hath given will he pay him again', which, with many other Biblical admonishments, was behind a strong Christian tradition of charitable giving. From the early Middle Ages, aristocratic men and women had established and endowed institutions to care for the ill and incapacitated poor, and thereby for their own souls. By 1500, there were some 580 hospitals or almshouses in England, often attached to a religious house of some sort. The medieval Latin word *hospitale*, meaning a place of reception for travellers or pilgrims, came to have a more specific meaning in denoting care for the infirm. Some of these medieval hospitals catered for specific illnesses, such as leprosy, and others for the poor of given groups, such as the clergy or converted Jews. Designed

to give spiritual as well as material support, large medieval hospitals such as St Cross in Winchester had a chapel, a hall for dining and sleeping rooms or cells for the beneficiaries. Normally they gave alms to the poor of the area as well as supporting a resident community of almsmen and women.

A great many of the medieval hospitals were attached in some way to religious houses. Come the Dissolution of the Monasteries, the hospitals shared their fate and a considerable number of the larger institutions were closed down. The second wave of the Reformation, in the reign of Edward VI, saw the closure of the chantries, endowments that involved prayers for the dead, which included many hospitals. The closure of these charitable institutions was largely an unintended by-product of the Reformation, and while a good number survived – among them St Bartholomew's Hospital in London, which was taken over by the City Corporation – many did not.

With charity an important element of the new reformed religion, and chantries no longer allowed, a wave of new charitable foundations came into being in the century after the Reformation. In some cases, the new hospitals or almshouses were created from scratch; in others, older institutions were refounded. Thomas Sutton established his great hospital in the buildings of the former Carthusian monastery, the Charterhouse in London, while in Lincolnshire the former Bishop's Palace at Lyddington was converted into

The circular plan of the Beamsley
Hospital is highly unusual. At its
centre is a small chapel lit by windows
below the raised central roof.

Margaret Clifford, Countess of Cumberland, the founder of the Beamsley Hospital, painted by an unknown artist c. 1585.

The 'Countess Pillar', erected in Cumbria by Lady Anne Clifford on the spot where she last saw her mother.

'Jesus Hospital' to house twelve poor men and two women. Come the reign of Elizabeth I, there were incentives for the creation of such hospitals and almshouses founded 'for the relief of poor people' were exempted from taxation under the 1559 religious settlement.

Into this context came the formidable Margaret Russell, daughter of the second Earl of Bedford. Brought up in Northampton and at Woburn, she married George Clifford, third Earl of Cumberland at the age of seventeen. Head of a great northern family, his seat was at Skipton Castle in the West Riding of Yorkshire. Highly intelligent, pious and a keen amateur chemist, Margaret was very different from her buccaneering husband. She was often alone as she bore three children of whom only one survived, a daughter born at Skipton Castle in 1590. Three years after Anne's birth the countess founded an almshouse for the poor women of Skipton, those decrepit and broken by age, who were reduced to daily begging. The hospital's income was to come from farmlands provided by the Countess. The Earl and Countess separated in 1600, and on her death in 1616, she left the Beamsley almshouse incomplete, but stipulated in her will that 'the almeshouse which I have taken order for may be perfected'. The task of completing the project was taken on by her daughter, Lady Anne Clifford, who added an additional building, enabling the foundation to accommodate thirteen women in number, a 'mother' and twelve 'sisters' (a common number of residents in an almshouse, echoing the number of Christ and his Apostles).

The form of the Countess of Cumberland's almshouse was highly unusual. Circular in plan, the building had at its core a tall circular chapel, 4.5 metres/15 feet in diameter, and around it seven lower wedge-shaped chambers. The circular plan was both an example of the Elizabethan taste for ingenious design, and an echo of the round churches inspired by the Holy Sepulchre in Jerusalem built after the Norman conquest. The inhabitants each had a 'handsome Roome' and a small garden, while the 'mother' had two rooms. The whole building stood in generous grounds with 'handsome walks sett with yew hedges for shade for the said widowes use'.

Circumstances had made both the Countess and Lady Anne into resilient, independent women. After Margaret's separation from the Earl of Cumberland, she fought a long and bitter battle, continued by her daughter, to try to regain Anne's inheritance from her male cousins. Mother and daughter had become devoted to one another. When Margaret died, Anne built a magnificent tomb to her in the parish church at Appleby, Cumbria. Years later, when she finally came into her inheritance, Anne erected an ornate pillar on the spot where she had last seen her mother forty years before. She recorded on it the endowment she had left for a sum of money to be distributed there to the poor of the parish every year on the anniversary of their parting. At Beamsley, mother and daughter created an environment where widowed women could live independently, and it was a place Anne cherished, calling it 'my blessed mother's almshouse at Beamsley'. She took her own daughters and granddaughters to visit the Beamsley Hospital, and would go on to found a second almshouse, the Hospital of St Anne at Appleby, again for twelve women and a mother, in the 1650s.

The establishment created at Beamsley had an extraordinarily long life. The seventeenth-century rules for the hospital set out the regime that would continue for almost four centuries. Prayers were said by a male reader in the chapel every morning, Holy Communion was taken four times a year and the women were enjoined to 'live Peacably and quietly amongst themselves'. An inventory of the building from 1810 shows that each room had a bed and chair, and a range on which the inhabitants prepared their own food, purchased with their tiny allowances. The income from the farms was paid directly to the mother and

kept in the chest in her room. From this, in the seventeenth century, the sisters received £6 a year and the mother and reader £8, leaving £2 for repairs and general outgoings.

The almshouse remained in use well into the twentieth century, still supported by its founder's endowment, until its remote location and the rise of the welfare state saw its last resident, Mrs Soare, leave in 1980. The buildings were still sound, but not in good repair, and in need of a new use. The Landmark Trust took the hospital on in 1983, and a programme of repair and refurbishment overseen by Martin Stancliffe Architects of York followed in 1985–6. The building was re-roofed, the chimneys rebuilt and partitions introduced in the 1960s removed, allowing the original configuration of walls and doors to be largely reinstated. The modern fireplaces were dismantled to reveal the large Elizabethan openings, the windows were re-leaded and new elm floorboards laid. The second building, added by Lady Anne Clifford, was converted into two cottages. It remains a monument to its formidable female founders and the resilient women who have inhabited it over the four centuries since. **AK**

The simple central chapel of Beamsley Hospital expressed the godly lives that residents were expected to live.

MANOR FARM
NORFOLK

C. 1597

THE GREAT REBUILDING

'Every man almost is a builder,' wrote William Harrison in 1577,
'and he that hath bought any small parcel of ground, be it never
so little, will not be quiet till he have pulled down the old house
(if any there were standing) and set up a new house of his own.'
William Harrison, *Description of England* (1577)

Other early modern commentators echo Harrison's
perceptions of 'a great amendment of lodging', and the physical
evidence of the surviving houses themselves also led English
local historian W.G. Hoskins in 1953 to a significant realization.
In a seminal article, *The Rebuilding of Rural England 1570–1640*,
Hoskins identified 'a revolution in the housing of a considerable
part of the population' in England. The thesis of a Great
Rebuilding, as it came to be known, has proved one of the most
enduring explanatory tools in English architectural history,
since challenged and refined, debated in chronology and
nuanced by region, but still essentially holding good as an
identifiable historical development in the period.

The rebuilding took three main forms: complete rebuilding
on an existing site; enlargement or adaptation that effectively
produced a new house; and building on a site for the first time.

It would be wrong to imply that the period of Hoskins'
hypothesis was unadulterated prosperity across the board: the
late-sixteenth century especially had periods of poor harvests
and increased vagrancy. Hoskins' third category of 'building on
a new site' was very largely cottages, often built by squatters on
marginal and waste land. An act of 1589 spoke of 'the erection
and building of great numbers and multitudes of cottages,
which are daily more and more increased in many parts of this
realm', and sought to prohibit such cottages on plots of less
than 1.6 hectares/4 acres without a licence. Few of these survive.

What does survive from the period is an increase in such
building activity among the middling sort, enabled by an overall
long-term increase in prosperity. 'Reconstruction' typically took
the form of inserting a ceiling into the open hall, along with a
new-fangled chimney stack, perhaps the most significant single
development in domestic architecture, its impact equivalent
to the arrival of screen culture in our own times. Increased
subdivision through use of partitions meant greater privacy;
more use of coal for heating where available and increased
production of cheaper window glass completed a revolution
in living conditions that is also apparent in contemporary wills
and inventories: there was simply 'more of everything and better
of everything and new-fangled comforts . . . as well'.

Several of the Landmark Trust's houses across the country
embody this building boom (Dolbelydr and Cowside among

Manor Farm today, immaculately
maintained with pink limewash, its
future secure in Landmark's care.

Wealthy seventeenth-century yeomen enjoyed a varied diet, served on affordable china and pewter.

New-fangled wooden stairs were still tucked alongside the chimney breast when Manor Farm was built.

them), but none more so than Manor Farm, near Pulham Market in Norfolk. Manor Farm's builder seems indeed to have 'pulled down the old house', since the parlour at the east end is thought to predate the main range, and be a remnant of an earlier building. The main house has been dated by tree-ring analysis to the first quarter of the seventeenth century. This stoutly framed house, thatched in long straw, has some traditional features – a service end below a screens passage and a ground floor hall – but the hall is no longer open to the roof as Purton Green had been (see page 26), for the house incorporates the period's innovative architectural features.

Manor Farm has stairs, and several bedrooms on a second floor with a corridor and a large, brick-built chimney stack (old men 'marvelled at the multitude of chimneys lately erected' in William Harrison's parish). The partition walls are, very unusually, formed of plank and muntin, a form of joinery common in the screen along a cross passage but rare to survive as walls, and suggesting plentiful supply of oak locally.

Discounting a further eighteenth-century extension, Manor Farm had eight rooms as (re)built around 1600. In the mid-sixteenth century, the average rural house in the Forest of Arden had just two to three rooms; 100 years later, this had risen to between six and seven. Floorplans had become more differentiated, the great space of the medieval open hall much better utilized, and such developments also required an injection of wealth.

This was the period of substantial yeoman farmers, benefiting from low rents as late medieval copyhold leases (under which buildings were held for a number of lives at the same, increasingly outdated rent) ran their course. The widening gap between costs and selling prices worked in farmers' favour and any yeoman worth his salt could accumulate money savings on a scale hitherto unknown. He used this cash to buy the freehold on his home and more land, and to build sturdy, well-appointed houses, in order to entertain.

Such was no doubt the experience of the Miltiwards who were living at Manor Farm in 1643 and were probably responsible for building the main range. This part of Norfolk was well-populated in these years, and generally prosperous, its rural wealth based on mixed arable farming with large areas of common land for grazing. Inflation (a new and accelerating phenomenon) was favouring the arable farmer. Grain prices rose eightfold in the sixteenth and early seventeenth centuries; the rate of increase for prices of animal products was half that.

The days of wool wealth were in decline, and the cloth market under pressure, as the medieval guilds struggled to survive. Pulham Market was a weaving as well as a farming village. When, in 1551, weaving was suppressed in many rural areas to prevent competition with the Norwich weavers, it was granted an exception for its 'Pulham work', a heavy furnishing material, and for its 'hats, dornecks [a stout linen] and coverlits'. In the timber framing of Manor Farm, there are fixation points thought to have been for a large loom, such as supplemented many a household's income through the winter months and lean times through weaving. It probably belonged to one Richard Baker, 'worsted weaver' who lived in the house after the Miltiwards, and whose name appears on one of the bells in Pulham Market Church.

This period also saw the birth of the consumer market. 'Costly furniture ... now ... is descended yet lower, even unto the inferior artificers and many farmers,' wrote Harrison, 'who by virtue of their old and not their new leases, have for the main part learned also to garnish their cupboards with plate, their joint beds with tapestry and silk hangings, and their tables with carpets and fine napery.'

Glass that had previously been so expensive that only the very wealthy could afford it – and so fragile that household retinues carried it around from place to place for use wherever their lord was in residence – became cheaper and affordable even for the middling sort, replacing the horn and lattice windows of the past. The great jurist of the era, Edward Coke, recorded an important legal precedent in 1579: 'Glass fixed by nails or any other manner cannot be moved, for without glass is no perfect home.' Glass had become a fixture, rather than furnishing.

The theory of the Great Rebuilding has proved seductive to mainstream historians and addictive to vernacular architecture enthusiasts, who still delight in tracing anomalies of the building boom by date and locality. One of the most intriguing applications has been that of social and anthropological theory, which traces the effects of the increasing 'enclosure' in both living spaces and the landscape on social, economic and cultural life, through to developing class and gender relations, and even political and religious sympathies.

No longer was life a communal one in an open hall: now, there was privacy in more numerous enclosed bedrooms, reached not through one another but off corridors. The master and mistress of the household became more remote from their servants, as social status even in middling homes became more differentiated. Some even speculate on whether such changes contributed to the eventual rise of radical politics and religion

Timber was still plentiful in Norfolk in 1600, and was used generously in all aspects of Manor Farm's construction.

The wealth to build sturdy houses like
Manor Farm came from all aspects of
the thriving Norfolk wool trade.

A wooden latch of traditional design
still serves its purpose today.

Landmark is replacing reed with more
traditional long-straw thatch as its
maintenance regimen proceeds.

The bedrooms boast a wealth of timber,
and sometimes a fireplace, too.

that led to the Civil War in the 1640s, given the opportunities provided by more private spaces for free-ranging and even seditious discussion. Women, perhaps, spent more time in their own private spaces than in the areas of household 'business'. Better living conditions may also have encouraged higher fertility and lower mortality – more of everything, and better of everything, for everyone, and such ideas make us think about how we live in our own houses today.

Of course, it is only through the very survival of such houses that we can formulate these theories of rebuilding, and they are much more likely to survive in the country than in the more frequently worked-over streets of towns and cities. Fast forward to 1948, and Manor Farm was bought by a junk dealer for demolition, at a time when numerous old houses across the country were being condemned as unfit for human habitation (Landmark's New Inn at Peasenhall was another such). Fortunately, the purchaser had second thoughts, and instead the house was inspected on a pouring wet day by Monica and Harry Dance, who subsequently bought it and carried out a painstaking and thorough restoration.

Monica was secretary to the Society for the Protection of Ancient Buildings for many years, and her indefatigable spirit in working to save and sensitively repair historic buildings was such that any building so directly connected with her attains a particularly special aura. 'The future of a building of this interest and quality is something which seriously exercises the mind,' she wrote in 1981, when she and Harry had decided to move on from Manor Farm to another equally challenging project in Methwold Old Vicarage (now also in Landmark's care). 'How can it be secured that a building continues for at least another thirty-two years and hopefully continues for much longer?' The answer, of course, was in the acquisition by Landmark, who carried out its own refurbishment thirty years after the original.

'Behind the evidence,' wrote Hoskins, 'whatever form it may take, one must strive to hear the men and women of the past talking and working, creating what has come down to us.' There is no better place than somewhere like Manor Farm to catch those echoes of past discourse, perhaps whispers of sedition in newly private rooms, or perhaps just the happy clatter of a rumbustious farming household. **CS**

A masonry stump, all that survives of Sir Baptist Hicks' Old Campden House, with the East Banqueting House to the rear.

Fantastical finials, spiral chimneys and elaborate strapwork in golden Cotwold stone surmount the West Banqueting House.

OLD CAMPDEN HOUSE
GLOUCESTERSHIRE

THE ENGLISH CIVIL WARS

'Before we started the Prince [Rupert] had given command to Colonel Bard, Governor of Campden, to march along with his regiment,' wrote Royalist soldier Sir Henry Slinsgby in his memoirs for 10 May 1629. 'When he had left it, being so near [Parliamentary] Evesham, ye Prince likewise commanded it to be burnt, which I set on a light fire before we marched off, a house as my Lord Campden says that hath cost £30,000 in building and in furniture.'

All that survives of this site of Jacobean ambition and achievement are a few outbuildings, and its most frivolous adornment, two gloriously exuberant banqueting houses now in the Landmark Trust's care. But unusually for this book, this section will focus not on what has survived from the seventeenth century, but on what was lost, and how.

Between these two pretty banqueting houses is a jagged stump of Cotswold stone blocks, coloured by fire in places, adorned with the ghost of ovolo mouldings and Mannerist strapwork in others, the sole remains of a once-great house. Beneath the Costwold turf, the outline of earthworks reveals the skeleton of gardens that once must have rivalled any in the country.

There are many reasons why buildings disappear: deliberate demolition, fire, decay, natural disasters – and war. Britain has been extraordinarily lucky in not having suffered an invading army on its territory for centuries, and that simple fact has done much to mould our national preoccupation with our past and leave us with such a rich architectural heritage to enjoy. True, the bombing campaigns of the Second World War in the 1940s inflicted serious localized damage, but the last time there was widespread destruction and killing right across the land was in the 1640s, when the struggle between Royalists and Parliamentarians for the soul of the country set communities and even families at each other's throats. It was a period of unprecedented, often pre-emptive, destruction of secular architecture, a period of national dislocation and architectural loss, perhaps even greater than the ecclesiastical desolation of the Dissolution of the Monasteries a hundred years earlier.

Old Campden House had been built just twenty years or so before its destruction, for a man called Sir Baptist Hicks, an incomer to the quiet Cotswold town of Chipping Campden in Gloucestershire. Hicks was a self-made man from London, an ironmonger's son who had made his fortune as a mercer, supplying the court, with its extravagant tastes, and the capital with fine cloths – and then bailing them out of the debts such extravagance incurred by moneylending. He lent to King James I too, which probably explains why he was one of 300 knighted by

James just before his coronation in July 1603; later he lent to Charles I from his accession in 1625, which in 1628 earned Hicks a viscountcy.

Hicks had already built two houses fit for a lord: a mansion in Kensington, west of London, and the great house begun about 1612 in Chipping Campden. The architect of this country seat is not proven, but the house blatantly took the town's fine fifteenth-century wool church as its backdrop and the beauty of the Cotswold hills as its prospect. The closest house to it to survive today is probably the central range of Hatfield House, built by Hicks' friend, Robert Cecil, Earl of Salisbury during the same years, and which Hicks certainly visited.

Hicks' career exemplified and to a significant degree enabled several of the key social and political trends that eventually led to civil war and the execution of the king. The period from 1550 to the outbreak of the war in 1641 was an era of exceptional social mobility, when the social structure teetered under the pressure to accommodate more and more new families, and the ideal of noble generosity became twisted into a frenzied competition in ostentation beyond the capacity of many a family to support. Death duties on inheritance could also be ruinous. Deposit banking did not yet exist in England. Surplus cash (if any) had to be stockpiled at home or else tied up in buying more land, and to tide over any temporary difficulties by borrowing. The system was a gigantic merry-go-round, with the great moneyed men of London in effect paying each other off every six months or so. It was in this game of lending at a higher rate than he had borrowed that Baptist Hicks excelled.

King James himself quickly developed tastes beyond his parliamentary-allocated means, a taste and mindset he transferred to his heir Charles, a sickly younger son who would never have inherited the throne had his handsome and accomplished brother Henry not died aged eighteen in 1612. The monarch depended on parliament to vote him much of his income through taxes; parliament resented this, and, when summoned to Westminster, demanded concessions in return, which the increasingly autocratic Charles I was reluctant to concede. Until about 1630, city moneylenders like Hicks enabled

The loggia of the West Banqueting House was filled in long ago to achieve additional living space.

the crown to survive with minimum intervention by parliament, but this was not sustainable.

Added to this potent brew of social and economic pressures was the still more emotive one of religion, as a stubborn monarch with a French Catholic wife and an extremely High Church Archbishop, William Laud, appeared to many to be intent on re-establishing Catholicism. Many had moved on from the retrogressive liturgical practices that Laud sought to reinstate in Anglican churches; their religion had become altogether more radical and puritanical. Historians will always debate the relative weight of such causes, but hindsight lends a sense of overall inevitability to the eventual descent into rebellion (some say revolution) and civil strife.

It was also a war of words. Thousands of books, pamphlets, broadsheets and newspapers were published during the 1640s, leaving rich eyewitness accounts. Propagandists sought to minimize the damage and disruption done by their own troops, whilst emphasizing the outrages of the enemy. Sir John Birkenhead wrote in his newspaper, *Mercurius Aulicus*, of the 'common Parliament practice, to set a House on fire, and then to runne away by the light of it'. Stung by criticisms of this kind, a Parliamentarian writer, looking back after the end of the second Civil War, reminded his readers of the damage done by the Royalists since 1642: 'the many streets they burnt downe in the suburbs of the City of York, many streets at Bristoll, Exeter, Worcester, many Townes in Wales, whole Townes in Buckinghamshire, at Banbury, and many other parts'. Meaner properties were considered entirely expendable in the improvement of existing fortifications; castles across the country not only suffered bombardment and siege but deliberate slighting once the battle had been won.

Chipping Campden's experience of garrison and raiding parties during the war was thus entirely typical of events across the country, and replicated at other Landmark Trust sites, like Astley Castle and Swarkestone Hall. Campden occupied an important strategic position, lying at the intersection of two main communication routes, between the Parliamentarian centres of Coventry and Gloucester, and between Worcester and Oxford for the Royalists. Garrisons like Campden House provided a satisfactory return on the manpower invested in them, both in cowing the local populace and in neutralizing the potential danger of occupation by a hostile force.

After Baptist Hicks' death, Old Campden House had passed by his daughter Juliana's marriage to the Noel family, who were, unsurprisingly, Royalists. Edward Noel died with the Royalist force at Oxford in 1643. His second son Henry died in July the same year, while a prisoner in Oxford. No doubt

The tomb of Baptist Hicks (1551–1629) and his wife in St James's Church, next to Old Campden House.

Prince Rupert, Charles I's nephew and commander of the Royalist cavalry, ordered the burning of Old Campden House.

Left: The East Banqueting House was derelict before the Landmark Trust's restoration in 1987.

Above: The Landmark living room in the East Banqueting House. The Earl of Gainsborough glazed the formerly open loggia in the nineteenth century.

embittered by the deaths of his father and brother, Baptist, third Viscount Campden, then became a very active Royalist partisan based on the family estates at Rutland, meting out much the same ravages there as Chipping Campden suffered at the hands of Colonel Bard, leader of the Campden garrison.

There were no niceties in this increasingly embittered conflict, and citizens and country dwellers were as likely to suffer as the soldiers. Colonel Bard was merely representative of the times in his proclamation to the parishioners of Twyning, just north of Tewkesbury: 'Unless you bring unto me . . . the monthly contribution for six months, you are to expect an unsanctified troop of horse among you from whom, if you hide yourselves, they shall fire your house without mercy, hang up your bodies wherever they find them and scare your ghosts.'

Bard's occupation of Campden was a threat to the Parliamentarians, who planned, but did not execute, an attack

The rear of the East Banqueting House reveals the building to be larger than expected. St James's Church provides a backdrop to the site.

on the site. In early May 1645, the garrison received their orders to join the king in his victorious march out of Oxford to relieve the siege at Chester and, like so many others across the country, Baptist Hicks' great house was fired. It conjures an eerie picture: the line of tense Royalist soldiers marching with the king's nephew Prince Rupert along the escarpment, no doubt speculating and wondering at the huge blaze visible in the vale below, in which one of the most renowned houses of its generation was consumed.

The jagged remnants of Sir Baptist Hicks' house today, scorched pink by fire, still bear witness to its violent end. The ruin was at first plundered for stone, but eventually it was carefully preserved as a feature in the landscape. When the wars ended, the entire mansion house site and its grounds were given over to grazing and orchards. The banqueting houses were used to accommodate humbler folk and keep animals, and even

to store apples. The former stable block to the mansion was converted into a house, and sheep were allowed to graze on the parterres and banks of the gardens.

The site remained in the ownership of Hicks' descendants and, in 1987, Landmark took a lease on the derelict East Banqueting House. The restoration respected the work of the Earl of Gainsborough, who had glazed its open loggia in the nineteenth century. In 1998, Lady Maureen Fellowes generously passed the whole site into Landmark's care, and restoration of the West Banqueting House and The Almonry followed. The West Banqueting House, by then in use as a lambing shed, had been adapted long before as a dwelling. Its loggia, though filled in, retained traces of its Jacobean interiors, so Landmark took a much softer conserving approach there. In today's peaceful scene, the days of unsanctified troops of horsemen and civil conflict seem distant indeed. **CS**

John Harpur, second Baronet of Calke Abbey, who was knighted when he inherited Swarkeston Hall in 1630.

Swarkestone Pavilion provides a grandstand view over a walled court, perhaps once a bowling green.

SWARKESTONE PAVILION
DERBYSHIRE

1632

THE DEVISING OF ELIZABETHAN AND JACOBEAN ARCHITECTURE

The late-sixteenth and early-seventeenth centuries saw the flowering of an extraordinary and uniquely English style of architecture, flavoured with foreign sophistication but firmly grounded in native vigour and circumstance. In Europe the preoccupation with ancient classical forms had already begun, but in Mark Girouard's memorable phrase, 'the Elizabethans approached the classical treasury in the spirit of pirates rather than disciples', a buccaneering approach that is apparent well into the following century. Stranded on the edge of a Derbyshire farmyard, Swarkestone Pavilion (also known as Swarkestone Stand) is a tiny, exquisite remnant of the glamour of pre-classical English architecture.

From the coats of arms on its frontage, it seems the pavilion was built to celebrate the marriage of a young couple with family connections to one of the greatest building families of the time, the Cavendishes of Welbeck and Bolsover. John Harpur inherited Swarkeston Hall in 1630 and was knighted the same year. A marriage was arranged for him with Catherine Howard, step-daughter of Sir William Cavendish. In the accounts for their wedding year of 1631–2 a payment of £111 12s 4d was

1534–1660: Forging Identities

made to Richard Shepperd, the mason for 'New Buildynge', together with a sum for 'Boardes' for the 'Bowle Alley house', probably the pavilion, which overlooked a walled parterre of some kind that could have included a bowling green. But on the basis of style, geography and family connections, the design of the pavilion is attributed not to Shepperd but to one of the foremost craftsmen and builders of the age, John Smythson,

The profession of architect hardly existed in sixteenth-century England. In his 1580 *Dictionarie*, James Baret defined an architect as 'the maister mason, the maister carpenter, or the principall overseer and contriver of the work'. In northern Italy, scholarly study of the rules and proportions of classical architecture was being revived (the Landmark Trust's Villa Saraceno, for example, was built by Andrea Palladio *c.* 1550). In England, however, the intellectual basis of Renaissance architecture was appreciated, if at all, only partially by a small circle of court intellectuals, as the first books on architecture began to emerge. Wondrous houses like Longleat, Wollaton, Hatfield and Burghley came to fruition through the shared inspiration of such gentleman owners and of the masons and devisers they employed, like Robert Smythson, father of John.

Such craftsmen were still the most influential force in the physical creation of the great houses of the age, which often evolved on site rather than being built to predetermined plans. Owner–connoisseurs selected what they wanted from their experience of Europe and the houses of others, and from books like Serlio's *Seven Books of Architecture* (from 1537) and John Shute's *First & Chief Groundes of Architecture* (1563).

There was a passion for architecture among the ruling elite in these years. Architecture became an expression of chivalric flirtation and desire to please in Court circles, as well as expressing the usual motivations to build: family, magnificence and posterity. The aristocracy tried out new designs and applied bits of Renaissance decoration. At first the results were somewhat tentative, but from the 1580s, Elizabethan style burst into self-confident stride with houses like Hardwick Hall, Lord Salisbury's Hatfield House and Walter Mildmay's Apethorpe. There was uninhibited delight in building design, based on circles, triangles, initials – especially 'E' for Elizabeth – with allegory and metaphor to be decoded by the initiated.

From the start of the seventeenth century, and with it the reign of James I, architectural emphasis shifted. There was less

The coats of arms above the loggia celebrate the marriage of John Harpur and Catherine Howard in 1631–2 .

The original staircase was lost so restoration architect John Bucknall designed this beautiful replacement in oak.

direct quotation from Serlio and other classical treatises, but rather a move towards a more compact plan and a delight in planes and blocking, with less emphasis on the glitter of whole walls of windows or classical decoration. Decorative effect was more likely to be Mannerist, with experiments in using decorative surface effects like strapwork to emphasize proportion and spatial relationships – the patterns drawn from many sources.

There was also a revival of medieval Gothic, a pull that has proved potent to English architects through the centuries. Bolsover Little Castle, begun by Sir Charles Cavendish in 1612 as a *capriccio* of a retreat from his main seat at Welbeck, was built partly on the footings of a twelfth-century keep and had 'a faintly castle air', being a tangled mix of medieval Gothic and classical sources. Robert Smythson started the work and his son John continued it after his death in 1614.

Stylistically, Swarkestone Pavilion samples directly from Smythson's work at Bolsover. The pavilion in particular shares the style of the Little Castle's entrance front: corner turrets with ogee domes, crenellated parapet and the rhythm of the windows. The pavilion's arcaded loggia of Tuscan columns beneath four-centred arches is similar to some of the fireplaces in the Little Castle. Rather than showing off the mason's skill at carving ornament, effect is achieved by the simple relationship of one plane to another: by projection and recession, proportion and silhouette. Tiny though it is, the pavilion's attribution to John Smythson is generally accepted as one of the last forays of this most exuberant period of English architecture. When John Smythson died in 1634, classicism was already in the air.

Swarkestone Hall survived the Civil War, but Sir John Harpur's branch of the family died with him in 1679. The estate passed to the Harpurs of Calke Abbey, and the hall was dismantled in 1746–8, leaving just a stable block to become a farmhouse, and the pavilion with its walled court.

Landmark first approached the Harpur-Crewe estate to take on the Pavilion as early as 1966, but it was not until 1985 that acquisition occurred. By then, it was a floorless shell. The lead had been stolen from the tower roofs and only their timber frames remained. Such was the dereliction that almost everything except the masonry is new work in today's Landmark. The profile of the cupola roofs was reconstructed, with the slightly more generous seventeenth-century profile fitted around later repairs, like an onion skin. Here you must walk across the roof to reach the bathroom, because one of the two roof turrets was the only place to put one. The staircase had long since disappeared and so a new one was designed in the position of the original, made to a quality to rival anything that John Smythson's joiners of the 1630s might have produced. **CS**

Swarkestone Pavilion was a gutted shell before Landmark commenced its restoration in 1986.

A drawing by John Smythson for an interior at Bolsover Little Castle. Swarkestone Pavilion may plausibly be attributed to Smythson, too.

TOLERATION & ENLIGHTMENT
1660–1760

The Restoration of Charles II brought hopes of reconciliation and religious toleration, not fully realized until Parliament took the succession into its own hands after the Glorious Revolution of 1689 and, once the line of the non-Catholic Stuarts ran out, turned to the Hanoverians. England was becoming a great trading nation and this made Scotland keen for a closer relationship, formalized by the Act of Union in 1707. Politics were still shifting alliances of personal interest. London saw a period of great expansion after the Great Fire, and fascination with Classical architecture took hold, as people sought solace in their landscapes, and enlightenment though their intellect. As Landmark's properties of this period testify, this was a period of prosperity, curiosity and experimentation.

Culloden Tower in Richmond, Yorkshire, was raised to commemorate Hanoverian victory over the Jacobites in 1746.

Wall paintings of biblical texts were discovered beneath paint at Cowside during Landmark's investigations.

Wall paintings of biblical texts were discovered beneath paint at Cowside during Landmark's investigations.

Cowside is a late seventeenth-century farmstead tucked in the lee of the high fells of the North Yorkshire Dales.

COWSIDE
NORTH
YORKSHIRE

1680

RELIGIOUS RADICALISM AND CONFORMITY

Many in the Dales who were converted to Quakerism by George Fox would meet secretly in their homes.

'Better is a dinner of herbs where love is than a stalled ox and hatred therewith.' Peering by torchlight through the shadows in the parlour of a boarded-up and derelict farmhouse in Langstrothdale in the Yorkshire Dales, Landmark's team unexpectedly glimpsed the shadow of this text from the Book of Proverbs beneath layers of later paint. The farmhouse was Cowside, near Hubberholme, derelict for forty years, without electricity or water, and positioned high on a fellside above the River Wharfe. We found matching texts from Corinthians and Romans on the opposite wall ('Whether ye eat, or drink or whatsoever ye do do all to the glory of God,' and 'For of him and through him, are all things: to whom be glory for ever. Amen.') The house was already interesting as an unaltered farmstead of around 1680; these monochrome wall paintings, set within scrolled frames and in a secular setting, made it exceptional.

They were also surprising to find in a corner of England that saw the birth of one of the most radical religious movements of Christianity – Quakerism – just a few years earlier. Given this wider local and national seventeenth-century context, the existence of these genial texts in a remote dale testifies to a

George Fox, shown here in the snow at Lichfield, was a charismatic itinerant preacher and founder of Quakerism.

Crown's property. In 1551, Sedburgh School was re-endowed as Edward VI's Free Grammar School, part of the redistribution of resources by royal will that explains why so many schools across Britain bear the young king's name.

The relevance of Sedburgh School to Cowside is that a William Slinger 'of Langstrothdale', born in 1656, was taught at Sedburgh and in 1672 went on to St John's Cambridge where he trained as a priest. The progression of this bright farmer's son was impressive but not especially unusual, the combination of free local grammar schools and closed scholarships representing a genuine route to upward social mobility. William eventually became chaplain to Henry Compton, Bishop of London: in other words, a pillar of the Anglican establishment. Perhaps it was William who persuaded his parents (or perhaps relatives) that Cowside deserved some embellishment. The presence of the biblical texts on the walls and the fact that the Slingers of Cowside were recorded in the registers of the parish church clearly indicate that this was an Anglican household.

This would not be especially noteworthy, were it not that Langstrothdale and the Yorkshire Dales were also the cradle of Quakerism. With the national church dislocated through the years of Civil War, many men and women took charge of their own religion and relationship with God. Quakerism (initially a term of derision describing the behaviour of those seized by the Holy Spirit) was also perceived as one of the most threatening of these sects to the social fabric due to its radicalism.

In May 1652, in the years of Cromwell's Commonwealth, a young man called George Fox came travelling on foot through the dale. Fox was born in 1624, the son of a Leicestershire weaver. While walking to Coventry in 1646, he experienced a religious revelation, of the direct, unmediated presence of the divine life in every person. From then on, Fox preached that the spirit of Christ to be found in the heart of each man was the final authority, without need of churches ('steeple houses'), priests, sacraments, rituals, nor even necessarily the Scriptures. The payment of tithes and fine clothes were blasphemous, and the faithful might gather to find their faith anywhere – indeed it was a Christian duty to disrupt church services and sermons. Only God merited a man to stand bareheaded before him, and everyone should be addressed by the familiar 'thee' and 'thou'. Disregard of such key indicators of common civility and respect became an identifying badge of honour for the Quakers, and an intense irritation to those in authority, as was the Quaker belief that the swearing of oaths, which underpinned the legal and political system, was forbidden by Christ. Most sinister of all, Quakers did not see themselves as a sect, but a movement to win all mankind. Far from religion being one of

community's ability to heal and coexist through moments of high tension and division, and also of literacy and social mobility among the yeoman class.

From the Hubberholme parish registers, we know that Jane, wife of Francis Slinger, died at Cowside in 1682. Slingers lived in the house until about 1730, one of the prosperous farming families of the dale. Thirty miles or so to the northwest, over the high and lonely pass into Cumbria, lies Sedburgh, where there is still a school, founded in 1456 by Roger Lupton, himself born in Sedbergh parish. Lupton rose to become Provost of Eton, and in 1525 endowed a chantry chapel at Sedburgh to pray for his soul after death. By 1528, an associated chantry school had been built, bound by its foundation deed to St John's College, Cambridge, to which Lupton endowed scholarships from the school. The Reformation outlawed prayers for the dead, and a 1547 act under the boy king Edward VI made all chantries the

the mainstays of social hierarchy, Quakerism aspired to make it the means to upend it.

Such views were extreme even in Cromwell's England and Fox had already suffered imprisonment for his ideas by 1652, when he set out for the north-west of England on a pilgrimage of personal discovery. His route through the Yorkshire Dales can be traced with topographical precision from *The Journal of George Fox*, dictated to his stepson in 1675. In late May 1652, Fox 'came through the Dales to a man's house, one Tennant and I was moved to speak to the family, and as I was turning away from them I was moved to turn again and to declare God's everlasting truth to him and he was convinced and his family, and lived and died in the Truth.' This was William Tennant, who lived at Scarhouse, just a few miles down the dale from Cowside, and which became one of the earliest and longest-lasting Quaker meeting houses and burial grounds.

Also in May 1652, at Pendle Hill, Fox had a vision of 'a great people in white raiment by a river's side coming to the Lord, and a vision of places where a great people would be gathered'. He travelled on to Sedbergh or, more precisely, to Briggflatts just outside the town. On 13 June 1652, Fox preached to an expectant crowd of 1,000 or so people at Firbank Fell between Sedbergh and Kendal, with far-stretching views on the

Westmorland side of the Lune. He recognized the crowd as the people in white raiment of his vision, and his message of prophetic authority answered the yearnings and hopes of this community of earnest-hearted followers. Within a few weeks, this solitary enthusiast gathered an eager band of disciples, and the Dales became a strong centre of Quakerism. The movement spread rapidly, as Fox and other leaders travelled the country. They began to present a significant threat even to a regime seeking a fairer and more equitable way to rule, and more imprisonment followed.

In 1658, Oliver Cromwell died ('people not much minding it', as an Essex clergyman recorded in his diary). By now the Quakers were a genuine political as well as religious force, on the margins perhaps but impossible to ignore for the socially iconoclastic implications of their views.

When Charles II was made monarch in 1660, the reign began as a period of hope. The Quakers hailed the king as 'a man of sober countenance', and he allowed them to wear their hats in his presence. Charles, for his part, initially found them 'quite entertaining'. But to most, Quakers were distasteful and ridiculous in their extreme behaviour, finding notoriety in going naked – or, like James Naylor in Bristol in 1656, posturing as Christ – and dangerous in refusing to moderate their behaviour.

The kitchen, or 'housebody', was severely dilapidated before its rescue by Landmark.

An inserted eighteenth-century fireplace was revealed in the massive kitchen hearth during restoration.

Cowside's residents were Anglicans. They worshipped here at nearby Hubberholme Church, whose rood screen is a rare survivor of the Reformation.

The insecure new regime, seeking to re-establish a broad Anglican church but fearing potentially treasonous Papists on one side and socially undermining Non-conformists on the other, resorted to legislation to shore itself up, requiring oaths of allegiance for public office, licensing all printing presses, requiring uniform adherence to the Book of Common Prayer, prohibiting Non-conformist preaching within five miles of a town, and finally, under the Conventicle Acts, making the gathering of five or more people for an unorthodox religious meeting an offence punishable by fine, imprisonment and, at the third offence, by transportation. Many Quakers did indeed flee, or were transported, to the New World, but even there they were outlawed by some early Puritan settlements.

The early Quakers in part found their identity through civil disobedience, which meant they suffered more than any other dissenting group. Thousands were imprisoned, but this too became a way of testifying their faith. Quakers were set on by mobs in the street, as, with swords and staves, in Richmond in 1660, but there was equally much quiet sympathy: in 1682, 'sum small quantitie of goods' were seized in Swaledale from Quakers Jeffrey Lonsdale and Anthony Pratt, 'all of which was given to the poore, but the poore did cary or send every man his owne again'.

At the trial of the York Assizes in 1663, George Wilson of Cray Farm, another neighbour to Cowside, was prosecuted for holding meetings in his house. James Tennant of Scarhouse died in York Castle, imprisoned for his faith. It must have been the Quakers' neighbours in the dale who informed the authorities of their activities, their antagonism stemming from a clash of radical new religion with nostalgia for pre-Reformation ways.

In Hubberholme Church is Catholic evidence of earlier religious controversy – one of two surviving rood lofts in Yorkshire, outlawed at the Reformation but smuggled into this tiny parish church, probably from nearby Coverham Priory. It was in front of this that the Slingers of Cowside worshipped bareheaded, while the Tennants and Wilsons wore their hats at their simple gatherings in their parlours and barns.

When Protestant William and Mary of Orange took the throne after the brief and disastrous reign of Catholic James II was ended by the Glorious Revolution of 1688, a spirit of religious pragmatism prevailed. The Act of Toleration gave freedom of worship to all Protestants willing to swear the oaths of supremacy and allegiance, with specific exemption for Quakers from the strict form of oath-taking. It was an end to persecution, and Quakers became less militant and more inward-looking, with more emphasis on the pacifism for which they are known today.

The Cowside wall paintings might indeed express this new spirit of toleration under William and Mary (their precise date being, after all, uncertain). Either way, 'better is a dinner of herbs where love is than a stalled ox and hatred therewith' is not a bad expression of tolerant neighbourliness in any age. **CS**

Now restored, Cowside once more offers a warm welcome in its isolated spot in the North Yorkshire Dales.

Until Landmark took it on, Cowside stood empty and boarded up, without water or electricity.

The view from Maesyronen Chapel west towards the Black Mountains.

The chapel keeper's cottage is attached to the north end of the chapel itself.

MAESYRONEN
POWYS

THE BIRTH OF RELIGIOUS NONCONFORMITY IN WALES

The chapel and cottage at Maesyronen just outside Hay-on-Wye in Powys, Wales, are a rare and magical survival. Still standing in picturesque open countryside, its name meaning 'meadow of the ash tree', this is the oldest active Nonconformist chapel in Wales and, together with its adjacent cottage, Maesyronen is a window on religious life here three centuries ago.

The civil wars of the 1640s in Britain were wars of religion, and in the decade that followed, under the English republic, the Anglican Church in Wales was dealt a blow from which it would never recover. Bishops were abolished by Parliament in 1643, and the particularly punitive terms of the 'Act for the better Propagation and Preaching of the Gospel in Wales' of 1650 saw hundreds of Welsh clergymen ejected from their parishes for alleged 'malignancy' by the new ultra-Protestant, Puritan regime. Among the many evicted was the Vicar of Glasbury, the parish in which Maesyronen stands. In this new world, a whole range of 'reformed' religious groups emerged, drawn into the vacuum created by the crushing of the Anglican Church. In some cases, a Puritan minister was given responsibility for a parish, proclaiming the gospel from the existing pulpits; in

others, itinerant preachers, or leaders of new reforming groups such as the Quakers or Baptists, drew less formal congregations to them. In 1653, the Puritan Richard Powell was appointed Vicar of Glasbury and set about preaching the reformed religion to the once-Anglican congregation.

After the death of Oliver Cromwell in 1658, the English republic began to disintegrate, and in 1660 the monarchy was restored. The young Charles II was open to a restored Church of England broad enough to encompass many of the new breeds of Christianity. But a conservative House of Commons and body of reinstated Anglican bishops were adamantly opposed. The result was the reinstitution of a narrow definition of Anglicanism, expressed in the Act of Uniformity of 1662. At a stroke, hundreds of ministers and their congregations were excluded from the restored church and, with the Conventicle Act of 1664, were more or less prohibited from meeting at all. They were now seen as 'Nonconformists'.

At Glasbury, Richard Powell was expelled and his predecessor, Alexander Griffith, was restored to the parish. Griffith set about rebuilding the medieval church on the banks of the Wye, which had been badly damaged by flooding. While this served the old Anglicans, those who had become convinced by a simpler form of worship that focused closely on scripture were left out in the cold. After the Restoration, the Maesllwch estate of Glasbury was inherited by the prominent Puritan

The timber frame of the much older building embedded within Maesyronen Chapel can be seen from the stairs.

The northern end of the cottage, known as the stable, was collapsing when Landmark took on the building, and had to be entirely rebuilt.

gentleman Charles Lloyd, who was connected to the charismatic Independent pastor, Henry Maurice. In 1675, Lloyd was identified as an elder of the Independents in Brecknock. It was with his arrival, if not before, that the buildings at Maesyronen began to function as an illicit religious meeting place – although it is possible they were being thus used during the interregnum. Maesyronen was then not a chapel but a comfortable house on the Maesllwch estate with an attached animal byre. Between the cottage and chapel today stands a large oak cruck truss, part of the timber frame of these earlier buildings.

The accession to the throne of the Catholic James II in 1685 was the disaster many had predicted, and in 1688 he fled to France and the Calvinist William III and Mary II were confirmed as his successors. Religious reform quickly followed, and with the Toleration Act of 1689, the lives of the worshippers in the barn at Maesyronen were instantly transformed as, with various provisos, they were now permitted to worship freely. Charles Lloyd quickly found the funds to rebuild the barn as a chapel proper, and the result is the simple but fine building that still stands today. The existence of an official chapel here in 1697 is confirmed by its being registered at the Presteigne Quarter Sessions. The chapel prospered, enjoying the continuing support of the affluent and generous Lloyd family. Lewis Lloyd, Thomas' son, included in his will a stipulation if any of his successors wished to sell the land at Maesyronen they would need to provide the funds to erect a new chapel elsewhere. The first minister to be installed at Maesyronen was David Price, who as a schoolmaster embodied the enduring connection between Nonconformity and education.

The chapel created at Maesyronen is a simple rectangular structure of six bays, measuring approximately 15.25 x 7.5 metres/50 x 22 feet. It is built from local rubble with a stone slate roof, and two small gabled pediments over the western door and eastern window of the entrance facade. The windows, although they have had replacement glass, are still the early casements. As with all early Nonconformist chapels, it is defined by its simplicity. Eschewing the traditions of the Catholic Church, these reforming groups sought to reassert the Bible as the source of all guidance on personal behaviour and worship, and to dispense with any practice without a specific biblical source. Religious paintings and icons, elaborate interiors and prescriptive religious hierarchies were largely disposed of. Instead, these chapels were plain preaching boxes where the words of scripture and their meaning could be clearly elucidated. At Maesyronen, though the building is on an east–west orientation, the focal point is on the north wall, and – as with other Nonconformist chapels – is defined by the pulpit and not an altar. The building retains a wonderful collection of very early furniture arranged as it must always have been. This includes three box-pews of vertical boards with seats, floorboards and book rests, fixed against the walls. In the body of the chapel is a series of benches, one dated 1728. The Communion table has six turned legs and may well have been here from the 1690s.

The small cottage at the chapel's west end replaced the larger, earlier house, and was certainly standing by 1720 when the 'little house' is mentioned in a deed. In the cupboard under the stair, the doorway through from the earlier house to what was once the barn can still be seen. The cottage seems from the first to have accommodated the chapel's caretaker. The Maesyronen congregation was never large, but the building needed to be kept clean and warm and be otherwise cared for. The small stone building with slate roof has two rooms on each of its two floors and a western extension that functioned as a stable. A fine moulded post-and-panel partition with an ogee-shaped door-head now forms the west wall of the kitchen, but was probably reused from the earlier structure. The last resident caretaker was Mrs Annie Lewis who lived at the Maesyronen cottage for fifty-two years. Twelve of her fifteen children were born here and she remained active until she moved out at the age of eighty-two in 1979.

After the departure of Mrs Lewis, it became clear to the Maesyronen congregation that the cottage needed urgent repairs. The stable was in danger of collapsing, lintels to doors and windows were rotten, the roof needed substantial repairs and the building was without running water. The Landmark Trust agreed to take the cottage on a lease from the chapel trustees and to fund its repair and renovation, allowing them to concentrate on the chapel itself. The works involved the repair of the roof, the reconstruction of the stable, the removal of a host of tin sheds and the creation of a new bathroom in the small northern extension. Running water and modern wiring was introduced and the internal arrangement reconfigured to allow it to sleep four people. The post-and-panel partition was repaired and new membranes and linings introduced to keep the building dry and warm. The building has been available for bookings since 1986. **AK**

The appearance and atmosphere of the seventeenth-century Nonconformist chapel are little changed.

London's crowded medieval streets were devastated by the Great Fire in 1666.

Princelet Street was built in the same years as Nicholas Hawksmoor's Christ Church in Spitalfields.

PRINCELET STREET
LONDON

THE BUILDING OF GEORGIAN LONDON

On the morning of Wednesday, 5 September 1666, the citizens of London awoke to a scene of fiery devastation. The acrid smell of smoke was everywhere, the pavements hot to walk upon. Fanned by an easterly gale, the Great Fire had raged for three days and nights through the ancient walled city, after starting in Pudding Lane in the house of Thomas Farriner, a baker. Viewing it from the top of Barking steeple, Samuel Pepys thought it 'the saddest sight of desolation that ever I saw. Everywhere great fires'.

Conspiracy theories of Papist arson soon sprang up, but today it is generally accepted that the fire started by accident through Farriner's negligence, and that it spread because of the authorities' indecision over demolishing adjacent streets. The fire laid waste an area of 177 hectares/437 acres. St Paul's Cathedral was destroyed, as were eighty-seven churches and 13,200 houses. It was a national disaster – but also an opportunity. London's jumbled, overhanging, overcrowded medieval buildings had been mostly swept away. The fire offered the chance for a new, more coherent street plan, and Christopher Wren, Robert Hooke and others proposed such schemes, although in the event, the state's powers were still too embryonic and most streets in the city were simply re-erected on their original medieval routes.

By 1702, the City and Westminster had connected up into 'a huge dragon of a town' along the north bank of the Thames, but today's London boroughs were still mostly satellite villages. South of the river, areas like Lambeth and Southwark grew organically around small industries, pleasure gardens and brothels. But more persistent, better-planned growth was also beginning. During the eighteenth century, London would double its geographic area, driven by speculative building.

Speculative building was not new at the start of the long Georgian period (broadly, from the accession of Queen Anne in 1702). Houses had been built speculatively in rows or 'rents' for centuries – including Cloth Fair at St Bartholomew, Smithfield, laid out for 175 new houses between 1598 and 1616 and now the site of another Landmark property. What did begin in the late seventeenth century, however, was the more carefully planned development of the aristocratic estates to the west and north of the City. These estates were usually entailed on a family and so could not be sold. The building lease was a convenient device through which development could be funded by others, and land could yield successive profits without being relinquished by its hereditary landlord. In Spitalfields – site of No. 13 Princelet Street – the investment resources of numerous very small investors were pooled for their mutual benefit.

The plain brick frontage of
No. 13 Princelet Street is
typical of the speculative
London housing in the
eighteenth century.

The Earl of Southampton's development of Bloomsbury was a key moment. His mansion, completed in 1661 (and sadly demolished in 1800), was to have a square in front of it. The first leases to build the houses around the square, also let in 1661, were building leases: the plots were let at low ground rents for periods of forty, and later sixty, years provided the lessee built a house or houses. When the leases ended, the buildings became the property of the ground landlord. Most of the Bloomsbury plots had a frontage of 7.5 metres/24 feet and this became the standard throughout London. Lord Southampton's square was the first in London to be developed in this way, and Bloomsbury became 'a little town' to grace his lordship's mansion. The conditions on which he let the land became the basis of almost all future development in London.

The broad shape of the great aristocratic estates of the West End, favoured in part because the prevailing wind blew eastwards to drive away the noxious fumes of city industry, can still be identified in their street names and often in the uniformity of their architecture. Further east, beyond the ancient city walls, the same basic form of building lease was usually employed, but the units for development were less likely to be aristocratically owned, and so were generally smaller. Here, too, began a spectacular multiplication of streets and houses.

Spitalfields, named after a twelfth-century hospital, was one such area outside the city walls, which ran more or less along today's Bishopsgate. In the early eighteenth century, rights of work and residency in the City of London were still tightly controlled by the livery companies and trade guilds, but these bodies also depended on enterprising foreigners who settled outside the walls. Many came as refugees from the Continent, especially Protestants following Louis XIV's revocation of the Edict of Nantes in 1685, which ended all leniency to French Protestants. This wave of French refugees, known as Huguenots, coincided with the early eighteenth-century building boom in London. Many were skilled craftsmen – silversmiths, jewellers and clockmakers – but the greatest number were silk weavers from Lyons and Tours, many of whom settled in Spitalfields. The immigrants were generally welcomed: 'Here they have found quiet and security, and settled themselves in their several Trades and Occupations,' wrote John Strype in the introduction to the 1754 edition of *Stow's Survey of London*. 'Also a great advantage hath accrued to the whole Nation, by the rich

Delft wall tiles in a fireplace at No. 13 speak of a cosmopolitan district.

The interior of No. 13 Princelet Street is simple but handsome in its proportions.

Manufactures of Weaving Silks and Stuffs and Camlets: which Art they brought along with them. And this Benefit also to the Neighbourhood that these Strangers may serve as patterns of Thrift, Honesty, Industry and Sobriety as well.'

A network of streets and alleys sprang up to meet the living and working requirements of the weavers, embroiderers, dyers, throwsters (silk twisters) and other craftsmen who were the first tenants. Spitalfields' street names still record their skills and French origins, among them Fleur de Lys Street, Petticoat Lane, Fashion Street and Fournier Street.

While in the prosperous and controlled West End the new streets were homogenously planned, in areas like Spitalfields development was more piecemeal, if no less dense. In 1700, Princelet Street was still a market garden known as Joyce's Garden, bordering other open ground, the Spital Field and a Tenter Ground, where new cloth was stretched out to dry.

Two businessmen, Charles Wood and Simon Mitchell, were acquiring Joyce's Garden piecemeal. They were small entrepreneurs typical of the building boom, and in 1718 they began to issue leases for plots on Joyce's Garden. In June 1719, a sixty-year lease on the plot for No. 21 (today's No. 13) was taken by Edward Buckingham, who was already building a house there. Buckingham was a mason, although bricklayers and carpenters were far more typical as speculative builders.

But 'build to let' was entirely typical. Such canny craftsmen were, in theory, regulated by building acts, passed both to prevent a recurrence of the Great Fire and to regulate the building frenzy. The acts required outside or party walls to be of stone or brick and specified the thickness of walls and scantlings for timber floors and roofs. Stone parapets were stipulated, so that roofs became half-hidden behind a parapet wall, reducing the impression of pitch. Window frames and doors were to be set back from the plane of the wall, as the newly invented sash window replaced the casement with its many leaded lights. Through such measures, the London house evolved into a certain uniformity.

Practically the whole population of Georgian London lived in such tall, narrow houses on long, narrow plots, whether in the unified terraces of the West End or the more artisanal dwellings of the outer orbit. The inflexible limits of party walls led to the insistent verticality of the city, which was commented upon by foreigners at the time.

The residents of No. 13 Princelet Street have been typical of the ebb and flow of this eclectic area. Through the eighteenth century, French silk weavers lived there, followed by an engraver, a jeweller and a fruit seller. By the nineteenth century, several families or tenants were crammed in, and Spitalfields

John Roque's 1748 map of London shows how Spitalfields developed east of the city walls, which ran along Bishopsgate at the extreme left.

became increasingly down at heel. After years of decline, in 1984 Spitalfields began to be revived in another of the great stories of twentieth-century conservation. In this context, No. 13 was bought in a dilapidated state by Peter Lerwill, who employed architect Julian Harrap to undertake its sensitive repair.

The Landmark Trust is incredibly lucky to have been left No. 13 Princelet Street through Peter Lerwill's generous bequest, the only way such a house in such a place could have come into the trust's possession, given the enduring popularity of the houses of Georgian London. **CS**

The east side of the Georgian House at Hampton Court, built by Colen Campbell as a kitchen.

George I by Godfrey Kneller, c. 1714. The German chefs he brought to England cooked in the Georgian House kitchen.

THE GEORGIAN HOUSE
SURREY

1719

A ROYAL KITCHEN AND THE RIVALRIES
OF A NEW AGE

On the shady north flank of Hampton Court Palace, across a narrow lane from the Tudor kitchens, stands an austere but handsome eighteenth-century building. Despite its domestic appearance, it was a great kitchen built for George I at the time he was engaged in a bitter struggle for popularity with his disaffected son, the Prince of Wales.

The new king of Britain, Georg Ludwig, Elector of Hanover, arrived in England on 18 September 1714, six weeks after the death of his second cousin, Queen Anne. With him travelled his mistress, their three young daughters and his adult son (the future George II), the Prince of Wales. While the new king and prince put on a performance of unity, behind the scenes things were quite different. George I had disgraced and banished his wife Sophia Dorothea when their son was eleven years old, and prevented the boy from seeing his mother again. The prince never forgave his father for this act of brutality and his loathing would soon become horribly apparent.

When George I visited Hanover in the summer of 1716, the Prince of Wales was furious that he was not made regent, but given only the largely titular role of 'guardian'. Politicians vying

King George I (left), his son, later George II (right) and young grandson, Prince Frederick, by James Thornhill. Each son loathed his father.

Hampton Court Palace from the south; the kitchens were behind the palace on the shady north side.

for position soon began to polarize around either the father or the son, and a dangerously competitive atmosphere developed when Robert Walpole and a gang of opposition Whigs allied themselves with the Prince of Wales. George I cancelled his planned summer trip to Hanover in 1717 and concentrated instead on making his stay at Hampton Court as splendid and sumptuous as possible.

During the three-month royal sojourn the palace was teeming with people: the council met every week on Thursdays, and on Sundays the king gave a dinner for large numbers of politicians and courtiers whose loyalty he wished to ensure. Evening receptions were hosted, as were morning levees, dances and card parties. Estimates were drawn up for a raft of improvements to cope with this new wave of court use, which included a scheme for 'an additional kitchen or side kitchen to be built'. The brief was for a modern kitchen to provide for the sustained lavish entertaining. The architect charged with designing the structure was almost certainly Colen Campbell.

In November 1717, relations between the king and Prince of Wales broke down altogether, and the prince was ejected from St James's Palace. He and his wife moved to a house on Leicester Square in the West End of London (but were forced to leave their young children behind), where they established a rival power base. The feud between the father and son raged for the following two years, during which time every effort was made to ensure the king's court outshone his son's. The following summer, the king was once again at Hampton Court. Here the Tudor Great Hall was being turned into a theatre – in direct rivalry with the theatre the Prince and Princess of Wales patronized in Richmond. The Jacobean tennis court was converted into a large reception room accessed from the great east front gardens, and the new detached kitchen was erected a few strides from the main body of the palace where the Tudor kitchens were.

The appearance of the new kitchen was not simply a piece of design whimsy but a statement. Colen Campbell was a Scotsman who had come to England following the Act of Union in 1707. Through his publication in 1715 of a lavish architectural book, *Vitruvius Britannicus*, Campbell was an exponent of a new, more sparsely classical form of architecture, which rejected the baroque exuberance and ornament of the previous generation, represented by Sir Christopher Wren's and John Vanbrugh's architecture. The book would be crucial in shaping British architectural history in the century ahead, and instilling a new classical simplicity inspired by the work of the sixteenth-century Italian architect Andrea Palladio. In 1717, however, this shift had yet to happen, and John Vanbrugh was busy building a new kitchen at St James's Palace. With his commission for a kitchen at Hampton Court, therefore, Campbell was not only meeting a functional brief, but had the opportunity to build a structure that expressed the architectural style of which he was the champion. The result is a building both sparse and imposing. Built of plain brown brick, seven bays wide, with two floors over a basement, its entrance is defined by a pediment over the three central bays. It closely resembled a house Campbell had built in Glasgow five years before.

While the external building was an essay in a new British Palladianism, inside it was highly functional. It faced the main palace kitchens and backed onto the palace's extensive kitchen gardens. Immediately inside was a serving lobby, behind which was a large single kitchen open to the roof, with large fireplaces on each side. On the far north wall, two tiers of windows let in cool north light. While the kitchen occupied the three central bays of the building, the two bays on either side provided domestic rooms for its very particular group of staff.

While George I had expected to succeed to the British throne for some time before 1714, he remained thoroughly German. He never spoke more than broken English and retained

The interior of the kitchen at St James's Palace, built by Colen Campbell's rival, John Vanbrugh, at the same time as the Georgian House.

many habits of his homeland until his death, not least his culinary tastes. He retained a large German kitchen staff including six cooks and three bakers and confectioners. George loved fruit, adored truffles and was a connoisseur of beer. The German way of preparing meats, sausages and hams was unfamiliar to most English cooks and he had such charcuterie imported to England. The Tudor kitchen at Hampton Court was now known as the 'English' kitchen, indicating that this new domain was now that of the German cooks.

The pattern of antipathy between father and son would be the curse of the Hanoverian dynasty, as each prince of Wales fought each king. Hampton Court ceased to be the stage for such family strife when, upon the death of George II, the court ceased meeting there. From the 1760s, the palace was gradually partitioned up into scores of apartments inhabited by palace officials and 'grace and favour' residents, given lodgings by the Crown in gratitude for some service. The kitchens were redundant, and in 1787 the western half of the Georgian house was converted into a home for the foreman of the gardens, a Mr Padley. He lived mostly in the two western bays, and the kitchen itself became the housing of a huge water cistern.

The eastern section of the building (now occupied by the Landmark Trust) was created in 1834, when instructions were given for 'Fitting up of apartments for the Clerk of Works within the Precincts of Hampton Court Palace in the wing of an old kitchen'. The house was created by making a new entrance on the east front from the walled garden, building a series of new internal partitions and inserting a staircase. Part of the north end of the original great kitchen formed part of this residence, reached through a door cut into the centre of the three eastern hearths. Shortly afterwards, the clerk of works, Mr C. A. Craib, took up residence.

This eastern half of the building continued to be assigned to the person responsible for the fabric of the palace until the 1980s, when it was home to the palace superintendent. The advent of the Historic Royal Palaces Agency in 1989 brought this position to an end, and so a new use was sought. The agency approached the Landmark Trust in 1991 and the charity agreed to take on two apartments, one in Fish Court (which the palace reclaimed in 2015) and the other the eastern half of the Georgian House. A repair and refurbishment project was undertaken by Feilden and Mawson architects, and Landmark determined the fitting out and furnishing of the building. The decoration of the interior now evokes the period of the house's conversion to domestic use, but in the house's kitchen, which still occupies a corner of the Georgian kitchen, something of the building's original royal function can still be read. **AK**

The Third Duke of Richmond with the Charlton Hunt, by George Stubbs. Fox Hall was built for the dukes to use during the famous fox hunt.

The single room on the first floor of Fox Hall was a bedchamber; the bed stood in a silk-hung alcove.

FOX HALL
WEST SUSSEX

1731

SPORTING LODGE OF THE WHIG NOBILITY

'About Three Miles to the East of Goodwood, lies Charlton, a small Village, remarkable for being the Seat of Fox-hunters; here are many small Hunting houses built by Persons of Quality, who reside there during the Season for Fox-hunting; but the most beautiful of these buildings, is that of his Grace the Duke of Richmond.' So wrote Daniel Defoe in a work published in 1738, describing how a tiny Sussex hamlet had shot to fame as the home of the new aristocratic craze of fox hunting and the prominence there of the building now known as Fox Hall.

Hunting animals for sport had been the favoured pastime of kings and noblemen throughout the Middle Ages, but this was usually stag hunting, with hares a secondary quarry. Enormous enclosed hunting parks were created adjacent to most great houses and castles in which large herds of deer were kept, while wild deer roamed the royal forests. Venison was highly prized and the pursuit of the statuesque stag was seen as a noble pastime. The culling of foxes, by contrast, was regarded primarily as a practical business undertaken to protect livestock. In the later seventeenth century, as deer herds diminished and hunting parks were divided, this began to change.

An important figure in the rise of fox hunting was Charles II's illegitimate son, James Scott, Duke of Monmouth. An 'indefatigable hunter' from childhood, he kept a large pack of hounds, which he took with him to Holland in 1679 to hunt with his cousin and friend William of Orange. That winter he was expelled from his father's court and became a leader of the new political party, the 'Whigs', campaigning for the future James II to be removed from the royal succession. Over the following four years he travelled across England, on the pretext of attending hunts and horse races, to drum up support for the Whig cause. In February 1683, Monmouth visited Sussex with his friend Lord Grey of Uppark, and participated in 'a very great hunting match for a great deale of Money' held near Chichester. This was the gathering that would become famous as the Charlton Hunt.

While Monmouth was executed for treason in 1685, the attraction of hunting in the beautiful downland around Charlton was untarnished and it drew his half brother, Charles Lennox, first Duke of Richmond, to acquire the Jacobean house of Goodwood 3.2 kilometres/2 miles south of the hamlet in 1697. Also a friend of Grey (now the Earl of Tankerville), the duke helped sustain Charlton's fame, and in the reign of George I, a 'great room' designed by his friend Richard Boyle, third Lord Burlington, was built there where 'the Gentlemen fox-hunters dine every day together'. But it was the duke's son, Charles Lennox, second Duke of Richmond, who would

oversee the apogee of Charlton's fame, and build the elegant hunting lodge now called Fox Hall.

A stalwart Whig and member of George II's privy council, the second Duke of Richmond was a man of real range. As well as being a serious and respected politician, he was a patron of the arts (employing Canaletto to paint his London house), an antiquarian, a fellow of the Royal College of Physicians and a benefactor of Italian opera. Greater than any of these amateur enthusiasms, however, was his passion for sport. Shortly after inheriting his title and the Goodwood estate from his father in 1723, he became joint master of the Charlton Hunt and commissioned an exceptional building for himself in the village at Charlton. A 'house', with yard and stable, it was a lodge designed to accommodate the duke in small-scale splendour for a night or two during the winter meetings. The structure was finished by 1731 and was paid for, in part at least, from the duke's winnings at the gambling tables at Royal Tunbridge Wells.

Fox Hall was a careful blend of form and function, perhaps the work of the architect Roger Morris, whom the duke also employed at Goodwood. An externally plain brick building of two storeys, it was not entered by the front elevation on the lane, but at the back of the building, opposite the stables that were built with it. On the lower floor was a simple service room and over it a spectacular one-room *piano nobile* (noble floor) Dressed with fine panelling and an overmantel with pediment, it incorporated a fashionable bed alcove framed by pilasters. This was, in the words of John Smith, 'Britain's premier bedsitter', a place where the duke spent the nights during the hunting season, and had breakfast, but little else. An inventory of the time lists equipment for breakfast including a coffee pot, a pair of candlesticks, teaspoons, a strainer and a cream jug. The wherewithal for the duke's dinner, including his silver cutlery, was kept instead in Burlington's 'great room'. The precise location of the 'great room' has never been established. It stood close to the Duke of Richmond's house, and it may be that some of the architectural curiosities of Fox Hall – such as the partly blind Venetian windows – were designed to balance features on this now-missing second structure.

While visiting noblemen needed somewhere to lodge during the Charlton Hunt, there was in truth no functional reason for

The plain but imposing brick exterior of Fox Hall; the entrance and stables are on this rear face.

Charles Lennox, second Duke of Richmond, the politician and polymath who built Fox Hall in 1730–1.

the second Duke of Richmond to have a house there at all, given the proximity of Goodwood. He was clearly drawn to do so in part by the pleasures of participating completely and conspicuously in the communal gatherings. But more than this for one who declared himself 'bred up from a child in Whig principles', the Charlton Hunt must have had real lustre in its association with the birth of the political party to which he was so devoted. The duke formalized his patronage of the hunt by buying the manors of Singleton and Charlton from the Earl of Scarborough in September 1730, so gaining control of the forests to the south. Within the village, he bought and demolished a cottage to 'make a beautiful Green before his hunting seat at Charlton' in 1735. Under his oversight, the Charlton Hunt became the most important meeting in the country, which it remained until his death in 1750.

In 1787, James Wyatt built new kennels for the third Duke of Richmond's hounds and the hunt moved permanently to Goodwood. Charlton settled back into obscurity and the duke's house, now known as Fox Hall, was leased to tenants and a series of alterations were made. By the early twentieth century,

it was used as the manager's office and flat for the local sawmill, and in 1961 its then tenant, Mr Tinniswood, bought the house from the Goodwood estate. In 1979 Mr Tinniswood's daughter put Fox Hall on the market, and John Smith decided that the Landmark Trust must acquire it.

The work undertaken at Fox Hall, overseen by Philip Jebb, was a mixture of straight repairs and the reinstatement, as far as could be deduced, of the original arrangements. Externally, the later stucco finish was removed to reveal the original brick, windows that had been opened were returned to a blind state and the gables were expressed as pediments on the assumption that they were originally so. Internally the panelling was repaired and regilded, the walls hung with silk and a new stone fireplace surround, carved in the Chichester Cathedral workshop, installed. The Lillywhite sawmill in Charlton supplied new oak for the upper chamber floor, while the damaged old boards were reused downstairs. In 2010 the weathervane was made to work so it now once again informs the inhabitants of Fox Hall of the conditions in the 'rich and beautiful Landskip' that Defoe so admired three hundred years before. **AK**

Fox Hall's main room as it was when Landmark acquired it in 1979.

New red silk damask was woven to line the bed alcove.

The mosaic ceiling of the Gothic Temple depicts the arms of Lord Cobham's claimed Saxon forebears, perceived bringers of natural liberty.

GOTHIC TEMPLE
BUCKINGHAMSHIRE

1748

TO THE LIBERTY OF OUR ANCESTORS

'Je rends graces aux Dieux de nestre pas Romain' (I thank the gods that I am not a Roman). This inscription, chosen by Richard Temple, Viscount Cobham, to run above the portal of the Gothic Temple in Stowe Gardens in Buckinghamshire, might well seem at odds with the prevailing classical mode of architecture in mid-eighteenth-century Britain. The temple, designed by architect James Gibbs and built from 1744–48, appeared when Palladianism — a codified and analytic architectural style founded on ancient Roman practice and considered well suited to the mood of the Enlightenment — was at its height. The Gothic Revival lay in the future, as did Horace Walpole's Gothick confection at Strawberry Hill, but a continuing current of Gothic survived in country churches and Oxbridge colleges, as Gothic was seen as the style most fit for religion and ancient learning. Set in the highly sophisticated, designed landscape at Stowe, however, Gibbs' design for Viscount Cobham's Gothic Temple was a radical new departure, loaded with political and cultural meaning.

By the 1740s, Stowe had long been a celebrated landscape. Alexander Pope's 'Epistle to the Right Honourable Richard Earl

of Burlington, Occasion'd by his Publishing Palladio's Designs of the Baths, Arches, Theatres, &c. of Ancient Rome', written in 1731, singles out Stowe in a famous passage advising on how to design a landscape: 'Consult the genius of the place in all; That tells the waters to rise, or fall . . . Nature shall join you; time shall make it grow, A work to wonder at – perhaps a Stowe.'

The landscape at Stowe reflects how tastes changed over almost a century, but its initiating and presiding impresario was Lord Cobham, born Richard Temple in 1675. As the first son of a noble family encumbered by debt, Temple was enrolled in the army at the age of ten. After surviving a court martial at eleven (for refusing to obey an officer), he went on to become a career soldier. When he received his inheritance in 1697, he was already serving as a member of parliament. He was a lifelong Whig by political persuasion; in the shifting sands of eighteenth-century politics, a Whig tended to favour parliamentary power and resist any increase of royal authority. The Whig stance is sometimes defined simply as 'opposition to the Tory party', or to factions that stood for religious and political conservatism. In the early eighteenth century, political faultlines were defined by attitudes to the overthrow of the Catholic James II in the Glorious Revolution of 1688, when the line of royal succession was derailed by parliamentary decision, and to the Hanoverian succession in 1715. Also significant was the tense relationship between the ruling monarch and the Prince of Wales, who became a focus of opposition for Whigs left out in the cold under Tory administrations. But such boundaries were far from hard and fast; they delineated groupings of interest rather than political parties as we understand them today.

Temple's politics interrupted his own career, even though he had proved himself a successful campaign soldier. In 1713 he was cashiered and stripped of his rank by Whig-turned-Tory Robert Harley, Earl of Oxford and Queen Anne's Lord High Treasurer. Temple subsequently retired to the family estate at Stowe and initiated a remodelling of its landscape. At first this was intended to be to Charles Bridgeman's design in the formal French style. The plans incorporated, perhaps for the first time, a ha-ha, a ditch forming an invisible boundary in a landscape. Temple had perhaps noted the potential garden use of this feature while contemplating trenches dug on the battlefields.

The Gothic Temple was designed by James Gibbs in 1741 to evoke medieval architecture.

George I's accession in 1714 brought rehabilitation for Temple, and he was created first a baron and then a viscount in 1717. In the same year, he opened the New Inn at Stowe to accommodate visitors to his country seat (the National Trust now employs it as a visitor centre). The mansion at Stowe had become one of the centres of political power in England, a Whiggish Buckinghamshire counterpoint to Robert Walpole's Tory stronghold at Houghton, Norfolk. As such, Stowe was no mere retreat for men of letters, but a centre of intense political activity for the talented younger relatives and rising stars that Cobham gathered about him. Known as 'Cobham's Cubs', they included relatives of the Grenville and Pitt families, names that would come to dominate politics. The Stowe landscape with its architectural surprises became a political crucible in which conversation and theorizing were elicited and developed.

Cobham was active within Robert Walpole's administrations through the 1720s but became increasingly disillusioned, coming to believe that Walpole's regime, mired in corruption, favoured royal Hanoverian interest at the cost of patriotic English mercantilism. When, in 1733, his opposition to Walpole's Excise Bill brought a definitive break with its proposer, Stowe became a more specific centre for Walpole's opponents. As patriotic Whigs defending Liberty and the Constitution, they railed against what they saw as a cynical policy of corruption by a self-interested subject who had raised himself to the improper position of 'prime' minister. Cobham's garden iconography at Stowe now became an explicit political manifesto, and in this he was now helped by landscape architect William Kent, whose more informal approach to the shaping of the natural scene would come to dominate English landscape gardening.

At this point, all the garden buildings and structures were unashamedly classical in style or reference, like the main house. Highlights included the Temple of Ancient Virtue, a celebration of four Greek heroes representing poetry, philosophy, law-making and military prowess; this contrasted with the Temple of Modern Virtue, a mock ruin, beside which stood a statue that was headless but easily identifiable as Walpole. Facing the Temple of Ancient Virtue across the 'River Styx' (actually the Alder) was the Temple of British Worthies, a showcase of the busts of sixteen recent luminaries claimed for Whiggish virtue. Cobham, by now an old man, was considering what should be the climax of his gardening campaign. He decided that, for his last and most combative restatement of the national moral compass Walpole had jeopardized, he would commission James Gibbs to design in a completely different, 'new' Gothic style.

There is no doubt that the Gothic was a multifarious phenomenon in the eighteenth century, being claimed by

Richard Temple, first Viscount Cobham, was a successful career soldier and mentor to the next generation of Whig politicians.

The Temple of British Worthies at Stowe displays busts of contemporary notables admired by Lord Cobham and his 'Cubs'.

contemporaries then, and historians since, as a receptacle for political and aesthetic interpretations of all persuasions. Cobham's Cubs (for they, too, had a hand in the Temple) were quite clear in the connotations they claimed for a building dedicated 'To the Liberty of our Ancestors'. On its ceiling are the arms of Cobham's claimed Saxon forebears (neatly also enhancing the pedigree of his own family); around it were placed statues of seven Saxon deities, representing the days of the week, and paths nearby were named the Gothic Walk and Thanet Walk. So what did all this mean, in this Palladian Age?

Before the Gothic Temple was built, and later on by others who also claimed Gothic for their own very different agendas, the style had been loaded with connotations of feudal and Catholic authority. Disparaged, it was used only to harmonize with existing medieval buildings; Christopher Wren designed his Tom Tower at Christ Church in Oxford, for example, only

'to agree with the Founder's work'. Palladianism was considered the official aesthetic of the Enlightenment — lucid, inherited from the ideals of the Renaissance and committed to the cause of rational enquiry.

The term Goth was synonymous with 'Vandal', a reference to the barbarian tribes from the north who sacked ancient Rome. For seventeenth- and eighteenth-century antiquarians and Whig propagandists, this connotation of the word Goth — and therefore the architectural style associated with it — encapsulated not the violent overthrow of a civilisation but the whole epic unfolding of liberties, from the arrival of the Anglo-Saxons in Britain to the Glorious Revolution of 1688, when parliamentary consensus triumphed over Catholic superstition and absolutist authority. Similarly, the Goths were conflated with the Jutes; when Hengist landed in Thanet, he was thought to have brought with him, not Roman imperialism, but the

A circular gallery beneath the Temple's dome gives superb views of the surrounding landscape.

democratic processes described by Roman historian Tacitus as typical of Germanic assemblies. From these evolved England's mixed government, often called 'our old Gothick constitution' in the eighteenth century, especially when it was under threat.

Veneration for such Anglo-Saxon Gothic is deeply embedded in English common law, even now. The law, based on Anglo-Saxon custom, was developed into precedent almost immemorial through the Middle Ages and refined through the authority of the courts as case law evolved pragmatically with improved understanding. This Whiggish procedure contrasts with other, non-English legal systems that trace their history through the Napoleonic Code to Roman law, and such resonances were familiar to Cobham's coterie. In their reinvention, 'Gothic' was adopted to embody all the moral and cultural values summed up in the Whig interpretation of 'Enlightenment', as they sought to limit royal authority and increase parliamentary power. The line above the door, 'I thank the gods that I am not Roman', not only describes the building, so defiantly un-Roman and un–Palladian, but also appeals to its builder and visitor alike to celebrate their Saxon birthright; Saxon virtue is contrasted with the perceived moral turpitude and political decadence of the day. This Whig appropriation of the Gothic 'For the Liberty of our Ancestors' would be echoed in the architectural brief for the Palace of Westminster after it burned down in 1834, even if others, as will be seen, continued to claim this style so resonant of ideas about the past to support their own very different beliefs.

Landmark's involvement with the Gothic Temple itself broke new ground. Stowe House and its landscape entered serious decline through the twentieth century. Much of the garden statuary, including the seven Saxon deities, was sold off, and in 1923 the house became the eponymous school. The Gothic Temple, in a use of which subsequent Romantic Goths would surely have approved, became an armoury. In 1966, the National Trust took on the gardens and launched a campaign to rescue the garden buildings. John Smith was a courageous pioneer in the campaign. Landmark took on a forty-year lease of the Temple and initiated its restoration as a first step in the National Trust's restoration of the landscape. Conservation of Stowe House eventually proved an insurmountable challenge for the school and, in 1997, Stowe Historic Preservation Trust took over its management. In 2012, a £40-million, multi-phase restoration was triumphantly completed, and the house and gardens are now in a better and safer condition than they have been perhaps since they were created in the eighteenth century. Safe, too, at the heart of this meaning-laden landscape, is the glorious Temple to the Liberty of our Ancestors. **CS**

Before Landmark's restoration, the Gothic Temple was in decline, used by a school as a weapons store.

Commitment to the Gothic style is apparent in every detail of the Temple.

Culloden Tower when just built (centre left) in a 1749 view of Richmond by Samuel and Nathaniel Buck. It stands in the grounds of Yorke House (on the river, centre, demolished in 1823).

Culloden Tower when just built (centre left) in a 1749 view of Richmond by Samuel and Nathaniel Buck. It stands in the grounds of Yorke House (on the river, centre, demolished in 1823).

Culloden Tower, built to celebrate the defeat of the Jacobites in 1746, was at first called the Cumberland Temple.

CULLODEN TOWER
NORTH YORKSHIRE

1749

CELEBRATION OF THE JACOBITE DEFEAT

On 23 July 1745, Charles Edward Stuart landed on the tiny island of Eriskay, off the tip of South Uist in the Outer Hebrides. The twenty-five-year old grandson of King James II, whose whole life had been spent in exile, had with him a tiny body of supporters and a single ship. On stepping ashore he explained that he had arrived to claim the throne, announcing with characteristic bravado, 'I am come home.' 'Home', however, was rather a loose term as he had never been to Britain before, and the kilt he wore when attending balls in Rome was little short of fancy dress. But after an inauspicious start, Charles Stuart attracted the support of a series of fiercely independent Highland clansmen who felt nothing but contempt for their English Hanoverian overlords.

On 15 September the Jacobites sailed into Edinburgh to the cheers of thousands. A week later some 2,000 defeated a government force at Prestonpans, just south of the city. Charles thereby earned himself the affectionate moniker 'Bonnie Prince Charlie', and the English establishment realized the extreme seriousness of the situation. Among those looking anxiously north was the Whig MP for Richmond in Yorkshire, John Yorke,

who would go on to build this picturesque ornamental building in Richmond, the Culloden Tower.

The Jacobite invasion was wildly audacious. For more than half a century the descendants of the deposed King James II (r. 1685–8) had lived in exile in mainland Europe, always maintaining they were the true sovereigns of Britain. A year earlier, in 1744, King Louis XV of France had toyed with the idea of backing them in their attempt to reclaim the throne and install an obedient dynasty. But just as his enthusiasm waned, the scheme lit a spark in the energetic and impulsive young 'Prince of Wales', who vowed he 'intended to come to Scotland next summer even if only with a single footman'. In the end he sailed without his father's consent or knowledge and with the flimsiest of forces and a minimal arsenal of weapons.

In 1745, almost sixty years since the Glorious Revolution and thirty since the uprising of 1715, a Jacobite invasion had seemed unlikely. But while card-carrying Jacobites were few, general disenchantment with a corrupt and self-serving Whig oligarchy was widespread. Nowhere was this more true than in Scotland, which had profited little from the union with England. England was, it was realized, remarkably easy to 'take'. There were virtually no government troops in Scotland, and the excellent military roads created by General Wade had made it easy for the gathering Jacobite army to march to Edinburgh. In the event, the news of the victory at Prestonpans sent shock waves through

the counties of England. The King and most of the army were abroad at the time of Charles Stuart's landing, and the government was extraordinarily unprepared to resist the invasion. The Duke of Cumberland, son of the King and commander-in-chief of the army overseas, was urgently recalled. The town of Richmond, standing on the great north road at the northern end of Yorkshire, had reason to worry; for the Jacobites, it was only a few days' march south from Edinburgh.

In 1745, Richmond's two Members of Parliament were both Whigs: Sir Conyers Darcy, member of a powerful political dynasty, and John Yorke, also of an established Whig family, married to Darcy's cousin. When it became clear that they could expect little help from central government in defending themselves, the principal men of Yorkshire formed an 'association' and pooled money and men to try to raise their own defensive army. But time was short. Four days after Carlisle surrendered to the Jacobites in November 1745, Darcy wrote to the Secretary of State, the Duke of Newcastle, advising that though they had raised 350 men in Richmond, they would be little use as they were 'very ignorant in military discipline'.

The expected attack would, he concluded, 'end in nothing but the loss of all our men'. The roads around Richmond were blocked to hamper the Jacobites' progress, and on 20 November government dragoons finally arrived at the town to intercept the anticipated rebel attack.

In the event the Jacobites swept past Richmond, surging as far south as Derby by early December. Here the tide turned, and a retreat began that would see them withdraw north. Finally, on a boggy moor at Culloden, outside Inverness, on 16 April 1746, the Duke of Cumberland crushed the Jacobite army in barely an hour of bloody fighting. Charles Stuart himself escaped to the outer isles, from where, after many months on the run, he would sail back to France.

English jubilation, tinged with not a little relief, at the defeat of the Jacobites was immense. Thanksgiving services were held, and a furious crackdown on those who had supported Charles Stuart began. While this would bring misery for many, the Whig gentry were delighted at the outcome, and over the following few years a number would embark on significant building projects that celebrated the victory. The Duke of Argyll, the

An Incident in the Rebellion of 1745, attributed to David Morier. The painting was probably commissioned by William, Duke of Cumberland, whose troops defeated the Jacobites.

The upper two storeys of the tower were rooms for entertaining, with the lower room Gothick (right) and the upper room classical in style.

The main door to the Culloden
Tower, still graced by its
original 1740s doorcase.

Top: Detailing of the highly ornate
decorative plasterwork.

Above: A view of Richmond from the
parapet of the Culloden Tower.

senior Scottish Whig, laid the foundation stone for a new castle,
more decorative than defensive, at Inveraray in 1746. At
Wentworth Woodhouse in south Yorkshire, the Earl of Malton
commissioned the Hoober Stand, an immensely tall 'pyramidall
building' to mark the victory, in 1748. In Richmond, John Yorke
commissioned an ornamental Gothick tower on the rising
ground above his seat at Yorke House, replacing an old tower
house on the same spot. The building, complete by 1749, was
first called the 'Cumberland Temple' after the victor at Culloden;
it was later known as the Culloden Tower. The name of the
architect is not recorded, but the building is strikingly similar
to the 'Temple' that Sir Conyers Darcy built in the grounds of his
house at Aske to a design by William Kent.

John Yorke's tower, an octagon set on a square base, was
built three storeys high with a single room on each floor. Clearly
intended for entertaining, it was a cocktail of classical and
Gothic in style, the latter being of the fanciful eighteenth-
century 'Gothick' variety. As such it is an important early
example of the new taste, and was already standing when
Horace Walpole began transforming Strawberry Hill, his house
on the Thames, into the famous 'little Gothic castle'. At
Culloden Tower the first-floor room has an exuberant Gothick
chimney-piece with classical enrichments, and a plaster vault
decorated in Gothick ribbing. The room above, on the other
hand, with its pedimented doorcases and ribbon-work stucco,
is entirely classical in detailing. Recognizing the delightful scale
of the building and the quality and sophistication of its
decoration, Nicholas Pevsner described it as 'glorious' when he
visited in the early 1960s, remarking that 'the building ought to
be far better known than it is'.

Yorke House changed hands after the Yorke dynasty died
out and was demolished in 1823, with another building on the

Top: The vandalized ceiling of the upper chamber as it was when Landmark acquired the Tower.

Above: The ceiling of the lower chamber on completion of Landmark's restoration work.

The eighteenth-century stone spiral stair.

estate, Temple View, becoming the main house. By the twentieth century the tower was being used as a cowshed with a hayloft above. The lead was stolen from the roof, to be replaced with asphalt that was soon damaged. In 1977 the architectural historian and broadcaster Alec Clifton-Taylor featured the sadly dilapidated structure in his BBC series *Six English Towns*, noting in the accompanying book that 'if it is allowed to become ruinous it will be a great loss'. This exposure prompted a number of people to write to the Landmark Trust suggesting it should step in. A visit was made by Landmark staff in 1978 and the condition of the building noted as 'vandalised and being vandalised'. After protracted negotiations, helped by the chief executive of Richmondshire District Council, a freehold purchase from the owner at a market sum was agreed in 1981.

The programme of repair, begun immediately, was masterminded by Martin Stancliffe of York. Most serious was

the dry rot that had established itself in the roof, eating the roof timbers and causing the collapse of much of the fine ceiling in the upper chamber. What remained had to be taken down to allow the replacement of the roof structure and was used to inform a careful reconstruction thereafter. Similarly painstaking reinstatement was necessary on the floor below, where the eighteenth-century plaster had been badly damaged. A new staircase was created to connect the lower part of the building with the originally separate, polite upper rooms. Within the basement two storeys were created, to contain the kitchen, bathroom and a second bedroom, while the two upper rooms became the sitting room and bedroom. Most prominent on the exterior was the replacement of the Gothick pinnacles, the originals having been kicked off by vandals, re-leading of the roof and the reinstatement of the weather vane on the onion dome of the tower's stone stair turret. **AK**

Dr Johnson and 'Bozzie' return from a night's carousing in Edinburgh: 'I can smell you in the dark,' Johnson is saying.

Lord Auchinleck, seen here in his judge's robes, was an altogether sterner figure.

AUCHINLECK HOUSE
AYRSHIRE

1760

THE FORGING OF THE ANGLO-SCOTTISH UNION

During a rainy week in November 1773, two educated and opinionated old men passed the time in the library at Auchinleck House, an imposing, west-facing room with views across Ayrshire. They were a retired Scottish judge, Alexander, Lord Auchinleck, and Dr Samuel Johnson, the celebrated man of letters. Auchinleck's son, the diarist James Boswell, had persuaded Dr Johnson to undertake a tour of his native country as far north as the Hebrides with him. He was longing to impress his friend with his family seat, and desperate for his two father figures to get along.

Unfortunately, the pair held politically opposed views. 'I was very anxious that all should be well, and begged my friend [Johnson] to avoid three topics, as to which they differed widely: Whiggism, Presbyterianism and – Sir John Pringle [a physician renowned for his questing philosophical views].' Lord Auchinleck was 'as sanguine a Whig and Presbyterian as Dr Johnson was a Tory and Church of England man'. Boswell, of course, was of the same political mind as Johnson.

Eighteenth-century views of the union between England and Scotland were complex, and in ways both familiar and unfamiliar today. England and Scotland had shared a monarch since the English invited James VI of Scotland south to become their king in 1603, applying the logic of Divine Right to a slender kinship. The later seventeenth century had brought a series of ruinous civil wars and poor harvests in Scotland, leaving its population exhausted and its resources reduced. The country's small economy and limited range of exports placed it at a disadvantage with England in an era of fierce economic rivalry, both in Europe and the New World. The Scots were reliant on English goods that had to be bought with sterling, and as their economic position deteriorated, so their clamour increased that Scotland become a great mercantile power like England.

The Darien Scheme of 1698, to colonize the isthmus of Panama as the gateway between the Atlantic and the Pacific, was seen as the means to achieve this. Two expeditions of many hundreds of emigrants set forth from Leith amid great excitement. They were financed by much of the Scottish population since England's powerful East India Company, fearing competition, had forced other investors to withdraw. A fifth of the country's wealth was wrapped up in the scheme, which proved a total disaster.

The failure of the Darien Scheme caused hardship throughout Lowland Scotland; many blamed the English, but the Scottish aristocracy and mercantile elites came to believe that their best chance of being part of a major power would be to

Auchinleck House, built *c.* 1760,
is a typical Palladian villa of the
Scottish Enlightenment.

share the benefits of England's international trade and the growth of empire. Scotland's future, they felt, could be bright only in unity with England.

Accordingly, the Scottish Court petitioned the English government for formal union, to wipe out the Scottish national debt and stabilize the currency. England sought a guarantee that the Hanoverian dynasty would succeed Queen Anne to the Scottish crown, to prevent the possibility of Scotland conducting a separate foreign policy through the accession of James Stuart, another of James II's offspring and a Catholic. Scotland looked for guaranteed access to colonial markets, and a more equal footing in trade. In 1707, Acts of Union were ratified by both Parliaments, although debate was fierce, especially in Scotland.

The Georgian Age began by force of parliamentary will, and James Stuart, 'the King over the Water', was a troubling focus for both Scottish nationalism and Catholic revivalism. The Jacobite rebellion in 1745 may have failed, but it made the British realize that more determined cementing of the Union on an equal footing was needed. 'Every Scotch man who had the zeal and the abilities to serve the King should have the same admission with the administration as the subject of England had,' wrote prime minister Henry Pelham in 1746. Legislation also followed to erase the cultural, political and economic distinctiveness of the Highlands: in 1747, an act made royal, rather than clan, jurisdiction supreme in all matters. The act's implications must have been hotly debated by Alexander Boswell, ennobled in 1754 with his non-hereditary peerage, and they no doubt underlay his instinctive Whiggism.

For the increasingly integrated British establishment, however, trade and patriotism became inextricably linked. Once Englishmen and Scots were working together on trade, Scottish appetite for foreign trade became no longer a nuisance but a resource for the emerging Empire. Many Scots made their fortunes and, returning, built fine mansions. In 1758, during the building of Auchinleck House, the steward James Bruce reported that progress was slow, 'the reason of which was ... masons was all taken up as a vast worke is carrying on in this country by these great Naboos [nabobs].'

The Palladian design of such houses represented both cosmopolitanism and intellect. The Scottish Enlightenment

The library at Auchinleck House, where Lord Auchinleck and Dr Johnson argued over their politics, before restoration.

Following restoration by Landmark, the library was furnished to evoke its appearance in the eighteenth century.

was in full flower, and the stock Scottish characters on the London stage in these years were a careerist and an intellectual – figures of envy rather than contempt. Scottish engineers like Thomas Telford and James Watt, working with architects like Robert Adam and William Chambers, were changing the way and look of life north and south of the border.

The emerging consensus was not without tension. Many Englishmen, especially in London, felt swamped by a flood of Scotsmen seeking their fortune. In 1762, a Scot, the Earl of Bute, became prime minister, ousting 'Patriot', William Pitt. Bute now controlled state patronage, which led to accusations that he favoured his Scottish compatriots who enjoyed the benefits of the Union without contributing their fair share of revenue. 'Into our place, state and beds they creep,' wrote radical member of parliament John Wilkes. 'They've sense to get what we want sense to keep.' Scottish aristocrats struggled to eliminate their origins in their pronunciation and prose. 'I am indeed from Scotland,' said Boswell when he first met Johnson in a bookshop in 1767, 'but I cannot help it.'

Dr Johnson 'allowed himself to look upon all nations but his own as barbarians', wrote Boswell. 'If he was particularly prejudiced against the Scots it was because they were more in his way; because he thought their success in England rather exceeded the due proportion of their real merit.' Boswell and Johnson, who thought that Mary II had derailed due male descent from her brother James, both 'had a kind of liking for Jacobitism' (a contrary, archaic view after 1745). 'We are both Tories,' wrote Boswell, 'both convinced of the utility of monarchical power, and both lovers of that reverence and affection for a sovereign that constitute loyalty.'

So when Boswell brought his friend home to meet his father, whose accent and idiom would have grated in many a London drawing room and whose no-nonsense politics and religion were diametrically opposed to his own, all these undercurrents were swirling unsaid, intensified by the dynamics of a disapproving father and a wastrel son.

'The contest began when my father was showing [Johnson] his collection of medals; and Oliver Cromwell's coin unfortunately introduced Charles First and Toryism. They became exceedingly warm and violent, and I was much distressed by being present at such an altercation between two men, both of whom I reverenced, yet I durst not intervene.' A gossipy snippet from Sir Walter Scott reveals that when challenged by Johnson to name one good thing Cromwell had done for his country, the old laird snapped back, 'God, Doctor! He gart kings ken they had a lith in their neck!' (He taught kings they had a joint in their neck – in other words, divine right or no,

kings were but men like everyone else.) The episode illustrates the enduring tensions between those who live north and south of the border. The perennial, central political debate between centralizing (then royal) power on the one hand, and devolved parliamentary organization on the other, still rages in this year after the 2014 referendum on the union between England and Scotland, if anything with greater intensity.

As for Auchinleck House, the house declined through the twentieth century. Uninhabited from the 1960s, its roof lead was stolen, water poured in behind the parapets and the building deteriorated rapidly as rot set in and the library's fine coved ceiling fell in pieces onto the floor. In 1986, the house was acquired by the Scottish Historic Buildings Trust, who made it watertight but struggled to find a use for it.

In 1999, they turned to Landmark. Funded mainly by the Heritage Lottery Fund and an enabling grant from Boswell scholar Lady Mary Eccles via the Royal Oak Foundation in America, the restoration, overseen by architect James Simpson, was Landmark's most ambitious in Scotland to date. **CS**

The elegant dining room has a ceiling with elaborate papier-mâché decoration.

THE PATH OF INGENUITY
1760–1840

The Industrial Revolution dawned as new inventions led to the first modern factories. The British Empire was growing, even as the American colonies went their own way. Two decades of war against Napoleon both stimulated ingenuity and created social stresses; engineers led a revolution in mining, manufacture and transport, building canals and then railways that transformed the country and the ways in which life was lived and commerce transacted. In this time of social change, the first steps towards a wider vote were taken, while others looked whimsically to the past, or sought escape in the thrills of landscape and sensibility. Many of Landmark's properties of this period are poignant survivors of this time of country-wide expansion in industry, transportation and foreign trade.

Danescombe Mine, an early nineteenth-century engine house in Cornwall, was formerly used to pump water from mineshafts deep below.

The Ruin was based upon this 'Design for a Roman Ruin' by Robert Adam.

THE RUIN
NORTH YORKSHIRE

1766

THE SOUTH SEA BUBBLE

'To Hackfall's calm retreat, where Nature reigns/In rural pride, transported Fancy flies;/Oh! Bear me, bear me, to those blissful plains,/Where all around unlabour'd beauties rise.' One of the apparently 'unlabour'd beauties' that inspired the anonymous author of this 1770 poem was a folly perched perilously above a wild and wooded gorge in North Yorkshire, overlooking one of the best views in the country. From soon after its construction in the late 1760s, this folly has been affectionately and ironically known as The Ruin.

Its design can be traced to a fanciful amalgamation of ancient forms by architect Robert Adam, whose seminal experience wandering the ruins of classical Rome in the 1750s set the tone of English architecture for the next half-century. But ruination comes in other forms. The miraculous flowering of Hackfall and its companion landscape at Studley Royal nearby, both masterpieces of the eighteenth-century English landscape tradition, were the work of father and son John and William Aislabie. While William, the son, was chiefly responsible for Hackfall, his father John created Studley Royal as a distraction after one of the most spectacular and notorious

The Ruin, now restored as a Landmark, offers excellent views of Yorkshire.

The Ruin

The
SOUTH SEA BUBBLE.

BUBBLE CARD.

The Headlong Fools Plunge into South Sea Water,
But the Sly Long-heads Wade with Caution after,
The First are Drowning but the Wiser Last,
Venture no Deeper than the Knees or Wast.
1720.

The Gathering of the Golden Fruit.

LONDON;

Thomas Boys, 7, Ludgate Hill.

1825.

Buying shares in the South Sea Company became so widespread that packs of cards satirized the collective greed.

The issue of shares became a financial 'merry-go-round' involving all levels of society, as depicted in this cartoon of 1720.

episodes of political and financial ruination in British history: the South Sea Bubble. It remains a cautionary tale even today, and Aislabie was one of its chief architects.

John Aislabie (1670–1742) was the fourth son of a Yorkshire gentleman of merchant stock. Of mediocre abilities, he was educated in the fashion of the gentry at Cambridge and the Inns of Court, and inherited the Studley Royal estate in 1693. He was Member of Parliament for Ripon from 1695 until his enforced retirement from politics in 1720 (a typical 'Country' member, he voted with consistency only in his own personal interest). Aislabie was a lord of the Admiralty for the Tories in 1710, and by 1714 treasurer of the Navy for the Whigs (although such party labels still meant little). Such coat-turning led to suspicion: Speaker Onslow found him 'dark', 'cunning' and 'suspected and low in all men's opinion', while also acknowledging Aislabie as of 'good understanding, no ill-speaker in Parliament and very capable of business'.

The government was dominated by the Earls of Sunderland and Stanhope, both of whom avoided anything to do with 'finance', which they saw as 'middle class'. Sunderland was First Lord of the Treasury, and in April 1717 he appointed Aislabie as Chancellor of the Exchequer, where he relieved the earls of the work and stayed obediently in the background. The stage was set for one of the biggest financial scandals of all time, known as the South Sea Bubble after the trading company at its heart.

At this time, the national economy was still based on hard currency, as western Europe groped its way towards a modern economy based on paper money. After decades of war against France and Spain, the English parliament was obsessed by the rising national debt. An unbalanced budget was still a novelty and no one knew how to get rid of it; traditional credit systems were creaking at the seams. In France, a Scotsman in exile after a duel, John Law, was executing a carefully controlled foray into a central bank using paper money; this supported another large speculative trading concern, the Mississippi Company. The bank's apparent spectacular success for the French regime boosted the credibility of similar proposals in England.

The South Sea Company had been formed in 1711 to exploit the supposed riches of South America, then controlled by Spain, with whom England was technically at war. However, the Company's directors were confident that peace terms could be agreed and the required trading privileges granted, and the Company traded successfully against its future expectations.

In 1719, a Company representative, John Blunt, inspired by Law's activities in Paris, came to Stanhope with a radical proposal to solve the national debt crisis. The South Sea Company would take over the entire £50 million national debt

by converting it into shares in their own company. Once the wondrous markets opened up in South America (as surely they would soon), everyone would make their fortunes. Sunderland considered himself too grand to be bothered with a tradesman and referred Blunt on to Aislabie. Together the pair refined the proposals so that 'only' the £30-million debt owed to the general public would be taken on.

When Aislabie introduced the proposals to the Commons in January 1720, 'a profound silence ensued for a full quarter of an hour'. But the scheme was accepted, helped by large Company bribes to numerous members of parliament, lords and ministers – even, it was said, the King and Prince of Wales. Royal assent was given to the act to convert the debt in April 1720. The stock had more than doubled since the beginning of the year and continued to escalate steeply. The whole edifice was entirely dependent upon the rise of the South Sea Company's stock value, as people holding former government stock gambled upon the future success of the Company.

The proposal was justified thus: if South Sea Company stock was valued at a par value of £100 a share, parliament would authorize £100 worth of new stock for every £100 of its debt the Company converted – already an inflation of 100 per cent. The current market value of the Company stock was £128, but suppose the market price rose to £300 (as it might when trade picked up again). If someone holding £1,200 of government securities converted them into Company stock, the Company would only be allowed to issue twelve new shares at £100 each. But the Company would only have to give the investor four of those shares to cover investor return if the market price of its shares had risen to £300. The Company would retain eight surplus shares for further sale, netting it a profit of £2,400. Everything depended on the rise of the stock, in itself based on mythical trading assets, but the Company had every confidence.

The Bubble's growth was further facilitated by the fact that the conversion price from government security to Company share was not fixed. The higher the Company share price, the more cheaply the government could refinance the government debt from its previous owners – and the more cash would remain for other purposes. Countless smaller schemes known as 'bubbles' were sold to investors, raising finance on the vaguest

John Aislabie, scapegoat for the bursting of the South Sea 'Bubble', retired to Yorkshire to create famous gardens at Studeley Royal and Hackfall.

Hackfall became so famous it featured in a Wedgwood dinner service created for Catherine the Great of Russia.

Top: The Ruin became a destination for tourists and picnics.

Above: The stonework in the arch of the 'ruined' dome became seriously eroded by wind and rain.

The urgency of Landmark's role was underlined in 2001 when this central arch collapsed.

of ideas, one satirized as a 'scheme of great benefit but no one to know what it is'. The frenzied increase in trades put pressure on their settlement, especially since only three days a week were appointed for settlements. Some were gambling on the value of yet unissued shares as people scrambled to invest in the imagined foreign markets. The Bubble finally burst in August 1720, and the year ended in scandal and an investigation by a Commons committee.

In January, Aislabie resigned his office, deeply implicated and called to account by the Commons committee. No one raised a finger to help him; he had no influential connections and was not much liked. It was alleged that he had made a personal profit of more than £1 million on the scheme, and when asked to produce the account book, he said he had burnt it. Aislabie was found guilty by unanimous vote, and expelled from the House. As his coach rolled through the city on the way to

token incarceration in the Tower of London, the delighted populace lit bonfires, having found a scapegoat.

Thanks to the influence of Robert Walpole, who rose to prominence in the aftermath of the crash, Aislabie was allowed to keep all the money and property that he had made before October 1718; he walked away with £120,000 after the crash, making him the equivalent of a multi-millionaire today. But his reputation was ruined and he was hated by the entire nation — 'so little respected that he fell almost unpitied by anyone', said Speaker Onslow. Retrospectively, it seems beyond belief that the government and nation would have staked their all on such an ill-conceived scheme, yet recent events demonstrate that credulity, recklessness and greed still stalk financial activity.

Thus it was that John Aislabie retired to lick his wounds in comfort at Studley Royal. For the rest of his life, he put his undoubted energies into developing its landscape: what he

The blue and white interior of the main chamber is based on paint analysis of the eighteenth-century scheme.

could not achieve in one sphere, he would achieve in another. Some earlier interest in waterworks and architecture may be detected in his serving on the commissions for the Navigation of the Aire and Calder in 1699 and for the Building of Fifty New Churches. To a degree, Aislabie succeeded in using Studley Royal to expunge the memory of the South Sea scandal, since today he is far more widely known for the estate than for the detail of his implication in the financial scandal. In 1731, John Aislabie also bought the land at Hackfall, reportedly for the escarpment's agricultural potential. Little was done besides felling and hedging before his death in 1742 and the gardens as created were the work of his son, William.

Landmark's involvement with The Ruin dates back to the 1990s, although it had been on its radar for some time already. In 1995, a cliff fall placed the already derelict folly in real peril, after which English Heritage stepped in to stabilize and

underpin the edge. This focused all parties' attention, and a lease was agreed in 1999. In 2001, while Landmark was still raising the funds to save the building, the central dome of the craggy 'ruinous' facade collapsed. Work had to start even though Landmark had not reached its appeal target. The mason John Maloney spent a painstaking winter stitching the external skeleton of the domes back together, and eventually Landmark was able to recreate William Aislabie's prospect room, crisply decorated in a Wedgwood blue and white as retrieved through paint analysis. The colour scheme was appropriate enough for a building already so renowned by 1774 that Wedgwood & Bentley depicted it in their famous Green Frog dinner service for Catherine the Great, Empress of Russia. More recently, Hackfall's picturesque landscape with its other structures and follies has been wonderfully restored by the Hackfall Trust. Here, at least, there shall be no more ruination. **CS**

Life in terraces like North Street was communal, here celebrating the crowning of a May Queen in the late nineteenth century.

Life in terraces like North Street was communal, here celebrating the crowning of a May Queen in the late nineteenth century.

Built in 1776, North Street in Cromford is the earliest example of industrial housing in the world.

NORTH STREET, CROMFORD
DERBYSHIRE

1776

INNOVATION & SOCIAL EXPERIMENT AT THE DAWN OF THE INDUSTRIAL REVOLUTION

Richard Arkwright (1732–92) was a businessman of great acumen and drive.

'Wanted at Cromford. Forging and Filing Smiths, Joiners and Carpenters, Framework Knitters and Weavers with large families. Likewise children of all ages may have constant employment. Boys and young men may have trades taught them, which will enable them to maintain a family in a short time.' This is Richard Arkwright advertising in 1776 to increase his workforce at Cromford, a village in the Derbyshire Dales. To help house his workers, just up the hill from his cotton-spinning mills he built North Street, a terraced street generally accepted to be the world's first industrial housing.

Home to these first experiments in the factory system, Cromford became a model settlement acknowledged and copied by contemporaries. Never before had people been set to work at fixed hours in such an organized and specialized way, on a mechanized process housed from start to finish in a single building. Arkwright transformed Cromford from a scattered community of lead-mining families into a tightly knit industrial village, providing work and amenities for all ages.

Arkwright was not a man to attract unqualified plaudits. 'A Tyrant and more absolute than a Bashaw' is a not untypical

North Street, Cromford | 173 |

The prototype for the revolutionary cotton-spinning technique designed by Arkwright and Thomas Hayes and patented in 1767.

In a matter of decades, Arkwright's invention was scaled up and refined, and mass mechanization came to transform the lives of workers in the British cotton industry.

description, yet the first Sir Robert Peel thought him 'a man who has done more to honour his country than any man I know, not excepting our great military characters'. Born the youngest of nine children to a poor Preston family, Arkwright began his career as a barber and peruke or wig maker, travelling the countryside in search of hair as raw material.

As he travelled the country collecting hair, Arkwright had ample opportunity to make contacts. He would have been well aware of the shortage of thread in England and the attempts to invent new textile machines. The jenny spinners had gradually improved their carding and roving mechanisms but failed to solve the 'holy grail' of fully mechanized spinning. In 1767, Arkwright took up with John Kay, a clockmaker, and Thomas Hayes, a reedmaker. Hayes' critical advance was the idea of using fluted rollers to card the raw cotton, rotating at different speeds to draw it out. Arkwright got Kay to make him a small model of Hayes' idea, which Hayes had kept secret. Hayes was poor and lacked the drive or funds to lodge a patent application, but not so Richard Arkwright. He and Kay set up a workshop in a rented room to develop the idea, refining it with weighted rollers to grip the fibres as they were driven forward.

In June 1768, Arkwright lodged a patent application for this spinning frame, and a year later, it was granted. All the operator had to do was supply the frame with rovings (loosely drawn-out fibres) at the back, replace the bobbins as they filled and join the yarn if it broke. This was unskilled labour, and the machinery's potential to run many spindles at once was also clear.

Patent in hand, Arkwright astutely only granted licences in units of a thousand spindles. He knew he could keep control of his invention only by centralizing the units of production. The power required to drive a thousand spindles meant the frames could operate only in water-powered mills, and the sheer cost of entry deterred many. The size of his machinery in turn determined the structure of his mills.

The scene was set for Arkwright to settle in Cromford, and to apply water power to the still far-from-perfect machinery. It was a daring experiment, and a turning point in the history of the British factory system. On 1 August 1771, Arkwright leased the land upon which the Cromford Mills would stand for £14 a year, and started building in the same month.

Relatively little is known about this first mill, but its plan and shape became the pattern for many that followed. The five well-lit rectangular floors, about 9 metres/30 feet wide, allowed space for two rows of frames, placed on either side of a central horizontal shaft driven by the waterwheel; there was just enough room for the child tenders to creep in and around the frames. Lavatory columns, stairwells and offices were attached to, or

alongside, the main building away from the factory floor space. By today's standards conditions were harsh.

The mostly teenage workforce, their fingers still young and nimble enough to re-thread the bobbins, toiled in two overlapping thirteen-hour shifts with an average of just forty-five minutes across two breaks, during which mothers or younger sisters brought in sustenance. Yet tourists found something heroic, even sublime, in the sight of the brightly lit mills in the landscape. 'These cotton mills,' wrote John Byng in 1790, 'seven stories high, and fill'd with inhabitants, remind me of a first rate man of war; and when they are lighted up, on a dark night, look luminously beautiful.'

Arkwright was soon prospering sufficiently to create a town around his factory site. North Street was one of the results: two parallel terraces of three-storey cottages of no-nonsense design in the local gritstone. Each had just one large, well-lit room on each floor. The ground-floor room, with its range, was both living room and kitchen; a bedroom was on the first floor. The top floor was a weaver's workroom, where finished thread was woven into cloth or knitted into stockings. Large gardens to the rear accommodated plots for vegetables, and sometimes a cow or pig. Compared to later industrial dwellings in the big cities, or contemporary rural hovels, these were attractive dwellings. Arkwright built other terraces, too, with the Greyhound Inn, shops, a chapel, a manager's house and a mansion for himself.

He instigated a local festival, an annual 'Candlelighting'. In short, he created a world in miniature where he was king, or 'a Colony', as Byng described it. Cromford and its mills provided a model of factory production and social organization that was instantly copied across the rest of Britain.

Perhaps because it was such an early example, the mills eventually outgrew the available waterpower; spinning ceased in Cromford in 1891. By the 1960s, most of North Street was badly in need of repair and modernization. In 1961, Matlock Urban District Council bought Nos. 4 to 9 in order to demolish them. A preservation order followed, and in 1965 the Ancient Monuments Society (AMS) bought them for £400. The AMS approached Landmark, and in 1974 Landmark acquired Nos. 4, 5, 6, 8, 10 and 11. Their refurbishment reinstated much of the original uniformity of the street, something Grade I status has helped to promote. Today, all the houses in Landmark's ownership except No. 10 are let to private tenants.

The Cromford mills, meanwhile, have also been conserved by the Arkwright Society and, since 2001, Cromford has been part of the Derwent Valley Mills World Heritage Site. As the mill workers sang to thousands of spectators from towns all around at the 1778 Candlelighting festival, 'To our noble Master, a Bumper then fill/The matchless Inventor of this Cotton Mill,/Each toss off his Glass with a hearty Good-will,/With a Huzza for the Mills now at Cromford:/All join with a joyful Huzza!' **CS**

Artist Joseph Wright of Derby captured the Cromford mills as a dramatic new presence in the landscape of 1783.

Arkwight's complex of water-powered mills at Cromford is preserved today as part of the Derwent Valley Mills World Heritage Site.

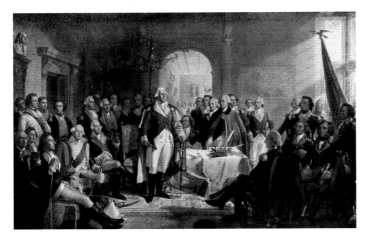

For George Washington and his compatriots, Lord Dunmore's promise of liberty to slaves who fought for the Crown threatened the colonies' very survival.

The folly is a botanically accurate representation of a pineapple executed in stone. Inside is a simple octagonal pavilion.

THE PINEAPPLE
FALKIRK

1777

LORD DUNMORE AND THE AMERICAN WAR OF INDEPENDENCE

John Murray, fourth Earl of Dunmore, painted in traditional Scottish garb by Joshua Reynolds in 1785.

'If that man is not crushed before spring,' wrote George Washington in 1775, 'he will become the most formidable enemy America has; his strength will increase as a snowball by rolling, and faster, if some expedient cannot be hit upon to convince the slaves and servants of the impotency of his designs.'

'That man' was John Murray, fourth Earl of Dunmore, last British Governor of Virginia and a key if unwitting catalyst of the endgame in the stand-off between the British Crown and American Patriots, which led to American Independence. George Washington's outrage was caused by Dunmore's proposal to arm loyalist slaves in return for their liberty. Dunmore had both swept aside the careful, if disintegrating, negotiations between Crown and colonies, and united North and South in defence of their social and economic structure.

Dunmore was also builder of one of Landmark's most iconic buildings, The Pineapple, near Stirling in Scotland. This prickly stone fruit was an addition to a pre-existing pavilion dated 1761, in the walled garden at Lord Dunmore's estate at Elphinstone. The fruit had been adopted as a symbol of hospitality in the eighteenth century, and it has always been said that when

Dunmore returned in disarray from Virginia early in 1777, he cocked a snoot at the world with this flamboyant folly.

Tensions between London and the thirteen American colonies had been simmering throughout the 1750s and 1760s. After Charles II's restoration, parliament claimed the right to control trade with the colonies and to tax their imports and exports. Yet 'no taxation without representation' had long been a key principle in Britain, fought for in the English Civil Wars in the 1640s and enthroned anew in the 1689 Bill of Rights after the Glorious Revolution. Far away in America, the colonists had no such representation in parliament and believed their rights as Englishmen were being denied. Taxation became a grievance, uniting both the more militant, formerly Puritan New England seaboard colonies and the otherwise loyalist, Anglican southern colonies of Virginia and the Carolinas. The ownership of African slaves was something else the colonies all had in common.

Tax collection in the colonies had always been lax and the colonists evasive. A prominent impetus behind the Seven Years' War between the major powers in Europe had been the struggle for empire. When the war came to an end in 1763, prime minister (and Scot) Lord Bute decided to leave a large standing force in the Americas. Burdened by crippling national debt, the administration of his successor, Lord Grenville, decided to ratchet up the British colonists' contribution to their own defence. The 1760s saw a series of provocative Acts seeking to impose import and trade duties on the colonies.

Lord Dunmore, meanwhile, spent most of the 1760s in London, making his own plans to go to America. Lady Shelburne recorded a journey in 1766 spent 'planning Lord Dunmore's Settlement in North America where he has a scheme of going some time or other . . . after tea Lord Shelburne read us some very curious accounts of the Indians in North America and after supper drew a plan of Lord Dunmore's habitation on the banks of the Ohio'. In 1770, Lord Dunmore was appointed governor of the Royal Colony of New York.

This was a plum posting, promising both honour and profit. The new governor and his wife entertained lavishly and were initially popular. However, in September 1771, Dunmore was promoted to Virginia. Despite the promise of a higher salary and a larger and more prosperous colony, Lord Dunmore did

In December 1773, rebels dumped a cargo of tea into Boston harbour in protest at its taxation without their consent.

all he could to avoid the office. 'Damn Virginia,' he wrote. 'Did I ever seek it? Why is it forced on me? I asked for New York – New York I took, and they robbed me of it without my consent.' He tried to have his appointment changed on the grounds that the climate was unhealthy and the social life inferior, but he did not succeed. The Virginians' first impressions of him were not good. The *South Carolina Gazette* stated in September 1772: 'In Virginia their new Scotch Governor began his Government with Negligence and Disregard to the Duties of his office. His Lordship was hardly ever visited, was very difficult of Access and frequently could not be spoken with . . . at last he agreed to name office hours . . . since which time all things have gone on very peaceably.' But such harmony was short-lived. When Dunmore finally convened the colonial House of Assembly in March 1773, he promptly dissolved it for proposing a committee of correspondence on colonial grievances.

Then, in May, news came from London of the Tea Act from London, requiring the colonies to buy their tea only from the financially troubled East India Company. The measure was intended both to reduce the Company's massive tea surplus in its London warehouses and to undercut the price of smuggled tea. It is a delicious irony that it was tax on this archetypally British staple that tipped the colonists into direct action. In December 1773, a whole consignment was dumped into Boston harbour, an event later known as the Boston Tea Party.

When news came in early April 1775 of an Act to seal the port at Boston until restitution of the duties was made, the House of Assembly at Williamsburg voted to set aside a Day of Fasting, Humiliation and Prayer in support of their fellow colony. Incensed, Lord Dunmore promptly dissolved the Assembly and, on the night of 20 April 1775, he clandestinely ordered barrels of gunpowder from the powder store in Williamsburg to be carried to HMS *Fowey*, anchored off Yorkton. It was, he wrote to London, 'prudent to remove some Gunpowder which was in a magazine in this place, where it lay exposed to any attempt that might be made to seize it'.

News of the move caused immediate uproar across the colony. Marching to the city, 150 men demanded the return of their powder or settlement, dispersing only when Dunmore complied with a bill of exchange for £330. It was in these hectic days that a group of slaves came to the Governor's residence asking for arms so that they might fight for the Crown, in return for their liberty. Dunmore, who owned fifty-six slaves himself, affected horror and told them 'to go about their business'. But the seed was sown. News arrived of the defeats of British troops by ragtag colonial militias at Lexington and Concord; the revolutionary War of Independence had begun.

In London, abhorrence of slavery had been mounting. Two years previously, liberal lawyers and campaigners united in defence of James Somerset, a slave kidnapped for bounty on London's streets. 'No man can be a slave being once in England; the very air he breathed made him a free man,' declared William Davey in Somerset's defence. Sensationally, the notoriously reactionary Lord Chief Justice Mansfield found in Somerset's favour, albeit on a narrow point of law. News of 'Uncle Somerset's' case also reached the colonies, giving further resolve to slaves who, more than anyone, had everything to gain and nothing to lose in these troubled times.

In May, Dunmore unilaterally decided to arm his own slaves 'and receive others that will come to me whom I shall declare free', he wrote privately. His motives, however, were not philanthropic; it was an entirely opportunistic, short-sighted initiative, a cheap gambit made in desperate circumstances. He hoped at the least to give the rebels pause, and at most to gain an army to defend the fort until British troops arrived. Crucially, only loyalist slaves might expect their freedom. The news spread

Lord Dunmore's Governor's Palace in Williamsburg was destroyed in 1781, but has now been reconstructed.

Tall trees shelter the walled
garden over which the
Pineapple presides.

like wildfire among the slave communities – but Dunmore's
strategy instantly backfired, for it also persuaded even back-
country loyalists to unite with militant Patriot leaders they had
hitherto seen as hot-headed ideologues. Revolution in the South
crystallized around the single, terrifying prospect of the
liberation of the slave force; social necessity united the South
with the North, where slaveholding was just as prevalent in
enterprises other than plantations. It was now a revolution as
much in defence of slavery as of colonial liberties. .

In June, Dunmore fled under darkness to the *Fowey*, from
where he conducted affairs as best he could, harassing the shore
with raiding parties. The Virginians declared that he thereby
abdicated his executive authority as Governor. Slaves came to
seek Dunmore in droves, and thousands more disappeared into
the swamps. A man of mediocre abilities and poor judgement,
he had become the unwitting patriarch of a great slave exodus.

On 7 November 1775, with still no word received from
London, Dunmore issued a formal proclamation, declaring
martial law and issuing a printed offer of freedom for 'all
indented Servants, Negroes or others (appertaining to Rebels) . .
. that are able and willing to bear Arms, they joining His
Majesty's Troops as soon as may be'. He was undermining the
whole fragile structure of the American colonies at a stroke, and
was vilified by the Patriots as 'arch traitor to humanity'.

Dunmore continued to operate offshore for another six
months as scenes of horror and slaughter unfolded. Among
other disastrous sallies, he was responsible for one of the most
suicidal British imperial epics, at Great Bridge in Norfolk. He
finally sailed for New York in August 1776, and thence back to
London, where, in these muddled times, he simply resumed his
political career in the House of Lords. He was even given a
second chance at colonial service, serving from 1787 as governor

The Pineapple was derelict and its stonework stained before Landmark's restoration.

The Pineapple glows golden in sunshine after restoration.

The folly is unique in architecture, but the pineapple was a common motif of hospitality in furnishings and interiors.

of the Bahamas, where pineapples, still a rare sight in England, were available for a dollar a hundred.

Sadly, sources are silent on exactly when his outlandish stone souvenir appeared at Elphinstone. The walls around The Pineapple are hollow, heated by hot air to encourage production of this and other exotic fruits in a northern clime. The walled garden of the estate flourished through the next century. By the 1970s, however, the garden was neglected and the gardeners' bothies roofless. The Pineapple itself, thanks to the quality of its craftsmanship and an ingenious drainage system, was remarkably sound when Landmark took a long lease on it from the National Trust for Scotland in 1973, going on to restore both it and its flanking bothies. The Pineapple immediately became an iconic member of the portfolio, such that an exhibition celebrating the Landmark Trust's twenty-fifth anniversary in 1990 needed only to be titled 'Not Just The Pineapple'. **CS**

William James, the engineer and
entrepreneur brought in to complete
the troubled Stratford Canal.

The men working on the canals
were known as navigators, or
'navvies' for short.

LENGTHSMAN'S COTTAGE
WARWICKSHIRE

1812

REVOLUTIONS IN TRANSPORT

When Daniel Defoe made his 'Tour thro' the Whole Island
of Great Britain' in the 1720s, he knew that creation of a better
transport system was essential for trade and a properly united
kingdom. Britain's road system was maintained grudgingly by
parish levy and labour. Carts sank in winter mud; roads were
clogged by packhorse trails and droves of cattle; and high
moorland routes were so perilous that passengers made their
wills before they mounted the stagecoach. While privately
funded turnpikes helped somewhat, it was the advent of the
canals that first revolutionized industrial transport. The South
Stratford Canal, on which Lengthsman's Cottage stands at
Lock 31, was part of this early network of waterways.

Carriage by water was the key to the expansion of trade.
As economist Adam Smith explained, 'By means of water-
carriage a more extensive market is opened to every sort of
industry than what land-carriage alone can afford it, so it is
upon the sea-coast, and along the banks of navigable rivers,
that industry of every kind naturally begins to subdivide and
improve itself.' Water carriage massively reduced the transport
costs of both raw materials and finished products.

As a small country with a long coastline and a deeply
penetrating river system, Britain had naturally favourable
conditions for such economic growth, but early improvements
to naturally occurring rivers could not unlock the nascent
industrial heartlands of the Midlands, left marooned by the
country's watershed. The first industrial canal in England
opened in 1757, cutting through from the River Mersey to
St Helen's. Other schemes followed, and with the opening of
the Duke of Bridgewater's canal in a blaze of publicity in 1761
the canal age truly gathered pace. Running from the Duke's
colliery at Worsley almost as far as Manchester, this canal
required an aqueduct across a valley and a tunnel through a hill,
both unprecedented features. It also cut the price of carrying
coal to the urban area by a third.

The full potential of canals was now apparent, and in the
1770s major trunk lines began to be built, eradicating the effects
of the watershed down the backbone of the country to create a
self-contained internal canal network to link England's
navigable rivers. By 1790, the network was much improved but
links between the north-west and Birmingham with London
were still poor, because after Coventry the canal first travelled
due south to join the Thames at Oxford. The Grand Junction
canal, the main link from the Midlands to London, was initiated
in 1793 and completed in 1805. The 258 kilometres/160 miles of
waterways linking Birmingham, Coventry and Stafford was the

Lengthsman's Cottage on the South Stratford Canal is a rare example of a barrel-roofed lock-keeper's cottage.

pivot of the whole canal system, opening up the central industrial region and the Midland coalfield to ports on all coasts.

All this threatened to make Warwickshire a backwater. The opening of the Oxford–Coventry canal in the 1770s caused a serious slump in Warwickshire, affecting both land- and water-borne trade, since it allowed the Avon to be bypassed to the east. In 1791, an act to build a canal to link Birmingham to the Severn near Worcester meant that Stratford-upon-Avon and the Avon would be similarly bypassed to the west. Faced with this new threat, a local group of promoters, the Stratford Committee, achieved their own act in 1793 for a Stratford canal as far as King's Norton: the North Stratford Canal.

Work began on the North Stratford in 1793, but its cost was massively underestimated. It was at this point, in 1797, that a local land agent called William James entered the scene. James came late to canal investment, as his father had lost most of his resources on the Worcester & Birmingham and Stratford canals. Canals had begun to appear less attractive as investments from the mid-1790s; Britain was at war with Napoleon and, as taxation increased and inflation set in, the price of metals rocketed. The

Stratford canal scheme was in deep financial trouble. The cost of the whole canal had been estimated at £22,000: five times this had already been spent on the North stretch and the value of a £100 share was now £20. William James re-surveyed the line in 1797, and a new act in 1799 permitted money to be raised to enable construction to continue. The North Stratford link with the Warwick & Birmingham was finally completed in 1802.

Astutely, James bought up defaulted shares in the Canal Company until, almost singlehandedly, he was able to pay for the southern section of the canal from Kingswood to Stratford. He appointed William Whitmore as his engineer, with the brief to tighten expenditure. Each lock on the Lapworth flight had cost around £1,600 to build, and each bridge about £500. It was Whitmore's ingenuity in slashing construction costs that gives the South Stratford Canal a quite unique character.

The first innovation was the use of cast-iron, prefabricated 'split bridges' for small farm lanes, rather than the more expensive brick crossings used so far. To avoid the need for the width of the cut to include a towpath, a narrow gap between the two decks of the bridges was left, so that the horse's tow rope

Lapworth cottage on the Stratford upon Avon canal also has the distinctive barrel roof.

could pass between the sections of the bridge while the towpath passed up over the embankment – an ingenious solution, which cost just £320 a crossing. Only at Lowsonford, where the road to Henley-in-Arden crossed the canal, was a more robust solution provided: a neat brick bridge with integral towpath.

James also bought 11.25 kilometres/7 miles of light-gauge railway, already commonly used at collieries, to speed up deliveries of bricks and shift the vast quantities of spoil and clay dug out for the channel. He then halved the cost of building a lock to just £800 by reducing the width of the canal at the lock to a single boat's width, requiring only single-leaf lock gates.

As for the cottages built to house the men who would maintain the canal, these were carefully stationed at the centre of the 'length' of canal that these men would look after. Their duties included keeping their locks in good working order, trimming hedges and scything banks, and keeping the towpath in good repair. They would maintain a constant level of water by adjusting the sluices governing its flow, and stop any minor leaks in the banks with clay puddle.

Here, too, a pragmatic approach was taken, adapting a simple bridge span to construct cosy, modular living quarters. They consist of a standard compartment, 4.8 metres by 10.6 metres/16 feet by 35 feet, on which iron bars were laid along the top of brickwork as a rectangular frame. A brick vault was then built as the roof, probably using the timber formers used for building tunnels. The South Stratford is one of the very few canals in the country where these barrel-roofed cottages are found. Just six were built on the canal, and only Lengthsman's Cottage and the Lapworth cottage at Lock 22 are unaltered.

Even as the link opened in 1816, however, the next great innovation in transport was already making itself felt. The turnpike campaign, high canal tolls and Robert Macadam's dramatically improved road surfaces were already combining to diminish what had been the disadvantages of carrying goods by road. Then, in 1825, the Stockton–Darlington railway opened, along which Robert Stevenson's *Rocket* was soon puffing. By comparison, canal transport was undeniably slow.

Canals hold a special place in Landmark's history: it was the thoughtless destruction of Thomas Telford's Junction House at Hurlestone on the Shropshire Union Canal that maddened the Smiths into starting the Landmark Trust. In 1960, the National Trust took on the by now near-derelict South Stratford Canal, which was then restored by volunteers in a pioneering conservation campaign. To help, Landmark bought the cottage at Lock 31, but it did not become a Landmark until 2006, by which time lengthsman Ned Taylor had lived out his eighty-four years in the very spot where he was born. **CS**

Split bridges were narrow, which kept costs down. The horse walked around the bridge, with its tow rope passing between the bridge leaves.

Ned Taylor was born in the cottage and lived out his life there as the last lock-keeper at Lowsonford.

The entrance of the Martello Tower is at first-floor level, reached by a bridge over the dry moat.

Napoleon Crossing the Alps, by Jacques-Louis David (1801). The threat of a French invasion in 1802–3 prompted the construction of the spectacular string of coastal artillery forts known as Martello towers.

THE MARTELLO TOWER
SUFFOLK

1812

ENGLAND'S COASTAL DEFENCE AGAINST NAPOLEONIC INVASION

The coastal defences built in Britain in the first decade of the nineteenth century to see off the rapacious Emperor Napoleon were without parallel in their extent and ambition. Prominent among these were the Martello towers, a string of 103 small artillery forts built between 1803 and 1812. The most northerly, and most sophisticated, of them all was that at Aldeburgh, an extraordinary building rescued from dereliction by the Landmark Trust in 1971.

The southern coast of England was always the country's soft underbelly, being long, perilously close to continental Europe and with many easy landing spots. Attempts had been made to provide it with a coherent string of coastal defences from the fourth century, when the Romans erected a series of high-walled fortifications along the 'Saxon shore', to the 1940s. In the 1540s, Henry VIII erected a line of artillery forts from Cornwall to Kent, and it was largely this infrastructure that was put on high alert when the Spanish Armada sailed a generation later.

In 1793, hot on the heels of revolution, the new republic of France declared war on Britain. Within just a few years a direct French invasion of Britain, led by its extraordinarily ambitious

Corsican premier, Napoleon Bonaparte, was considered a near certainty. This was not a trade war or dynastic skirmish but the work of a regime intent on European, perhaps even world, domination. In 1802, following a temporary hiatus, Britain found itself standing almost alone against Napoleon, who, having sold Louisiana to the United States for 12 million dollars, was in more than usually bombastic mood. He started to prepare a gigantic invasion fleet, and began construction of a series of enormous new harbours along the Channel coast at Boulogne, Calais, Dunkirk and Ostend. In 1804 Napoleon crowned himself emperor of France. It was clear that something substantial had to be done to stave off disaster.

Throughout the eighteenth century, the received wisdom about defending strategic positions was based on the work of the seventeenth-century French military engineer Sébastien Le Prestre de Vauban, who had fortified scores of towns and ports for Louis XIV in the 1670s and 1680s. His approach to defending a place was to encompass it with elaborate zigzags of ditches and squat walls, with a series of further triangular bastions

England's Martello towers were inspired by the success of the tiny sixteenth-century Tour de Mortella, on Corsica's northern coast, in holding off British naval vessels in 1794.

protecting each corner. When deployed at ports and harbours, the purpose of such elaborate and expensive defences was principally to deter attack rather than to repel a landing force. Should an enemy actually land, the expectation was that ground troops would be despatched from barracks elsewhere.

In 1794, while serving against the French in Corsica, the soldier and military writer Major-General David Dundas had witnessed a small, round sixteenth-century tower at Mortella holding off a British naval attack for some days. The event made a deep impression on him and three years later he wrote a highly ambitious and completely new proposal for British coastal defence: a string of small towers built along the southern coast. Placed close together and hard on the beaches, the towers were designed to hold off an active enemy attack for up to forty-eight hours. They were to be 'strong towers, favourably situated . . . mounting two or three large guns'. These, he argued, 'would answer this purpose better than larger batteries and expensive low works'. Each would cost only £700, so at least a hundred could be built.

Dundas's scheme was put into action by the Board of Ordnance in 1803 in the face of the acute French threat. The towers were to be built close enough together to produce effective crossfire with the next building in the line, and to stretch from Seaford in East Sussex round to Aldeburgh in Suffolk. The towers on the southern coast were built first, each to an identical circular plan, standing 10 metres/33 feet high with brick walls that tapered inwards. Internally they were two storeys high, the lower floor housing gunpowder and supplies and the upper floor a barrack room for the garrison. On the roof stood a 24-pounder gun that pivoted centrally to provide a complete field of fire. Access into the buildings was through a first-floor door reached by a drawbridge when there was a surrounding ditch, or by a ladder if not. The second phase of building saw the erection of towers to a similar, though slightly improved, design along the Essex and Suffolk coasts. Built between 1808 and 1812, this second section of the Martello chain was to end at Aldeburgh in Suffolk.

The Aldeburgh Martello Tower is an exceptional building among an otherwise largely homogenous group. Considerably larger than the rest of the towers, it is clover-leaf rather than round in plan, and was designed to take four guns on its rooftop. While the other Martello towers have a large brick column running up the centre of the building, at Aldeburgh there is instead a substantial central chamber, off which are four projecting lobes. When it was built the tower was part of the village of Slaughden, but relentless coastal erosion destroyed that settlement before the Second World War, and the Martello

Tower itself only survives thanks to the defences erected immediately in front of the building in the 1950s.

The building was complete by 1812 and, together with a long-gone gun platform immediately to its east, was poised for action until Napoleon's spectacular defeat at the Battle of Waterloo in 1815. Accommodation on the first floor allowed for eight double berths for private soldiers, five single berths for non-commissioned officers; a partitioned area probably housed the officer in command. On the lower floor general supplies and gunpowder were housed in separately accessed areas.

Minor modifications were made to the tower in the century after it was built, but by the 1920s it had fallen out of use, and in 1931 the now-derelict tower was sold by the Ministry of Works. Five years later it was acquired by Miss Audrey Debenham, of the Debenham and Freebody department store dynasty, and for her an elegant concrete structure was erected on the roof by the architect Justin Vulliamy, allowing it to serve as a stylish beach house. This polite use was short-lived as the building was requisitioned as an anti-aircraft post in the Second World War. After that it sank into dereliction once more, with erosion from the sea tides and winds severely damaging the buildings' earthworks and the 1930s' additions.

When the Landmark Trust bought the building in 1971, it was in a sorry and dangerous state. Vandals had long since pushed the stone copings on the parapet into the moat, which had allowed water into the body of the walls, causing the external skin of the brickwork to come away in large areas. Internally the building was derelict, the southern and central areas of the barrack-room floor had been destroyed and the storeroom floor beneath was buried under a mass of rubble. John Smith asked his architect John Warren to repair it to its original early nineteenth-century form and create 'the very simplest open-plan habitation inside'. The damaged fabric of the tower was repaired. Internally the oak timbers of the original basement floor were hauled out from under the rubble and used to repair the barrack-room floor. Off-cuts were used to make the tables and benches with which the building is now furnished.

The building first opened for bookings in 1975, and has been much used ever since, its comfort improved by a programme of additional renovations undertaken in 2002. Almost two-thirds of the original 103 English Martello towers have now been destroyed, and of those that survive fourteen are 'At Risk', many suffering the same sort of fate from which the exceptional Aldeburgh Martello Tower was delivered in 1971–5. **AK**

The Martello Tower in 1970, by which time much of the outer brick face had fallen off.

Swiss Cottage at Endsleigh epitomizes the Picturesque estate buildings popular in the Regency period.

Georgiana, Duchess of Bedford, was the presiding spirit in the creation of Endsleigh's Picturesque landscape.

Swiss Cottage was built to be a convincing replica of dwellings in the Swiss Alps.

SWISS COTTAGE, ENDSLEIGH
DEVON

1815

THE PICTURESQUE

'It is impossible to divest myself of the feeling, that the most Picturesque subject on which I have ever been professionally consulted, should have been reserved to so late a period of my life.' The author of these words in 1814, an elderly man confined to a wheelchair after a carriage accident four years earlier, was generally acknowledged to be the finest landscape designer of his generation. His name was Humphry Repton, and he was writing the introduction to his 'Red Book' for John Russell, sixth Duke of Bedford. Repton's Red Books were detailed watercolors with flaps that lifted from the existing landscape to show how he proposed to improve it. Russell himself owned Endsleigh, an estate in Devon where nature provided everything a practitioner and theoretician of the Picturesque could wish for.

Repton first came to Endsleigh around 1809, summoned chiefly by the twenty-eight-year-old duchess, Georgiana. The Bedfords' main seat was at Woburn Abbey in Bedfordshire, where they led a life of extravagant and opulent formality. Georgiana, beautiful youngest daughter of the socially ambitious Duchess of Gordon, had grown up less conventionally in the Scottish Highlands. She was said to

be engaged to the fifth Duke of Bedford, but he died tragically and suddenly in 1802 of a strangulated hernia after playing tennis. Georgiana was whisked off by her mother to recover in Paris, where the newly widowed sixth Duke, delivering a lock of his late brother's hair to the erstwhile fiancée, also fell in love with her; they, too, became engaged.

The marriage was a long and happy one. The couple complemented each other: Georgiana a vivacious and accomplished hostess who loved to entertain and dance a reel; the Duke a quieter man, fifteen years her senior. Georgiana bore the Duke twelve children (even if the last, Lady Rachael, was said to be sired by her lover, the artist Edwin Landseer). They led a happy, romping family life, with guests expected to be entertained by plays and entertainments put on by the children.

This was the background to the Bedfords' decision to create a seat at Endsleigh; distant from centres of power, the estate had been owned by Dukes of Bedford since the Dissolution. Here the family could relax in a sylvan setting, and the grand house Georgiana aspired to build was to be known as Endsleigh Cottage, with a separate wing for her children and follies dotted about the landscape. All were to evoke the 'association of ideas' so sought after by aficionados of the Picturesque.

The ideal of the Picturesque came into focus through the altogether sterner aesthetic of the Sublime. In 1757 philosopher Edmund Burke wrote a seminal essay, 'A Philosophical Enquiry

Designed by architect Jeffry
Wyatt (later Wyatville), Swiss
Cottage stands high on a hillside
overlooking the Tamar Valley.

into the Origin of our Ideas of the Sublime and Beautiful'. Burke
was analyzing the sensations provoked by craggy, perilous
alpine landscapes, all rocks and waterfalls, spirit-challenging
and awe-inspiring, yet also uplifting. Burke found beauty in such
unmistakable signs of the Earth's dramatic decay, and dubbed
this aesthetic the Sublime. He contrasted such scenery with the
calmer sensations prompted by smoother and more tamed
natural landscapes, which he termed Beautiful. So far in the
eighteenth century, William Kent and Capability Brown's
naturalistic approach to English landscape design – smooth
slopes with belts or clumps of trees and glassy expanses of still
water – largely fell into the latter category. The Beautiful had
become perhaps over-familiar to the eye, while the Sublime
offered altogether stronger and wilder inspiration, and appealed
to many. Burke's theories were an essential manifesto for those
able to travel to the Alps, and also for the Romantic era of

painting and literature, but they were perhaps harder to put into
practice on an English country estate.

The Picturesque therefore emerged somewhere between the
Sublime and the Beautiful, being an aesthetic that sought nature
as pleasingly composed, as if in a picture. The term itself comes
from the Italian *pittoresco*, meaning 'in the manner of painters',
and the theorists drew inspiration from the great landscape
painters Salvator Rosa, Claude Lorraine and Nicholas Poussin.
These artists' works often featured religious or mythological
subjects within a dramatic landscape, and their narrative scenes
prompted the desired 'associations'.

The Duke and Duchess originally hoped that Repton could
design both landscape and buildings, but he was not an
architect. His 1809 design for a 'Picturesque cottage' was soon
abandoned, and architect Jeffry Wyatt was commissioned
instead. Wyatt came from an extraordinary architectural dynasty

Pond Cottage is another Landmark
building by Wyatt to adorn the
Endsleigh landscape designed
by Humphry Repton.

Like Swiss Cottage, Pond Cottage
includes many rustic details, like
the porch's gnarled supports.

that sprang from Staffordshire farmers. He served his
apprenticeship in the London office of his uncle, Samuel Wyatt,
designer of neoclassical country houses, model farms, cottages
and lodges. In 1792, Wyatt moved to the practice of another
uncle, James Wyatt, an even more prolific and renowned
architect. In 1824, at the peak of his career and with the express
permission of George IV, for whom he had worked at Windsor
Castle, Jeffry Wyatt changed his name to Wyatville, seeking to
distinguish himself from his famous uncles. The Bedfords'
appointment of the young man to work in partnership with
Repton at Endsleigh was inspired, and the partnership produced
one of the finest expositions of the Picturesque.

In the wider world, the late eighteenth and early nineteenth
centuries brought uncertain times. Colonies were being lost.
Dangerously close across the Channel, a French king and
aristocrats had been guillotined in violent revolution for *liberté,*

egalité, et fraternité. Napoleon's revolutionary armies were
rampaging across Europe and Russia, and Britain was at war on
land and sea. Change and modernity were stirring across the
land under a new breed of engineers, industrialists and
scientists. Factories were springing up and iron bridges flung
across undreamed-of spans. Enquiring minds were probing the
possibilities of steam and electricity.

The Picturesque movement was, at some level, a rather
typically British reaction against external threat and internal
change, a whimsical withdrawal to a fantasy world of other eras
and foreign lands, such as you might find in a picture. It began
in the playgrounds of the landed aristocracy, but its appeal was
such that it soon permeated all levels of society.

Wyatville's own early career had stuttered in these uncertain
times. War with France from 1795 made building work scarce,
and he worked on government and institutional contracts. Such

The views from Swiss Cottage across the Tamar gorge are worthy of Switzerland.

Humphry Repton, shown here surveying with a theodolite, was the landscape designer of choice for Regency gentry.

utilitarian projects were dismissed by established architects like Sir John Soane, who criticized those 'architects who chose to lose that high distinction and degrade themselves and the Profession by becoming Contractors'. In fact, here were the seeds of the modern building professions. From his Uncle James's office, run in a 'shambolic manner' with 'haphazard accounts' and 'extreme disorder', Wyatville learnt the need for methodical bookkeeping, and contract procedure. He also learnt the importance of surveying, measuring, costing and supervising building works, as well as draughtsmanship. It was Wyatville's insistence on fairness and rigour of practice that eventually led to the establishment of the separate profession of quantity surveying.

In the early 1800s, Wyatville was introduced to the Marquess of Bath at Longleat, and through him to a network of aristocratic Whig families. Wyatville first worked for the sixth Duke of Bedford at Woburn Abbey in 1810, and his success both there and at Endsleigh gave his career a crucial boost. A commission at Chatsworth for the Duke of Devonshire followed, and that led to Wyatville's most famous work, the extensive alterations to Windsor Castle. At the time this was a bleak, cold, authentically medieval building, and additionally it was judged to have an uninspiring skyline. Wyatville transformed it into a unified Picturesque whole with new towers, wings, chambers, staircases, entrances and linking corridors. It was this confected icon of England's history and monarchy that cemented Wyatville's seminal role in the architecture of the Picturesque.

In 1810, the Endsleigh estate, with its steeply wooded hillsides giving into an intimate wooded valley, provided the perfect setting for an essay in the Picturesque. It offered Repton unlimited scope, a natural canvas where he could unleash his imagination: mass arboreal swirls of judicious planting threaded by silvery cascades; a Chinese bridge; a Dairy Dell with a smooth expanse of water, beside which his friend Wyatville could design a rustic cottage and an exquisite model dairy where the Duchess and her children could play at making butter and cheese, within a minute's walk from their so-called Cottage, all castellations, gables and pinnacles.

But the climax of this setting is the view across treetops of a bend in the River Tamar. Neither Switzerland nor France could offer a finer view, and here Wyatville and Repton planned a separate, smaller Swiss Cottage for the Bedfords. In time, Swiss Cottages would become a subgenre of the Picturesque in their own right, disseminated through countless pattern books across both landed estates and suburban villas. The one at Endsleigh was arguably the first, however, and through its association with glamorous partnerships, both that of the owners and the designers, its fame spread fast. The Endsleigh Swiss Cottage is convincingly rustic and 'authentic', and its simple lines and proportions avoid the whimsy of later variations on the theme. The detailing of its overhanging eaves and wide veranda is remarkable: for example, much of the directionally laid timber was installed complete with its bark. French windows in the Bedfords' sitting room on the first floor give directly onto a veranda, with breathtaking and precipitous views of the Tamar winding below. There are no alpine mountain peaks, but here for once the English Picturesque nudges the Sublime.

Landmark has been involved at Endsleigh since 1977. In 1962, the large house at Endsleigh and its park were sold by the trustees of the Bedford Settled Estate to a syndicate of friends and neighbours, who subsequently founded the Endsleigh Fishing Club. The Club owned and ran the estate until 2005, retaining much of the original furnishing in the main house and many of the staff. The Swiss Cottage, meanwhile, marooned at the edge of the park and increasingly derelict, was judiciously sold by the Fishing Club to Landmark to ensure its survival.

In 1984, a similar deal was struck to preserve the Dairy and its 'dell' environs. The Dairy, too, was in a parlous state, and it was only to secure its preservation as an object in the landscape that Landmark also acquired Wyatt's nearby cottage, by now known as Pond Cottage. It is particularly hard to secure the future of delightful but diminutive playhouses like The Dairy, because its fittings as well as its size make it unsuitable for commercial use. Yet care of such ancillary buildings is an important, if often overlooked, aspect of Landmark's work, and is enabled by the letting income from the main property on the site.

Attempts to define the Picturesque prompted surprising vehemence among contemporary commentators. Repton's own writings represent the voice of practical reason, favouring experience above its artistic representation. 'Painting and gardening are nearly connected,' he wrote, 'but not so intimately related as you imagine . . . The comfort of a gravel walk, the delicious fragrance of a shrubbery, the soul-expanding delight of a wide extended prospect . . . are all subjects incapable of being painted.' At Swiss Cottage, the endlessly changing lights and seasons across the view prove his point entirely. **CS**

Before it was acquired by Landmark, Swiss Cottage was neglected and threatened by encroaching vegetation.

The tiny, exquisite model Dairy, where Georgiana and her daughters played at being milkmaids, is also in Landmark's care.

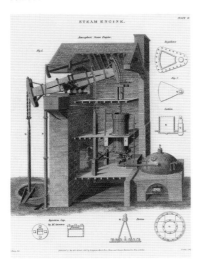

A nineteenth-century section of an engine house and its beam engine, showing how water was removed from mines.

The Danescombe Mine engine house was built in the early nineteenth century in densely wooded grounds on the Cotehele estate in Cornwall.

The buildings of Danescombe Mine, which switched from copper to arsenic extraction, show signs of numerous alterations and adaptations.

DANESCOMBE MINE
CORNWALL

1820

REVOLUTION IN MINING TECHNOLOGY

At the very beginning of the eighteenth century, Thomas Newcomen, a Baptist from Dartmouth in Devon, made regular visits to mineral mines in Devon and Cornwall in his work as a dealer in iron tools. A practical, ingenious man, he observed the huge difficulties the mine owners and workers faced in keeping the subterranean shafts from filling with water. Together with his assistant, a plumber, John Calley, Newcomen applied himself to the problem and in 1712 they unveiled 'a fire machine for drawing water from the mines'. The invention was the world's first true steam engine, in which mechanical work was performed by a piston propelled by steam moving in a cylinder. This, the 'atmospheric steam engine', would go on to transform British industry, and the buildings of Danescombe Mine on the Cotehele estate would use refinements of this technology in drawing copper and then arsenic from the Cornish earth.

From the Middle Ages the wealth of the far south-west of England had come in part from the exploitation of minerals. Since prehistory, copper had been a desirable substitute for stone. Malleable, strong and with an attractive reddish hue, it combined with tin to make bronze, harder and stronger still.

While other materials, notably iron and steel, superseded copper and bronze for strength, copper was still prized both for its decorative qualities and for its resistance to corrosion. The Romans had undertaken rudimentary shallow copper extraction in Wales, but exploitation of the deeper Cornish copper deposits started in earnest in the later sixteenth century. In the 1560s, experienced miners from Germany were brought to England and in 1580 mining rights in Devon and Cornwall were leased to the new Society of Mines Royal. A century later the Crown monopoly on copper mining was abolished, and with the advent of steam-engine technology Cornish copper production moved from a local to an industrial scale. The depth of the copper deposits made the problem of water particularly acute, and so the impact of the steam engine was pronounced. By the 1770s, sixty Newcomen steam engines had been built in Cornwall, and many of those that followed featured a modification devised by James Watt to reduce the engine's coal consumption.

Exactly when Danescombe Mine was established is not certain. The buildings stand in dense woods on the Cotehele estate, close to the picturesque Tamar river and just west of the border with Devon. The Cotehele lands, property of the Edgcumbe family, like so much of this part of the two counties, covered land in which were buried rich mineral deposits, here tin and copper veins running in a belt 19.3 kilometres/12 miles long. The estate was inherited in 1795 by Richard, second Earl of

Mount Edgcumbe, and in 1837 he granted a new operating lease on an already established copper mine at Danescombe. The mine was worked for just five years under this arrangement, then reopened after a few years' disuse as part of what would become Calstock Consols, to be operated with a group of mines for the next twenty-four years. Life for the miners here was hard and hazardous. Half of the county's subterranean miners were very young men, aged between fifteen and twenty-five. There were numerous deaths, some involving the powerful machinery, but most from tunnel collapses or accidents in the darkness deep beneath the surface.

At Danescombe, as elsewhere, the steam engine was set up in a tall engine house with a chimney. The upward and downward force it generated, by means of steam in the cylinder, was applied to one end of an elevated pivoting iron beam, at the other end of which were the rods that transferred the motion down into the mine – hence the name 'beam engine'. At Danescombe, one end of the beam was within what is now the elevated upper bedroom, the mid-point rested on the sill of the large opening and the other end projected externally. There

were once 3,000 engine houses along similar lines in Cornwall, of which remnants of some 300 now remain.

Other structures were also erected to support the business of copper extraction. After the metal had been liberated from the seam, it had to be refined; this involved crushing and grinding, then subjection to heat through roasting and smelting to burn off impurities. The crushing occurred on site, and buildings for crushing the copper ore still stand at Danescombe. The mineral was then taken to a smelting works near a plentiful supply of coal. When, in 1717, the currency of Great Britain was first coined from British copper, the first smelting works had opened in South Wales; the minerals taken from Danescombe on the river Tamar were mostly smelted in that area.

For a century from about 1760, copper was the most heavily mined mineral in Cornwall. With the new pumping technology, mines could become deeper, reaching depths of 760 metres/ 2,500 feet and, at their peak in the 1850s, the Cornwall and Devon copper mines were producing almost 40,000 tonnes of copper ore each year. But this boom was to be followed by a dramatic collapse. The establishment of new sources of minerals

When the Landmark Trust took on Danescombe Mine it had been abandoned for over fifty tears and was in a highly ruinous state.

The engine house after the restoration works of 1972–3, standing among the picturesque, ivy-clad remnants of ancillary buildings.

in South America, and the advent of large-scale steamships that could bring vast quantities of copper from Chile and elsewhere with relative ease, severely undermined the Cornish copper industry. By 1870 production had contracted to a quarter of its former size. Danescombe was among the scores of mines that closed down, and in 1872 its machinery was sold off.

There was a small reprise for the Cornish copper mines in the form of a growing demand for arsenic, which was found in the mines in association with copper ore. Formerly discarded as part of the refining process, this poisonous element now had its own market as an ingredient in the insecticides being applied to the enormous cotton fields of North America. Danescombe reopened as a copper and arsenic mine in 1888 and continued to be active into the early years of the twentieth century.

Between the wars the sixth Earl of Mount Edgcumbe, whose only son was killed in the First World War, proposed that the Cotehele estate be accepted by the Treasury in lieu of death duties and passed to the National Trust. This finally happened in 1947; it was the first country house and estate to be 'saved' in this way. The derelict buildings of the Danescombe mine lay untouched until, in 1968, Michael Trinick, the National Trust's Regional Secretary for Devon and Cornwall, and John Smith discussed the possibility of Landmark leasing and converting the building. Smith had long wanted a Cornish engine house, and they agreed that 'this is probably as good an engine house as you are likely to find, and in a lovely setting'. Landmark took a forty-two-year lease on Danescombe from the National Trust in March 1971. Paul Pearn of Pearn and Procter architects of Plymouth, who also worked on the Egyptian House in Penzance, oversaw the renovation project in 1972–3.

The buildings were in a highly dilapidated state, with only the exterior walls of the engine house standing and the interior gutted. The restoration was undertaken with great feeling for the original configuration and use of this industrial structure. New floors were inserted at the levels of the collapsed internal platforms and a new roof contructed, covered with random-width Delabole slates. Cast-iron window frames were reinstated, made from old moulds by Iron Brothers of Wadebridge. The only significant change to the historic arrangement was the creation of a new window in the gap where the beam of the main engine once protruded. This allowed for the creation of a spectacular elevated bedroom on the top floor, the glazing on the window arranged in small overlapping pieces, echoing windows in historic industrial buildings the country over. This thoughtful conversion was completed in 1973, making it a pioneering venture at a time when hundreds, if not thousands, of industrial buildings were falling out of use. **AK**

The replacement cast-iron windows at Danescombe were re-cast from surviving historic moulds.

The bedroom was created in the upper chamber where once the great beam rocked back and forth.

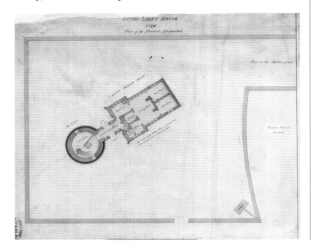

OLD LIGHT, LUNDY
BRISTOL CHANNEL

1820

A SHORT HISTORY OF LIGHTHOUSES

People often think Landmark has several lighthouses in its care, but in fact – so far – there is only one: Old Light on the island of Lundy, at the mouth of the Bristol Channel. When it was built in 1819 it was not, of course, 'old'; that name came later, in 1897, when its role was replaced by the current North and South Lights.

Despite the best efforts of successive monarchs, until the late eighteenth century Lundy would embody the twin and terrifying hazards of piracy and shipwreck in one of Britain's most important shipping lanes. Piracy was long entangled with human trafficking: for five years from 1627 the island was held by Barbary pirates, who terrorized the south-west coastlines of England and Wales, seizing Christian slaves that they spirited away to labour on the palaces of the Dey of Algiers. The Barbary threat gradually receded, but from 1744 Thomas Benson, a merchant of Appledore and member of parliament for Barnstaple, leased Lundy as a holding point for the deportation in his ships of convicts bound for Virginia; he used them as his personal slave labour on the island in the interim.

By the 1770s, Lundy was in the more honourable hands of Sir John Borlase Warren, who rose to the rank of admiral. By

Old Light stands on Lundy's west coast, with a handsome accommodation block for its keepers and their families.

Old Light, Lundy | 201 |

In 1759, civil engineer John Smeaton successfully built the third Eddystone lighthouse using stone. It was the start of a revolution in lighthouse design.

Old Light, here seen at dusk, helped to protect seafarers from the rocks of Lundy Island for nearly eighty years.

now the danger of shipwreck had became a greater preoccupation than piracy for those sailing the Bristol Channel, whose tidal range is one of the highest in the world. Though Lundy is small, ships were constantly forced close to its granite cliffs by dangerous and shifting shingle banks.

Merchants and traders from Bristol, Cardiff and Bideford began to petition for a lighthouse on Lundy, even offering to pay for its construction and maintenance themselves. They needed permission, not just from the transitory lessees of the island, but also from Trinity House. This independent corporation, still responsible for lighthouses and pilotage today, dates back to a Royal Charter issued by Henry VIII in 1514 to 'the Guild, Fraternity or Brotherhood of the most glorious and undivided Trinity [of Father, Son and Holy Ghost] and of St Clement in the parish of Deptford Strond in the County of Kent'. A guild was the traditional medieval means of organization for all manner of trades, and this seamen's guild was disturbed by the poor conduct of unregulated pilots in the Thames. Henry therefore charged his 'trewe and faithfull subjects, shipmen and mariners of this our Realm of England' to 'begyn of new and erecte and establish a Guild or Brotherhood of themselves or other persons as well men as women . . . so that they might regulate the pilotage of ships in the King's streams'. The organization became named Trinity House after its headquarters, and to this day its trustees are known as Elder Brethren.

In 1566, a Seamarks Act added to their pilotage duties, calling on the Guild 'at their wills and pleasures, and at their costs, [to] make, erect and set up such, and so many, beacons, marks and signs for the sea . . . whereby the dangers may be avoided and escaped, and the ships better come into their ports without peril.'

At this historical point, seamarks were mostly on land and not expressly created as navigation aids – they were clumps of trees, church steeples, houses and so on. The Seamarks Act gave Trinity House the right to regulate as well as create such marks; a merchant who had cut down a clump of trees that spoiled his view, for example, was upbraided for 'preferring a tryfle of private benefit to your selfe before a great and general good to the publique,' and threatened with a fine of £100.

There were no lighthouses in the sixteenth century: occasionally a pole might be driven into the seabed and a lantern placed on top, but it was unclear whether Trinity House had authority to create marks in the water until 1594, when rights of beaconage and buoyage were officially ceded to them by the Lord High Admiral. In 1609 Trinity House built their first lighthouse at Lowestoft – a pair of wooden towers, with candle illumination. However, when three hundred ship masters, owners and fishermen petitioned them to build another at Winterton in 1614, they did nothing. While this undermined confidence in their competence, private promoters were encouraged to step in. None of the ten lighthouses built in the next sixty years was built by Trinity House. The structures were by definition hard to build, and even harder to maintain – but it transpired that they could still be turned to profit.

The Crown connived at such infringements of Trinity House's authority by issuing letters patent (written orders) permitting both the erection of private lighthouses and the levy of tolls upon ships benefiting from them. As the great lawyer Sir Edward Coke put it to parliament in 1621, 'projectours like wattermen look one waye and rowe another: they pretend publique profit, intend private'.

In the event, Trinity House, too, turned royal fiat to their advantage, by petitioning for their own letters patent and then issuing leases to build lighthouses to private individuals, thus avoiding financial risk while allowing the projecteers to profit. In the early days, construction techniques did not match up to

ambitions, whether private or public. The famous Eddystone lighthouses, 22.5 kilometres/14 miles offshore from Plymouth, were first mooted in a petition to Trinity House in 1665; their comment was that such a thing, while desirable, 'could hardly be accomplished'. A first wooden tower, put in place by 1699, was swept away in a storm in 1703; its successor lasted until 1755, when it was destroyed by fire. The task of its replacement was given to the great engineer John Smeaton, who decided to build in stone. This was a significant breakthrough, and set the scene for increasingly urgent petitioning by the Bristol merchants for a lighthouse on Lundy. They chose Beacon Hill as their preferred position, and it might indeed seem obvious to place a lighthouse there, the island's highest point. In the event, it caused endless, and ultimately unresolvable, difficulties. The merchants got the foundations laid, but went no further.

In 1797, their campaign was given fresh urgency by the wreck of the *Jenny*, a ship returning from Africa with a cargo of ivory and gold dust. Lost in fog, she was dashed to pieces on the rocks in a Lundy bay still called Jenny's Cove, with the loss of all

Alexander's elevation of the Lundy lighthouse, prepared for the Elder Brethren of Trinity House.

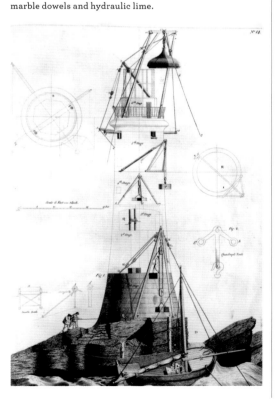

Smeaton fixed the stone blocks of the Eddystone Lighthouse tower with marble dowels and hydraulic lime.

Before its restoration by Landmark,
the lantern of Old Light was rusted
and without glazing.

Drifts of sea thrift flourish on Lundy's
granite cliffs, with Old Light standing
sentinel behind.

hands save the mate. Finally, in 1819, Trinity House was granted a 999-year lease on the site for £500 at a peppercorn rent. Daniel Asher Alexander, surveyor to its Elder Brethren, was appointed architect. Alexander had succeeded Samuel Wyatt to the post of surveyor in 1807, and had applied his own expertise to utilitarian and public buildings such as prisons, bridges, dock infrastructure and warehouses.

Alexander's buildings are characterized by design based upon fitness for purpose, principles clearly apparent in the stately Old Light and its ancillary keepers' cottages. He and his builder, Joseph Nelson, constructed the lighthouse in a year using granite from the island quarries. Its walls are 1 metre/3¼ feet thick at the base, narrowing to 60 cm/2 feet near the lantern. At 29 metres/95 feet tall and 122 metres/400 feet above sea level, Old Light was the highest light in England when it was completed in February 1820. Its upper beam revolved by clockwork, once every sixteen minutes, with an attention-

grabbing flash every two minutes. The beam was visible 5.5 metres/18 feet above sea level for some 52 kilometres (32 miles). A secondary arc of lights, displayed beneath a canopy lower down the tower, was a last warning visible only to ships 6.5 kilometres/4 miles or less from the shore.

Unfortunately, this last measure proved a hazard in its own right, because to ships within 13 kilometres/8 miles of the shore the two illuminations merged. In 1828, *La Jeune Emma* bound for Cherbourg from Martinique mistook the Lundy lights for Ushant and foundered on the rocks with the loss of thirteen lives, including the niece of the Empress Josephine. There was a further problem. The lighthouse stands so high that even if the island is clear, its lantern is often capped by fog or cloud. From 1862, in foggy conditions it was supplemented by a battery, and two 18-pounders sounded a warning every ten minutes.

The Lundy keepers were resourceful and redoubtable men, required to produce bursts of heroism among days of uneventful

A tight stone spiral staircase winds
up the centre of the lighthouse to the
lantern room at the top.

The lighthouse is constructed
throughout from granite
quarried on Lundy.

routine. Keeper John McCarthy arrived on Lundy with his wife
and seven children in 1884; eight years later he masterminded
the rescue of twenty-one people from the wreck of the French
steamer *Tunisie*. During a snowstorm over seven hours,
McCarthy shot a rocket line over the ship to improvise a rescue
apparatus in which the crew were transferred ashore in a coal
sack. It was no less than his due that two Elder Brethren from
Trinity House came to Lundy expressly to award him a
testimonial for 'his gallant and successful exertions'.

In 1897, Old Light was definitively superseded by two new
lighthouses, the current North and South Lights (two of the
sixty-nine lighthouses still operated by Trinity House). These
were built nearer sea level and are still in action today, though
their operation is now fully automated.

Old Light passed to the island's owner, the Reverend Hudson
Heaven, who for many years rented out its associated living
quarters for holidays. In 1947, then-owner Jack Harman gave the

Old Light grouping to the Lundy Field Society, those most
passionate aficionados of the island, who used it as their
headquarters and ran the keeper's cottages as a hostel.

By the time Landmark came on the scene in 1969, Old Light
needed major refurbishment, which is not straightforward for
such a tower. In 1976, even replacing its windows required the
construction of external platforms; contractor Mike Haycraft
worked from a harness as he screwed the frames into the granite
with a hand drill in the absence of an electrical supply. Three
years later the lantern was repaired and the weather vane
regilded, and further works to the lantern room were necessary
in 2012. Such a building in such a setting will always present a
challenge, but while Daniel Asher Alexander's lighthouse may
not have been flawless in operation, its monumental structure is
still sound. Looking out from the lantern room over the white
horses that mark the spot where the Atlantic Ocean meets the
Bristol Channel counts as a highlight of any visit to Lundy. **CS**

William Beckford as a handsome young man at the age of twenty.

Beckford's Gothick Fonthill Abbey was an overweening folly and the prodigy house of its day.

Opposite: Beckford's tower echoes the form of a Tuscan campanile, and refers to the Athenian Tower of the Winds in its gilded belvedere.

BECKFORD'S TOWER
SOMERSET

1827

A MONUMENT OF REGENCY BRIO

'Some people drink to forget their unhappiness,' wrote William Beckford. 'I do not drink, I build.' Beckford was one of a kind and he appears here for his enduring cultural significance, and also as a representative of a different strand of history, always present, but until very recent decades charting its course only subversively through subterranean channels, forbidden by law and outlawed by society. The social consequences of Beckford's sexuality defined his life, but he is remembered for much else besides. Beckford was a maverick, a hedonistic figure claimed both by devotees of the Picturesque and Gothic Revivalists, and his influence still resonates in architecture and literature. He commissioned two great buildings in his lifetime: the first, Fonthill Abbey in Wiltshire, is the stuff of legend. The second, an old man's folly but more enduring than the great abbey, is Beckford's tower, standing above Lansdown Crescent in Bath.

Born in 1760, William Beckford grew up at the family mansion in Wiltshire, so prodigiously magnificent it was known as Fonthill Splendens. It was built with vast wealth from Jamaican plantations by his domineering father, an ebullient sugar merchant. His only son was highly intelligent, sensitive and precocious: an eight-year-old Mozart gave William piano lessons when he was five, and Sir William Chambers, architect to the King, taught him drawing and the principles of architecture. Beckford also loved writing letters and diaries from an early age, and later developed (or possibly affected) a counter-tenor voice and was a willing performer.

Beckford's wealth, inherited when he was just ten, cushioned him from both hardship and censure. Educated at home, he soon adopted an extravagant lifestyle, throwing legendary parties, and indulging his taste in fine arts and architecture. He was attractive to, and attracted by, both sexes, although his preference lay with his own. In 1778, when he was eighteen and visiting relations at Powderham Castle, he developed an all-consuming 'wayward passion' for ten-year old the Hon. William 'Kitty' Courtenay, a relationship which developed over the next six years.

Beckford is seen on his Grand Tour in 1780, aged twenty, in Romney's famous portrait of him as a handsome, languid, melancholy young man. His coming-of-age party at Splendens the same year is one of the set pieces that have entered the legend of his life. Staged by a celebrated theatrical impresario, scenes of sunsets, volcanic eruptions and moonlit glades were projected through the halls and corridors by strategically placed lanterns. There were braziers of scented coals and incense; unseen in the semi-darkness, castrati sang eerily.

Like the whorl of a shell, a spiral staircase painted in its original soft pink ascends Beckford's belvedere.

Beckford's tomb is in the graveyard that later grew up around the tower. Today, it provides a suitably Gothic setting.

It was 'the realization of romance in its most extravagant intensity', Beckford was to write years later.

Such house parties (and there were others) scandalized society, and also inspired Beckford to compose a lengthy Gothic novel, *Vathek*. This begins as a light-hearted pastiche of Arabian life but moves to a vision of Hell, the author maintaining a position of strict neutrality over extremes of good and evil. The veil of Arabian myth confers an air of spurious plausibility. *Vathek* ran to nine editions during Beckford's lifetime and influenced authors as diverse as Byron and Jane Austen.

Then, in 1786, Beckford and Kitty were discovered by a house guest while staying at Powderham. The scandal this time was intractable. A marriage to Lady Margaret Gordon had been arranged by Beckford's mother in 1783, and the couple now fled to Switzerland. It was a happy marriage, and Margaret bore him two daughters before her death in 1786, but Beckford remained ostracized by English society.

The young man travelled obsessively through the next few years, enjoying a trail of glamorous (and amorous) adventures through Venice, Lisbon and Madrid and acquiring a vicarious taste for Catholic religion and its ritual. He created a still-famous park around his villa at Monserrate in Portugal; escaped revolutionary Paris in 1793; and played the role of a minor Scarlet Pimpernel in Switzerland.

Meanwhile, Kitty's father, Lord Courtenay, had died in 1788, making it safer for Beckford to return intermittently to Fonthill Splendens and direct its refurbishment and landscaping. His collections benefited greatly from the bargains made available by the disintegration of the French aristocracy and he began to plan a further project at Fonthill, a building of a scale and grandeur hitherto unseen in England. He commissioned architect James Wyatt – brilliant and celebrated, but also unreliable and dilatory –to build Fonthill Abbey, a monastic-style building topped by an enormous tower.

Hundreds of workmen were employed and Beckford enjoyed the sense of purposeful activity around him. Wyatt, on the other hand, rather lost interest once plans were drawn up, and the building proceeded in fits and starts over the next seven years. Inactivity alternated with furious activity, which led to hasty and skimped work of ad hoc design. In 1797 a spring gale brought the central wooden tower crashing down. A new structure was built, this time of a new compo-cement claimed to be everlasting, but this, too, collapsed in 1800, just before Lord Nelson was due to visit at Christmas with his mistress Emma Hamilton, also part of Beckford's coterie. Beckford orchestrated the visit carefully so that only the parts of the building fit to be seen appeared, and then to their best advantage.

Beckford moved into the Abbey in 1807, although building continued until 1818. Fonthill Abbey was the prodigy house of its generation, famous for its vast tower, 85 metres/280 feet high, the huge octagonal hall at its base and the wealth of its interiors. Yet it was not a comfortable place to live, and by the early 1820s He was in financial difficulties, obliviously defrauded for years by unscrupulous lawyers and agents. Beckford found himself £145,000 in debt and Fonthill became less a great adventure than a millstone, its great tower moving and groaning in the wind. The place filled him with melancholy and foreboding. There was no reason to stay and every reason to get rid of it.

In 1822, the entire Fonthill estate was put up for sale. The public flocked for a glimpse of this notorious treasure house, and 72,000 catalogues sold at a guinea each. Then, the sale was cancelled at two days' notice: estate, house and contents had been sold by private treaty to a John Farquhar, an elderly man who had made his fortune selling gunpowder.

Fonthill deserves its own postscript. Later that same year, it tumbled down. Miraculously, no one was hurt, and old Farquhar declared with great amiability that now the house would not be too big to live in. All that are left today, as reminders of the boldest architectural exposition of the Romantic movement ever erected in the English countryside, are one small wing and a few fragments.

And so, aged sixty-three, Beckford arrived in Bath, a city whose glamour and intensity were fading as the eighteenth-century passion for classicism yielded to the Picturesque. He bought a house on Lansdown Crescent, and then its neighbour,

too, for privacy. In 1827, he commissioned H.E. Goodridge, a young and relatively unknown architect, to build a belvedere on the hill behind the crescent, to be a casket for his treasures and a shrine to St Anthony of Padua, patron saint of lost trifles (including hearts). The tower was one of the earliest introductions of the Picturesque to post-Georgian Bath, combining its accommodation block with innovative gestures to both Tuscan *campanili* and Greek Revival architecture. Beckford filled it with his collections of fine furniture, paintings and *objets*, and commissioned watercolours of the interiors from Willes Maddox, later published as lithographs. Increasingly reclusive, each day Beckford rode up a specially created walk with his dogs and dwarf servant to the tower, to contemplate his collection, sit in his tower and enjoy the view.

William Beckford died, a very old man, in 1844. His tower became a funerary chapel for a fittingly Picturesque graveyard that grew up around it. In 1972, it was bought by Leslie and Elizabeth Hilliard, who converted it to live in and opened a small museum room. In 1977, they established the Beckford Tower Trust, to which they gifted the tower. By the late 1990s, the tower was in urgent need of restoration. The trust shared a trustee with Landmark in Bath surveyor Theo Williams, who suggested that Landmark could help by taking on a long lease on the rooms at the base of the tower. It was to be an unusual project for Landmark, one of just a handful where it has taken an explicitly 'restorationist' approach, guided by the Maddox lithographs, to evoke the true spirit of one man's remarkable contribution to Regency taste and brio. **CS**

In 1843, Beckford commissioned watercolours from Willes Maddox of the tower's interiors, here the Scarlet Drawing Room.

Landmark used the watercolour (below left) as a template for the refurbishment of the Scarlet Drawing Room.

In provincial adaptation, the
window dressings in Penzance
look more like ship's figureheads
than Egyptian goddesses.

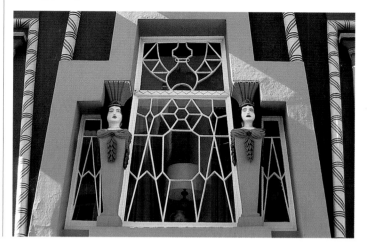

Inspired by Napoleon's Egyptian
campaigns, the Egyptian House
stands incongruously in a quiet
Cornish street.

THE EGYPTIAN
HOUSE
CORNWALL

1835

EGYPTOMANIA

Engravings of the sites (here the
Temple of Philae) discovered on
Napoleon's campaign of 1798–1801
were widely disseminated.

In a small street in Penzance stands a brightly coloured,
exuberant building that looks as though it has landed, Tardis-
like, from another planet in this Cornish fishing town. Originally
called The Egyptian Hall, it was built in 1835 by John Lanvin,
a local bookseller, as a museum and shop for semi-precious
stones and fossils that he bought, sold and exhibited as his
main business. There is nothing quite like it in the country for
wholehearted Egyptiana and gaudiness. But how did such a
building come to land in a quiet Cornish street in the 1830s?

As with so much in the Regency period, its origins lie in the
Napoleonic Wars. In May 1798, Napoleon Bonaparte invaded
Egypt, ostensibly to liberate the Egyptians from Ottoman rule
but in reality to protect French trade interests. He took with him
a Commission on the Sciences and the Arts: 167 artists, scholars
and scientists as well as the more predictable military engineers
and surveyors. Their mission was to record what they found.

The French spent three years in Cairo, and it is a remarkable
story. Three months after they landed, Nelson destroyed their
fleet in the Bay of Aboukir in the so-called Battle of the Nile,
leaving Britain in control of the Mediterranean and the French

Campaign draughtsmen and artists,
such as Dominique Vivant Denon, were
inspired by what they found in Egypt.

The Egyptian Hall on Piccadilly,
designed in 1809 by P.R. Robinson
to house William Bullock's Museum
of Natural Curiosities.

army land-bound. Unperturbed, Napoleon set himself up
as absolute ruler in Cairo and campaigns in Syria followed.
The expedition, beset by plague and guerrilla warfare as well
as resistance, eventually petered out in 1801, when Napoleon
decided France needed him more. Such events were, of course,
much in the public eye in Britain, too.

Meanwhile the Commission, doing its work in the most
hostile conditions, had been awed and inspired by the ancient
remains it encountered. 'Since I came to Egypt, fooled by
everything, I have been constantly depressed and ill,' wrote one.
'Dendera has cured me; what I saw today has repaid me for all
my weariness; whatever may happen to me during the rest of
this expedition, I shall congratulate myself all my life for having
been part of it.'

Among the Commission members was Dominique Vivant
Denon, an artist and archaeologist who, in 1802, published a
two-volume set of engravings called *Voyage dans la basse et la
haute Egypte* (Journey in Lower and Upper Egypt). An extended
grand tour was now taking in Turkey or Egypt, and English
upper-class imagination was seized by the romance of the East.
French pillaging from Luxor and Karnak made Egyptian objects
increasingly desirable among the European elite, fuelled indeed
by earlier collections of engravings, although none of these
reached wide circulation. Denon's work soon became the source
book *du jour*, and an English pocket-size edition was even
published – 'attainable to all classes', according to its preface.

This passion for the Egyptian initially manifested itself
chiefly in aristocratic interiors. In 1802–6, James Wyatt built a
new wing at Goodwood House for the third Duke of Richmond
and created a dining room sumptuously decorated in the
Egyptian style, recently triumphantly restored.

In the same period, Thomas Hope had settled in London
after an extended, seven-year grand tour that had included
Egypt. He bought a neoclassical house in Duchess Street and
set about remodelling it. Hope was immensely wealthy and an
influential and eclectic arbiter of taste (the phrase 'interior
decoration' itself is attributed to him). One of his rooms at
Duchess Street was in the Egyptian style, and was included in
his *Household Furniture and Interior Decoration* (1807).
Sphinxes, winged discs of Horus, lotus buds and papyrus
columns began to appear on clocks, candlesticks, vases, dinner
services, bookends, wallpapers and fabrics as the fashion spread.

Then, in 1809, a Liverpudlian impresario named William
Bullock arrived in London with his Museum of Natural
Curiosities. To house it, he commissioned from architect
Peter Frederick Robinson a museum in the Egyptian style at
170 Piccadilly, right opposite Burlington House. This Egyptian

Hall's spectacular frontage was the first major public building in England with an Egyptian exterior, and defined the key elements that would be borrowed and diluted in hundreds of Victorian civic buildings – and funerary monuments and cemeteries, too, as it was felt that the ancient Egyptian preoccupation with the afterlife made the style especially appropriate. Features that instantly allow something to be identified, even vaguely, as 'Egyptian' – tapering pylons, columns modelled on bundles of papyrus reeds with lotus or palm capitals, the winged solar disc 'guarding' the entrance, the concave cornice with battered sides, the monumental supporting figures – were all present on one of London's premier streets, housing a collection of Egyptian exhibits to match.

By the 1820s, however, the London vogue for the Egyptian had peaked. When, in 1818, Louis XVIII presented the Duke of Wellington with the magnificent Sèvres Egyptian dinner service, still on display at Apsley House today, there were fears that it was out of fashion. The Piccadilly Egyptian Hall survived as an exhibition space until 1904, when it was demolished to make way for bland offices.

Perhaps fashion travelled slowly to Penzance, but we cannot but believe that John Lanvin, bookseller and purveyor of minerals, had visited William Bullock's Egyptian Hall, or at least seen an engraving of it in a book or newspaper. When he bought two adjoining cottages on Chapel Street in 1834 with the intention of building Lanvin's Museum, he aspired to bring some of the glamour of Piccadilly to Penzance.

There was already great enthusiasm for the study of minerals and fossils, especially in England's south-west. The Royal Geological Society of Cornwall was founded in Penzance in 1814, second only to the London Society. The mining industry in Cornwall made it a centre of scientific knowledge and enthusiasm, and many of the rare specimens sold by Lanvin in Chapel Street were found by miners in the Cornish mines. It must have been a thriving business for Lanvin to be able to commission such a building, raising the height of the cottages for extra effect.

The architect of The Egyptian House is not known; P.R. Robinson has been suggested; more plausible but still unproven is John Foulston, a Plymouth architect of eclectic tastes who built the Civil and Military Library in Devonport in 1823 in a spare, Egyptian style. The proportions of the Penzance Egyptian House are striking, good and true. It is the mouldings that betray it as an enthusiastic but essentially provincial foray into the Nile delta, more folk art than Pharoanic. The female figures on The Egyptian House seem formed by someone more used to carving the figureheads for ship's prows; the window dressings replace the disc of Horus with a sort of beribboned fruit; and the eagle looks as though he has landed from somewhere else altogether. It was long assumed that the jaunty embellishments were Coade stone (a fired ceramic), but a Coade craftsman would have had a keener eye for the true nuances of the style, and manufacture of Coade stone was dying by 1835. In 2011, it was confirmed that the Egyptian House mouldings were not a Coade stone, but rather a cast cement.

John Lanvin ran his geological shop and museum for nearly thirty years. His son, Edward, carried on the companion stationery, bookbinding and printing business in The Egyptian House but it seems he was less keen on geology. In 1863, soon after his father's death, he sold the entire collection of minerals for £2,500 and built a large hotel on the esplanade. The Egyptian House was let to various tenants and remained in Lanvin ownership until 1910, when it was bought by a draper; he sold it in 1951 to the Cornish Stone Company, who sold it to Landmark in 1968. Landmark created three flats, one on each floor, and upped the Egyptian atmosphere by reglazing with windows based on engravings of the Piccadilly Hall and Foulston's Library. The bright colour scheme is based on paint scrapes and colours known to have been used in the Regency revival.

Walking down Piccadilly today, there are only the merest hints of Egyptian architecture in its buildings, and even these are now more likely to belong to twentieth-century Art Deco than Regency influences. In Chapel Street, Penzance, however, John Lanvin's Egyptian House will continue to delight and intrigue in all its glory, its future safe in Landmark's care – whatever the vagaries of fashion. **CS**

The Egyptian House in Penzance was in a sorry state when it was taken on by Landmark in 1968.

DESIGNING THE
MODERN AGE
1840–2015

Mass production, and with it greater leisure and choice, led to increasing fragmentation of life as governments struggled to adapt to a fast-changing society. Christian evangelism was increasingly vehement across all denominations, especially after it was realized that religion's hold was slipping. Peace and prosperity at home was threatened by greater adjustments in Europe, and eventually two world wars transformed Britain. Architecture changed and developed at a faster rate than ever before, as nostalgia for the past ceded to modernism, and digital technology transformed the world. The Landmark Trust has preserved key properties of this era, and has embraced cutting-edge reworkings of earlier buildings that are too ruinous to be restored conventionally.

Goddards, built by architect Edwin Lutyens, was commissioned as a peaceful place for the rest and recuperation of the poor.

Pugin's 'substantial Catholic house . . . convenient and solid', next to the church he also built at his own cost.

THE GRANGE
KENT

1844

TURNING TO THE PAST TO FACE THE FUTURE

Augustus Welby Northmore Pugin's description of his plans for a family home in Ramsgate in 1843 – to erect 'not . . . a Grecian villa but a most substantial Catholic house not very Large but convenient & solid' – captures in a single phrase the shifting plates of English society at the time. The first half of the nineteenth century were years of social disorder and riot; high grain prices and poor harvests; and the growing pains of an electorally disenfranchised, rapidly industrializing society readjusting after a long war. Pugin, inspirational architect and designer for the Gothic Revival, Catholic convert and vehement social polemicist, was not a politicized man, but he lived in an age when religious creed and politics had become deeply entwined, amid a general sense of dislocation and unease.

The word 'Catholic', for anyone living in England in the 1820s and 1830s, was a portmanteau of swirling social and political, as well as religious, concerns, as half a million destitute and mostly Catholic Irish arrived in England looking for better times. Catholics remained objects of suspicion in the popular imagination and their freedom to worship openly, build churches or hold public office was still prohibited by law.

In addition, many non-Catholics thought the religion to be synonymous with the absolutist monarchies of contemporary Catholic countries like Spain and France.

In practice, however, the provisions of the Popery Act were increasingly ignored. Many Irish and Scottish Catholics served quietly and valuably in the army despite the Oath of Allegiance. And then there was Ireland, where the English Reformation had never taken hold, and where the Catholic majority was largely excluded from their own government by the requirement to subscribe to the Anglican Church to hold office. Ireland boiled over into open rebellion in 1798. The Napoleonic Wars were by now in full swing and Ireland was always a back door into England in times of war. The rebellion was quashed, and resulted in the 1801 Acts of Union, which merged Great Britain and Ireland to create the United Kingdom. Catholics could now vote if otherwise qualified, but were still barred from a seat at Westminster and any other public office.

But the country was changing, and the issue of wider electoral reform was becoming pressing, with Catholic emancipation a particularly emotive element. 'No Popery' remained the Tory cry, but the Whigs were increasingly in favour of Catholic emancipation and opinion began to swing in its favour. Emancipation bills were passed in the House of Commons in 1821 and 1825, only to be rejected by the Lords. There was a sense of waiting for old men to die, and a sense,

too, that the whole social fabric was in danger. The Catholic question involved all the important issues of the day: royal authority, the right to vote and hold office, and the place of religion in the constitution.

In Ireland, a Catholic nationalist, lawyer and orator called Daniel O'Connell was leading a mounting campaign of civil disobedience. In 1828, O'Connell was elected to Westminster in a by-election in his home county of Clare – but was debarred from taking the seat. Outright rebellion again threatened. In this atmosphere of crisis, the Duke of Wellington (himself of Irish origin) was appointed prime minister, with a young Robert Peel as his henchman in the Commons. But not even this national hero could restore order to British politics without decisive legislation. The otherwise ultra-right Iron Duke came to the conclusion that if he were to win over the Irish army and police upon whom he depended to restore law and order, there was no alternative but to repeal the anti-Catholic legislation.

In 1829, the Roman Catholic Relief Act was forced through parliament. From now on, Catholics were counted equal citizens, free to hold public office, worship openly and build churches for

the first time since the 1530s. The Relief Act was also a first tentative step towards the wider electoral enfranchisement of the Great Reform Act of 1832 and beyond.

Augustus Pugin was an adolescent in this period of feverish intellectual and religious turmoil when, in political theorist John Stuart Mill's words, 'the old doctrines have gone out, and the new ones have not yet come in'. Many shared William Cobbett's sentiments: in his journal, *Rural Rides*, one morning in Salisbury Cathedral, he contrasted the beauty of its soaring medieval architecture with the paltry religion carried on inside, with the comment that 'we are living in degenerate times'.

Pugin had grown up in the Picturesque tradition; his father's widely published drawings did much to popularize the style. He inherited Romanticism's trust in truths taught by intuition and faith rather than the cold empiricism of reason. By the early 1830s, however, he was sick of the Picturesque's evolved Regency form and over-eclectic vocabulary. He, too, sensed an imminent moral and spiritual crisis in the country, and like many others of his generation Pugin looked not to the future for a resolution of the crisis, but to an idealized view of the Middle

Pugin applied Gothic design to everything, even light fittings.

The rich Gothic detailing of Pugin's churches is nowhere more apparent that at St Giles in Cheadle, Staffordshire.

Ages. All around him he saw ugly, unchristian architecture and a disturbed social order. Conversion to Catholicism was a logical conclusion for Pugin, the Pre-Reformation Catholic Church offering the only salvation. Equally importantly for him, a revival of Gothic architecture was the only way 'the grand and sublime style of church architecture can ever be restored'.

Pugin's decision to convert in 1834 was a courageous act, despite the 1829 Act. Catholics remained objects of popular suspicion, and as late as 1850 Pugin's third wife, Jane, was bolting the doors at The Grange against anti-Papist disturbances in the town. The Act did, however, have a profound effect on his career through its permission for Catholics to worship openly, and therefore to build churches. Pugin's earliest architectural commissions were ecclesiastical; his early patrons were wealthy Catholics like Lord Scarisbrick and the Earl of Shrewsbury, who were at last able to express their religion fully by endowing churches and seminaries. Pugin's fees enabled him to design and build his own home at the age of just thirty.

There can be few, if any, middle-class homes in England where the hallway was surveyed by a life-sized statue of the Virgin and Child; where the Magnificat is painted above the fireplace in the dining room and diners are perpetually blessed by St Augustine; and where a private chapel leads off the back stairs. Pugin believed that Gothic architecture, even domestic Gothic architecture, was a vehicle for the sacred in the physical world. The Grange was, for a few years, a happy family home, before his descent into madness and early death.

Pugin's aesthetics, triumphantly displayed in the Medieval Court at the Great Exhibition in 1852, caught the imagination of the age. Victorians were forging solutions to the uncertainties of the emerging modern world: religious revivalism based on medieval Romanticism; ancient tradition in design, even if executed in new materials and mechanized in production; familiar medieval forms applied to meet new needs. Like the new Houses of Parliament that Pugin designed with Charles Barry over the same period, The Grange has all these, additionally infused with layers of personal meaning.

In the twentieth century, The Grange was subsumed into the monastery also intended by Pugin. Eventually disregarded and decaying, the house was acquired by Landmark in 1997, just as a whole new Gothic revival stirred after a seminal exhibition on Pugin at London's Victoria & Albert Museum in 1994. Landmark's acquisition and restoration of The Grange was enabled by grants from a new influence in the conservation world, the Heritage Lottery Fund, also founded in 1994, and whose funding had a transformative effect on this and other Landmark projects. **CS**

The hallway at The Grange had become plain and institutionalized in the twentieth century.

After Landmark's detailed research and restoration, the house has been restored to its rich appearance during Pugin's lifetime.

PRIVATE

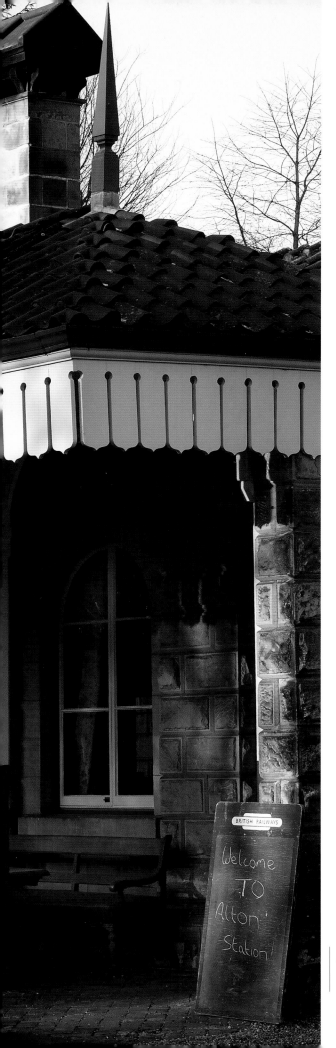

ALTON STATION
STAFFORDSHIRE

1849

THE COMING OF THE RAILWAYS

'You see, Tom ... the world goes on at a smarter pace now than
it did when I was young fellow ... it's this steam, you see.' By the
time George Eliot published her novel *The Mill on the Floss* in
1860, railways were part of daily life. The transformation had
been swift, and old Mr Deane was speaking for the modern age
in expressing his sense of the acceleration of life. Railways had
infiltrated all parts of Britain in the thirty years since passengers
first travelled in George Stephenson's steam locomotive on the
Stockton and Darlington railway in 1825. How lives were lived
was changing in every respect, but whether this was a good
thing was by no means apparent to everyone in the early days.

The railways' eventual predominance required profound
changes in attitudes: for many, the steam engine with its plume
of smoke puffing through the countryside on iron tracks was a
threatening and alien symbol of all that was disagreeable,
vulgarizing and mercenary. The early Victorian railway
promoters and engineers were relentless as they forged their
way through the countryside, and any landowners concerned
more with the tranquillity of their own estates than with the
public good complained vociferously. People feared physical

The platform at Alton Station has
changed little, but trains have not
stopped here since the 1960s.

The sixteenth Earl of Shrewsbury was initially suspicious of the railway coming through Alton.

J.M.W. Turner's famous painting, *Rain, Steam and Speed – The Great Western Railway* (1844), captures the romance of steam engines running though the countryside.

damage to a person travelling at such speeds (48 kilometres/ 30 miles per hour by 1840); it was believed that sheep's fleeces would be ruined by belching smoke and livestock near a rail line might die of fright, if not from suction. The railways' potential for making rural corners of the land more accessible brought out the worst in paternalistic snobbery, a sense that the rural idyll of 'true' England would be contaminated by an influx of vulgar humanity, the depraved poor of the towns.

'The Border peasantry of Scotland and England,' wrote influential critic John Ruskin as late as 1876, 'painted with absolute fidelity by Scott and Wordsworth, are hitherto a scarcely injured race; whose strength and virtue yet survive to represent the body and soul of England, before her days of mechanical decrepitude, and commercial dishonour. There are men working in my own fields who might have fought with Henry the Fifth at Agincourt, without being discerned from among his knights . . . What effect on the character of such a population will be produced by the influx of that of the suburbs of our manufacturing towns there is evidence enough, if the reader cares to ascertain the facts, in every newspaper on his

morning table.' The Poet Laureate, William Wordsworth, famously wrote to Prime Minister Gladstone, enclosing a sonnet protesting about the proposed Kendal to Windermere railway, with the line: 'And is there no nook of English ground secure from rash assault?' Echoing Ruskin's romanticism, Wordsworth held that the working class lacked the sensibility to appreciate his beloved Lake District, and that the landscape would be irreparably scarred. The perceived vandalism by the railway promoters of ancient sites – most famously the passage of the railway close to Furness Abbey in Cumbria – also contributed to the building preservation movement.

The sixteenth Earl of Shrewsbury was initially similarly suspicious of the North Staffordshire Railway running past his seat at Alton on its way up the Churnet Valley, a branch of the main Potteries' line to Stoke-on-Trent. 'Good Earl John', otherwise renowned for his local philanthropy, instructed the Revd Jones, Vicar of Alton, to speak up on his behalf at a public meeting in January 1841, and to say that the Earl would oppose the line in and out of Parliament. 'The Earl and his predecessors had expended a million and a half of money on what was

formerly a wilderness,' said the vicar, reported in *The Staffordshire Advertiser*. 'They had adorned it as far as art could go and had erected one of England's finest palaces. Was it likely that the Earl could submit to the beauties of the place destroyed by the cuttings and embankments of a railway?'

But the Earl became more amenable once he received £1,000 a year as a sweetener from the North Staffordshire. The pretty Italianate station at Alton was built in 1849, the first trains passing through the same year. As well as securing commercial advantage, the railways were an unstoppable force for democratization: in 1839, the Great Western Railway (GWR) had not decided how to transport 'the very lowest order of persons'; a year later, such persons were allowed to travel on goods trains, and by 1844 an act was passed to ensure that each line must run at least one train a day at a fare of just a penny a mile.

The railways revolutionized working lives, and surprisingly quickly. Augustus Pugin, for example, kept up punishing itineraries that would test even today's timetables. On his honeymoon in August 1848, in four days he travelled with his third wife from Ramsgate to Cambridge, Peterborough, Lincoln,

Passengers at Alton Station wait on the platform for the next train in this early photograph.

The railway track sometimes became a watercourse for flood water, with a disastrous effect on the timetable.

The former ticket office, off the
waiting room, is now a bedroom.

By the 1930s, Alton Station was so
well-used that holding pens were
created to control passenger flow
onto the platform.

Nottingham, Skegness and Hull, stopping off all the while to look at churches and cathedrals.

Railways even changed perceptions of time, turning it into a standardized commodity instead of a relative concept. Until the late eighteenth century, the time of day was typically set locally by sundial; no matter that the sun rose twenty minutes earlier in Norwich than it did in Swansea. On long journeys, watches were adjusted by a few minutes at a time as the coach made its laborious way across country, the differences having little effect. With the advent of the railways, such discrepancies came to matter a great deal: there were trains to catch, timetables to set, rail points to change. Forging its line through from London to Bristol, the GWR first set a standardized time in 1840, and not without controversy. 'Railway time' was different from local time and was fiercely resisted by some towns, where two clocks were often displayed. The station staff, it was argued, might run to railway time, but not necessarily the other inhabitants, and some grumbled about stolen minutes. The advantages of standardized time did gradually catch on, but it was not until 1880 that Greenwich Mean Time was adopted by parliament as the standard time across a single time zone.

A counter argument was also made in favour of the architecture associated with the railways having aesthetic potential to adorn rather than deface the landscape. No less than model villages and aristocratic estates, here was an opportunity to bring the architectural pattern books to life, just as I.K. Brunel and other railway engineers created their own works of unprecedented engineering elegance. Mass publications like Bradshaw's railway guides and J.C. Loudon's travel articles for *The Gardener's Magazine* popularized the new aesthetic. Travelling north in May 1839, Loudon wrote: 'The stupendous cuttings in some places, and high embankments in others, the lofty bridges crossing the road every now and then, the tunnel in which all is darkness, the beautiful and extensive views from the embankments and viaducts, render this [rail] road, which might hypothetically be considered dull and monotonous, actually full of variety.'

Station architecture could bring whiffs of other climes and ages, of ancient Greece, the Tudor, the Jacobean, the Gothic – or, as at Alton, the Picturesque Italianate. It may seem strange that Lord Shrewsbury did not choose Gothic for his station; Pugin, who was working on Alton Towers at the time, did submit drawings for the station and the North Staffordshire would have been happy to implement them had Pugin supplied the by-now customary detailed specifications and completed a tendering process for the contractor. This was not how Pugin worked. With no formal training, he relied entirely on his builder, George Myers, to translate his sketches into buildings. Pugin was being left behind by the new professionalism of the railway age, and had to content himself with building a Gothic lodge across the road for the Earl at the same time as Alton Station was being built. The station, attributed instead to H.A. Hunt, was perhaps even a propagandist gesture on behalf of 'cosmopolite practice' in the architectural 'battle of the styles', being a successful and provocative infiltration into the Gothic opposition's very heartland.

The Churnet Valley line opened in 1849, but it was not until 1850 that the main station buildings were ready to receive passengers, mostly day visitors who came in their droves from the pottery towns to visit the famous gardens at Alton Towers, to marvel at its temples, pagodas, glasshouses and monoliths. As many as 27,000 visitors came out each year and, at a penny an entry, this was a helpful income boost for the estate. In 1884, £200 was spent on lengthening the platforms to accommodate the numbers, with a special pathway built from the platform to the road up to the Towers, called 'The Avenues'. By 1937, holding terraces were necessary to control the flow of passengers onto the platform. Even in this narrow, wooded valley, the railway had become an essential and accepted part of life, all overseen by

the station master from his house, distinctively Victorian, both serviceable and fanciful with its prospect stone balcony, but not so grand that the station master might neglect to turn out in the early hours of a January morning to see off the milk train.

But after nationalization of the railways in 1948, use of such local branch lines declined dramatically. In 1960, Dr Beeching made his report for the rationalization of the nation's rail network. The Churnet Valley line was reduced to a single track, and then closed completely in 1965. The station master lived on in his house for a year or two, but the waiting room soon began to suffer from neglect and vandalism. Staffordshire County Council bought the station buildings in 1969, and in 1970 approached Landmark, who in 1972 took on the station master's house. The waiting room was initially mothballed, but in 2008 it was incorporated into the Landmark as its sitting room.

Now in commercial ownership, Alton Towers has become Britain's most popular theme park: on the other side of the estate from Alton Station, adrenaline-filled rides have replaced a stroll around aristocratic gardens as a visitor attraction. About 2.5 million visitors come each year, but the age of railways has ceded to the age of the car, and now they come by road. The once-busy railway cutting is a quiet cycle and walking way. **CS**

Closed in 1965 as a result of the Beeching Report, the station quickly became overgrown.

In Landmark's care, Alton Station again stands bright and trim. The former trackway is a walking and cycle route.

An early postcard of Fort Clonque.

Lord Palmerston (1784–1865) was famous for his 'gunboat diplomacy' and robust defence of British interest on the seas.

FORT CLONQUE
CHANNEL ISLANDS

1855

DEFENSIVE OUTPOST OF BRITAIN'S SHORES

'Generally, when Lord Palmerston talks of diplomacy, he talks also of ships of war.' Palmerston, one of the titans that bestrode mid-nineteenth-century British politics, was one of Britain's greatest foreign ministers and prime ministers; his Cabinet career spanned four decades. Diplomat Henry Bulwer's assessment of his foreign policy is, of course, over-simplistic but it captures the essence of Britain's engagement with the outside world for much of the nineteenth century. The British navy roamed the seas, taking an active and often interventionist role in the disputes and internal unrest of other nations across Europe and beyond – the phrase 'gunboat diplomacy' originates with 'Lord Pumicestone'.

The natural corollary to such a policy was the need for security on British shores, and Landmark has three forts in its care that owe their existence directly to Palmerston's policies: Fort Clonque (1856) on Alderney in the Channel Islands, West Blockhouse (1857) in Pembrokeshire and Crownhill Fort (1863–6) in Plymouth. All were built, primarily, through direct fear of French expansionism, at a time when memories of Napoleon Bonaparte's rampages across the Continent were still fresh.

By 1848, the disposition of European boundaries settled by the Treaty of Vienna in 1815 was being challenged from all sides. The vast, absolutist Austrian, Russian and Ottoman Empires were destabilized by nationalist and liberalist movements; Spain and Portugal's decaying monarchies augured power vacuums; Prussia was flexing its territorial muscles; and the Dutch, Belgians, Danes and Italians each sought self-determination as unified states. The balance of power, whose perpetuation or gentle recalibration was ultimately the aim of British foreign policy in Europe, was wobbling dangerously. And everywhere, there was growing frustration among the masses at the lack of universal suffrage.

Palmerston was a master of pragmatism in defence of British interest: 'We have no eternal allies, and we have no perpetual enemies. Our interests are eternal, and those interests it is our duty to follow.' But he also believed in constitutional principles. 'The independence of Constitutional states,' he said in 1832, 'never can be a matter of indifference to the British parliament, or, I should hope, to the British public.' Such principles, he believed, gave him carte blanche for Britain to intervene wherever he deemed it necessary, always with good intentions but sometimes to the despair of parliament and the young Queen Victoria and Prince Albert.

The French, equally suspicious of Palmerston's cavalier language and actions, were building a similar string of coastal

Fort Clonque is reached across a
causeway and is often cut off at high tide.

defences, as Anglo–French relations followed their usual roller-coaster course. The French prime minister in 1848, François Guizot, characterized English foreign policy as 'ambitious and proud, permanently and passionately self-preoccupied, [with] a burning and single-minded need to play its part and take its place everywhere, regardless of cost to anything or anyone.' The British often forget to consider how their policies might appear to others.

The 1848 revolutions that swept across Europe had few immediate lasting results but served as a warning regarding the instability of the region as a whole. In France, however, the Second Empire fell, and Orléanist monarch Louis Philippe was replaced by Louis-Napoleon Bonaparte, nephew and heir of the former Emperor, as president of the Second Republic. When a *coup d'état* three years later abolished the Republic, he declared himself Napoleon III of the Third Empire, nominally confirmed by a constitutional vote of consent. The outlook was ominous.

It was in this febrile atmosphere that the British government began to look to defences in its own backyard, the English

Channel. Lord Palmerston pointed out to the Cabinet that France needed to outmanoeuvre Britain's seapower in the Channel for only a week or so to be able to land sufficient forces from her vast armies to destroy dockyards and paralyze British resources for years to come. He proposed, among other measures, the fortification of British dockyards both seaward and landward. He also recommended the immediate construction of defences for the Channel Islands. Alderney, the nearest of the group, was already especially significant, both strategically for its location just off the north-west point of Brittany and as a re-fuelling point near the maximum range of the new steam-powered warships. Its harbour had already been fortified from 1847, but more was needed.

In 1852, a chain of eighteen forts and batteries was proposed, and a company of Royal Sappers and Miners, under the command of a brilliant young captain and engineer named William Jervois, was despatched to survey the sites and prepare the plans. Clonque Rock, on a narrow peninsular frequently cut off at high tide, was selected as the site for a battery of guns to

Clonque Rock was selected for a battery to protect Alderney's sea roads from attack by the French under Napoleon III.

protect Hannaine and Clonque Bays, supported by another, much larger fortification, Fort Tourgis (1855), to the east. The Clonque site was a challenging one: two prominent outcrops joined to an outlying rock by a natural arch. Jervois produced several designs, but permission was finally given for four batteries and a barrack block to accommodate two officers and fifty-five men. Construction in local granite started early in 1853, and the fort was completed in 1855, costing nearly double Jervois's initial estimate of £5,000.

Soon after Fort Clonque's completion, Britain's pragmatic policy led it to join France as an ally, fighting the Crimean War against Russia. But tensions in Europe were also at breaking point. In 1859, the Risorgimento, the movement for Italian unification and independence from the Austro-Hungarian Empire, again boiled over, and France entered the fray, nominally in support of the nationalists but also with its eyes on annexing Nice and Savoy. In May, the French army invaded Italy in support of the Piedmontese nationalists. Faced with this proof of resurgent Napoleonic ambition, Palmerston, by now prime minister for the second time, set up a royal commission to examine the state and efficiency of British land-based fortifications against naval attack. Its secretary, by now a major, was William Jervois.

Then, in November 1859, the French launched *La Gloire*, the first ocean-going ironclad warship. The British admiralty, who had started construction of their own first ironclad warship, HMS *Warrior*, the previous year, were seriously alarmed. British naval superiority was threatened. With absurd exaggeration, it was said that the new French ships alone would be able to mount an invasion of England. When the commission published its report in 1860, work began immediately on a range of forbidding and expensive fortifications.

And yet, in retrospect, Anglo–French suspicion and animosity had peaked. Palmerston died in 1865 and the royal commission's fortifications were soon dubbed 'Palmerston's follies'. Indeed, like all of Landmark's three forts, they saw little or no military use until the world wars of the next century. Advances in steam technology also brought the Channel Islands within easy reach of the mainland, reducing their strategic importance as re-fuelling stops. In any case, their harbours were too small to hold a fleet of steamships.

The fiercely contested strides in naval technology similarly came to little in themselves. Ironclad HMS *Warrior* was a transitional design, a product of the Industrial Revolution meshing with centuries of naval tradition. It had steam-driven engines but also three masts and a full set of sails for world-wide cruising range. The ironclad hull was lighter than a solely

Napoleon III's expansionist policies and French advances in naval technology in the 1850s alarmed the British government.

HMS *Warrior*, the first British ironclad warship, was powered by both sail and steam, but was soon obsolete.

The former German bunker at
Fort Clonque is now a sunny
bedroom with fine sea views.

wooden one of the same size and shape, offering more capacity
for guns, armour and engines, but it still contained a great deal
of wood, and had a wooden figurehead. For the crew, life on
board was little different from that at Trafalgar. *Warrior* was not
intended to stand in the line of battle, as the Admiralty was
uncertain about her ability to withstand concentrated fire from
wooden two- and three-deck ships of the line. Instead, twice as
long as a typical clipper ship, whose form she mimicked, she was
intended as the ultimate machine of aggression, fast enough to
force battle on a fleeing enemy. She could also control the range
at which a battle was fought to her own advantage. But warship
design was to evolve rapidly, and within ten years *Warrior* was
becoming obsolete.

Fort Clonque and the other Alderney fortifications met a
similar fate. Despite their combined firepower of 222 guns, all
were vulnerable to fire from the sea. Jervois, returning to assess

them in 1871, reported that the magazines were unsafe, and that
'there is so much exposed masonry in most of the works that
they would be difficult to fight, even if their armament were not
obsolete'. Remodelling works to the sum of £75,000 were
recommended, but 'since there is now nothing much to defend
at Alderney, it may probably be taken for granted that no such
sum will ever be spent'. By 1890, Fort Clonque was disarmed,
never having fired a gun in action, and by 1900 it had become a
private residence. Lieutenant-Colonel Jervois went on to serve
successively as governor of the Straits Settlements in South East
Asia, South Australia and New Zealand.

Ironically, when Fort Clonque's moment finally came, it
was used for hostilities against British shipping. The Channel
Islands were the only British territories to be occupied by the
Germans in the Second World War. Invading in 1940, the
Wehrmacht brought Fort Clonque into service as part of Hitler's

This lookout tower surveys the approach lanes to Hannaine and Clonque bays.

Alderney's fortifications soon fell out of use when steamships expanded their range, but their rough-hewn stone has stood firm.

'Atlantic Wall'. Fort Clonque was turned into a stronghold, codenamed 'Steinfeste' (rock fortress). From 1942, the Third Reich's civil and military engineering Organization Todt carried out an intensive programme of fortification, using thousands of forced labourers. The causeway was concreted and a casemate or bunker was constructed in the barracks to house the artillery. Today it does, at least, offer wonderful sea views.

The preservation of Britain's military heritage poses particular problems in a variety of respects: the difficulty of adapting buildings for new uses, precarious physical sites and a tendency to prioritize more glamorous, non-military candidates when allocating funds for restoration. There is also the risk that they might still be requisitioned for their original purpose. Being a particular kind of curious and overlooked challenge, such sites appealed greatly to John Smith. His new trust barely existed when Landmark bought Fort Clonque in

1966, still indiscriminately encased in German barbed wire, asphalt and concrete. This was at a time when most of the other Channel forts were abandoned and falling into ruin. Once it was restored (a heroic task, carried out almost single-handedly by islander Arthur Markell), Fort Clonque rapidly became one of the best-loved buildings in the Landmark roster.

And there is a postscript. When Landmark was buying West Blockhouse, on the Pembrokeshire coast, in 1969, John Smith became aware of a sorry, mastless hulk, Oil Fuel Hulk C77, moored at the Milford Haven Refinery depot. Barely recognizable, it was HMS *Warrior*. A campaign to save her began, and ten years later she was taken to Coal Dock at Hartlepool for a triumphant £9 million restoration as a museum ship, largely funded by the Manifold Trust. In 1985, she was brought to Portsmouth, where she remains, a proud reminder of the days of Palmerstonian gunboat diplomacy. **CS**

St Tygwydd's Church in the 1980s, already without its steeple and tower, with Church Cottage beyond.

This traditional view of the Victorians as universally devout was revealed to be false by a census in 1851.

Church Cottage, the first Landmark, exemplifies John Smith's belief that unremarkable buildings also deserve protection.

CHURCH COTTAGE
CARDIGANSHIRE

C. 1860

ANOTHER LAST STAND

Church Cottage, in the little village of Llandygwydd, has a special place in the history of the Landmark Trust because it was the first building that was restored and opened to guests for holidays. Its plight summed up the disregard in the heady, modernist days of the 1960s for the small, apparently unremarkable and 'outdated' buildings that contributed so much of the character of Britain's landscape.

The houses of Llandygwydd (pronounced 'clandiggwith') cluster around a wooded bowl near Wales's most westerly coast, a landscape of ancient sanctity. Llandygwydd means Tygwydd's place or dwelling, and at least four churches dedicated to St Tygwydd, an early Celtic saint, have stood here. The last of these, which the cottage was built to support, was built in 1857, part of the last great building campaign by the Church of England and Wales (as it then still was). In Cardiganshire, and across Wales, the Anglican Church was threatened by the rise of Nonconformists, those who refused to worship according to the Book of Common Prayer of the Church of England.

St Tygwydd's last church survived until 2000, when it was reduced to just a footprint and solitary font. With the church gone, its memory and history are now kept alive only by John Smith's prescient championing of its cottage.

The received image of the Victorian Age is of a religious nation, godly and dutiful each Sabbath day in its chosen place of worship. This was not so. As patterns of employment changed, and workers sought employment in the new factories and mines that sprang up in this newly industrialized age, congregations rapidly outgrew the seating capacity of existing churches, and ancient parish boundaries became meaningless. The Anglican Church, the Established Church supported by monarch and parliament, had become stagnant and ineffectual.

Ironically, despite the wholesale reform of ritual and doctrine in the English Reformation, the administration of the churches continued largely unchanged, so that old abuses continued. Ecclesiastical incomes were appropriated and distributed by the well-connected; many clergy held several livings and lived like minor gentry, while underpaid curates struggled to fulfil their duties across multiple congregations. Foreigners commented upon the swathes of deprivation and depravity born of despair across whole districts of Britain's overcrowded cities and ports.

The disturbances of the 1840s, when frustration at the lack universal suffrage led to organized public protest under the Chartists, frightened the Establishment, and the Anglican Church, traditional instrument of the rule of the gentry and those associated with them, was losing ground. In the half-

century to 1850, Nonconformists – Congregationalists, Methodists, Baptists and other sects – created more than three times the number of new places of worship (16,000 churches) compared to Anglicans, and more than four times as many 'sittings' (over 4 million).

On Sunday, 30 March 1851, everyone in a place of worship was recorded in a remarkable Census of Religious Worship. Of a population of 18.2 million in England and Wales, only 40 per cent were found to be in church at all that day, and only 52 per cent of those who did attend went to Anglican churches. Contemporaries were profoundly disturbed: it had been a universal assumption that everyone went to at least one service. Now it was clear that a large part of the population – 'the dark masses of our uninstructed people', as Bishop Selwyn put it in 1854 – had no contact with any Christian body.

The Cambridge Camden Society and Oxford Architectural and Historical Society, meanwhile, had spent the previous decade carrying out a systematic study of Gothic architecture. Despite state funding for new churches through the 1820s, the expected Anglican revival had not happened. Something was

Simple furnishings reflect the modest origins of this former church caretaker's home.

missing in the Anglican religious experience, and Gothic architecture was identified as the key missing ingredient. Those who supported this revival became known as Ecclesiologists, whose adherents across the country were encouraged to fill in lengthy forms capturing accurate and detailed architectural descriptions of churches. The Ecclesiologists' belief in the redeeming power of Gothic architecture would frame the physical identity of mid-Victorian religion.

Llandygwydd, though far from the centre, was entirely representative of the national situation; it was even, in some ways, ahead of the game. It had acquired a new church, its third, as early as 1804, 'a neat, modern edifice' that cost £300 to build. Llandygwydd was a large parish and the 1804 church accommodated seventy persons, or just 6 per cent of parishioners. This might seem a realistic assessment of likely attendance, but, spurred by the 1851 census, the pillars of local society came to feel it was too small.

The census showed that the overall provision of places of worship had risen dramatically in Cardiganshire – but this increase was not provided by the Established Church, who now accounted for just a third of the county's places of worship. The Calvinist Methodists were now the largest provider of seatings in the county; in Llandygwydd, the Congregationalists had built their Bethesda Chapel in 1840, but only one new Anglican church had been built in the whole county by 1841, at Llangorwen. This proved an additional spur to the Ecclesiologists' activities: not just to provide suitably handsome buildings to worship in, but also to increase seating capacity for the Anglican revival they sought to achieve.

After 1851, scarcely a year went by without an application to build a new church in Cardiganshire. Leading architects of the day were drawn to the county to help in this initiative; they built, rebuilt, extended and restored Cardiganshire's churches with evangelical zeal. The 1804 St Tygwydd's did not please the roving reporter for *The Church Builder*, who found it 'mean, neglected and unsightly . . . All within and without seemed to say that it was the least cared for house in the whole village'.

Four local landowners, the Brigstockes of Blaen Pant, the Joneses of Penylan, and the Llwyndyrus and Webley-Parrys of Noyadd Treffawr, put up £1,500 for a new church, and commissioned Robert Jewell Withers – an Ecclesiologist retained as architect to the Corporation in Cardigan from 1856 to 1859 – to build it. Local anecdote has it that it was these four landowners who were responsible for the ambitious height of the spire that topped the new church tower, so that each of them could see it from their house. Decades later, this tower and its spire were to prove the church's undoing.

In the late 1850s, however, there must have been great excitement in the village as the new church slowly rose, all in 'the Early English style of the thirteenth century', as *The Ecclesiologist* reported approvingly. The interior was adorned with pink and white marble and now seated 265, more than three times the capacity of the church it replaced. One later description summed it up as 'a good mid-Victorian church with unusually good stained glass and fittings'. Budget provision was even made for a cottage for a caretaker, someone to oversee the fine new creation and double as sexton when the occasion arose.

Unfortunately, within fifty years the fine spire was giving concern, and in 1913 it was dismantled. The Cardiganshire Antiquarian Society reported in its Transactions that St Tygwydd's had been 'somewhat pretentious with its tall slated spire [and] was ill-constructed . . . the tower is now more appropriately finished by a stopped battlement'. By the 1960s, Church Cottage was empty and derelict.

One task of the architect Leonard Bedall Smith, who lived in Cardiganshire, was to advise John and Christian Smith on the Church of St. John the Baptist on the Shottesbrooke estate. John Smith discussed his ideas for his new charity with Bedall Smith, who suggested some candidates from his own local area, including the derelict cottage beside the church at Llandygwydd. After restoration, a small advert was placed in *The Sunday Times* and Church Cottage welcomed its first visitors on 27 May 1967.

The church, meanwhile, was still in a bad way, even without its spire. In 1980, the top two storeys of the tower were demolished, leaving only its ground-floor chamber. But settlement problems continued, and, faced with an estimated repair bill of £300,000, the commissioners decided to close it. In 2000, the decision was reluctantly taken to demolish it altogether. Two years later, one of the two schoolhouses in the village was consecrated as St Tygwydd's. The calling bell that has rung to worshippers since the fourteenth century is now hanging outside it.

The site at Llandygwydd sums up much about the plight of the Anglican Church, and of Christian religion in general in the modern age. The melancholy presence of redundant churches across Britain today is one of the most pressing and poignant conservation concerns. Bodies like the Churches Conservation Trust and Friends of Friendless Churches do sterling work with ever-diminishing resources, but churches are rarely suitable for conversion to Landmark use. By saving Church Cottage, Landmark was at least able to keep the story of St Tygwydd's alive. The cycle of high hopes for religion and dwindling congregations continues to be played out in Britain today. **CS**

Despite the fine new church in the background, a young curate is unsuccessful in 'Attempting to Convert the Natives' in this cartoon.

Today, the church that these windows once looked out upon in Llantygwydd has gone.

Georgiana Naylor and her husband John were bought the Leighton Estate by John's rich uncle as a wedding present.

POULTRY COTTAGE & THE FOWL HOUSE
POWYS

1861

VICTORIAN MODEL ARCHITECTURE

In 1834, a Scottish farmer's son called John Claudius Loudon, botanist, garden designer, author and journalist, published *An Encyclopaedia of Cottage, Farm and Villa Architecture* and announced his intention 'to improve the dwellings of the great mass of society, in the temperate regions of both hemispheres; a secondary object is to create & diffuse among mankind, generally, a taste for architectural comforts and beauties'.

Loudon's encyclopaedia was the first of many such pattern books, and each eclectic scrapbook of architectural styles, plans and elevations was accompanied by earnest descriptions of how dwellings and the multiple outhouses required for self-sufficiency might best be ordered. These pattern books of so-called model architecture spawned an entire genre of Victorian estate architecture. They were generated partly by the prevailing desire of benevolent landowners to improve the living conditions of estate workers, and partly by the same landowners' wish to create a picturesque landscape in which to exist and to show off to their friends.

There was no doubt that rural living conditions, just as much as their urban industrial equivalents, needed improvement.

The palatial Fowl House dwarfs
the elegant cottage for the
poultry-keeper located behind it.

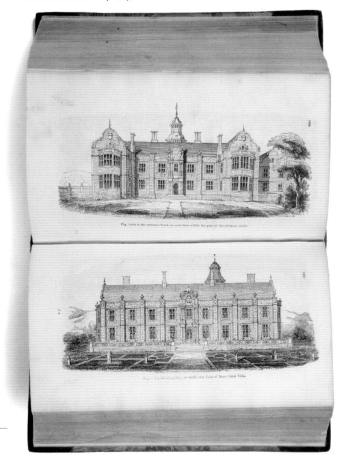

Readers of Loudon today, absorbing his flowing prose about piggeries and privies, along with Helen Allingham's picturesque watercolours, might easily forget the squalor of much nineteenth-century rural life. At the time, many shared Loudon's aspiration, expounded in his encyclopaedia, to provide 'all that is essentially requisite for health, comfort and convenience, to even the most luxurious of mankind. In such dwellings, every labourer ought to live, and any nobleman might live'. Loudon was careful to include accommodation for the animal kingdom in his designs and commentary, and just about all his 'farmeries' included purpose-built provision for cows, pigs, horses – and, of course, various kinds of poultry.

Louden discusses poultry houses at length, and although Landmark's Fowl House, on the Leighton Hall Estate near Welshpool in Powys, may not appear in his encyclopaedia, its probable architect, W.H. Gee of Liverpool, would have imbibed the spirit of the pattern books, like countless other provincial architects of the day, and so too did their patrons.

John Naylor, who transformed Leighton into a model of Victorian agricultural efficiency, came, on his mother's side,

Leighton Hall model farm offered the latest in agricultural efficiency, including its own broad-gauge railway and circular piggeries.

from two families of Liverpool bankers, the Leylands and the Bullins. Of his father's family, originally Lancashire yeomen, his grandfather Thomas Naylor was Mayor of Liverpool in 1796, but it was a great-uncle, Thomas Leyland, who provided the vast fortune that enabled John and at least one of his brothers to become landed gentry on a grand scale.

Leighton was bought for John as a wedding present in 1845, but no record survives of the old house that stood there. John set about the construction of a new Leighton Hall in the Gothic Revival style almost immediately, and it was largely complete by 1851. The architect, W.H. Gee, is otherwise unknown apart from his rather undistinguished church in Liverpool, but his work, if rather heavy-handed, is certainly competent. The detail of the stonework, to select one aspect alone, shows considerable skill.

The Hall was only the beginning, however. Soon afterwards came the church, the village school and its hall, innumerable farmworkers' cottages and, of course, the whole immense layout of the model estate, with its own gasworks, railway siding, workshops and elaborate system for distributing manure, plus the acres of purely agricultural buildings of the Home Farm. The cruciform arrangement of the buildings meant a mechanized water-powered shaft drive was available to all the buildings, including a novel, circular piggery. So large was the site that the buildings were linked by their own broad-gauge railway.

Not all the buildings were entirely utilitarian, however. When he built the Fowl House in woodland elsewhere on the estate, John Naylor was happy to emphasize an ornamental aspect of farm husbandry. A building as grand as the Fowl House was clearly about more than simply having fresh eggs for breakfast. It is perhaps more accurate to think of it as an aviary, since the birds it housed would have been valued as much for their decorativeness as for their egg laying. And in setting up such a thing, Mr Naylor was as fashionable as he was in the improvements being carried out all over his model estate. No lesser person than Queen Victoria herself had initiated the vogue for ornamental poultry keeping, and she took a close personal interest in the poultry house or aviary she had built at Windsor in 1843. Victoria also sparked off what came to be called Cochin Mania for collecting different breeds of poultry (named after the Cochin birds from China, with their endearing

A design for a fowl house from Loudon's *Encyclopaedia*.

'baggy-trousered' feathered legs). As the mania took hold, poultry breeding became a pastime as suitable for women as men; for his part, John Naylor was entirely typical in giving over nominal supervision of the Fowl House to his daughters. By long and deeply ingrained tradition, poultry, whether practical or ornamental, were seen as very much a woman's interest.

The Poultry Yard and Fowl House were built in 1861, and are said to have been a birthday present for John Naylor's fourth daughter, Georgiana, born in 1854 and later an artist and sculptress. The everyday care of the birds (who needed attention and protection day and night) was under the supervision of a poultry-keeper, who lived in the cottage just beside the yard; this building, now called Poultry Cottage, is today's Landmark. It was originally a plain cottage dating from about 1800, but Naylor smartened it up in 1861 by adding bargeboards and stone windows, perhaps elements left over from building the hall.

Inside, the Fowl House was divided into compartments for the different breeds and types of birds. Several of the nesting boxes survive, showing that large birds such as turkeys and geese were kept there, as well as hens and ducks. Each was

segregated from the other, even when let out into the yard to scratch, or onto the pond to swim. A storm shed was provided for wet days, and the complex was surrounded by a fence.

The Naylor family continued to live on the Leighton Hall Estate until 1931, when it was sold in separate lots by John Naylor's grandson. The Fowl House was included with the plantations bought by Major Charles Ackers, who had a keen interest in forestry, for which the estate was already famous. Poultry Cottage was used to house one of the woodmen, but the Fowl House, inevitably, was left to decay. The woodland changed hands again in 1977, and in 1987 the whole Poultry Yard was put up for sale, and bought by Landmark. Although they were dilapidated and overgrown, both cottage and Fowl House were relatively straightforward to repair. The Fowl House was re-roofed using the original slates, and its ornamental timberwork was largely renewed. Complete with the stained glass installed for the pleasure of its former inhabitants, the Fowl House has reverted, for now at least, to being simply an object of ornamental pleasure, one of several such exquisite ancillary estate buildings in Landmark's portfolio. **CS**

Poultry Cottage was a simple eighteenth-century cottage, later dressed with barge boards and stone windows to look more picturesque.

Many of the nesting boxes and other internal fittings survive inside the Fowl House today.

The Prince of Wales, later Edward VII, acquired Sandringham in Norfolk as a private house when he came of age in 1862.

Built in 1877 as part of a new water system for Sandringham House in Norfolk, Appleton Water Tower was both functional and decorative.

APPLETON WATER TOWER

NORFOLK

1877

A SAFEGUARD AGAINST TYPHOID

The house at Sandringham was rebuilt for the Prince and Princess of Wales, who were famous hosts, in 1869–70.

At the end of October 1871, the Prince of Wales, Albert Edward, was travelling south from Balmoral to his house, Sandringham, in Norfolk. He broke the journey by spending a few days with his friend Lord Londesborough at his villa in Scarborough. A week later the prince arrived at Sandringham in time for his thirtieth birthday party. He felt unwell and within ten days he was diagnosed with typhoid fever – the illness that was believed to have killed his father, Prince Albert, exactly a decade before. One of the prince's grooms was also found to have the disease, and died shortly afterwards; and on 1 December another of the people who had been at Lord Londesborough's house, the Earl of Chesterfield, was pronounced dead. The water at Londesborough Lodge had carried the deadly bacteria.

For the following fortnight the prince's life hung in the balance. The Princess of Wales nursed her husband, helped by his sisters, while Queen Victoria came to Sandringham for the first time and kept an anxious vigil for eleven days. The condition of the patient and the events of ten years before made the outcome seem a foregone conclusion; as Lord Granville put it to the queen, 'There hardly seems to be hope left.' A week

A nineteenth-century watercolour of Appleton Water Tower.

The flue from the fireplaces at Appleton runs up through the centre of the water tank, an ingenious way of stopping the water from freezing in winter.

later, to widespread surprise, the prince started to recover, and by Christmas he was pronounced out of danger. The queen published a heartfelt letter to her subjects, thanking them for their 'touching sympathy', while the prince decided something had to be done something about the Sandringham water supply.

It was Prince Albert himself who had wanted his son to have a private and unofficial house of his own when he came of age in 1862, and had ensured that a large sum was made available from the Duchy of Cornwall for that purpose. After an extensive search, Sandringham in west Norfolk had been lighted upon. The nearby historic estate of Houghton, erstwhile home of Sir Robert Walpole, was considered, but in the event it was the 5,666-hectare/14,000-acre estate belonging to Charles Spencer Cowper that found favour. The scale, privacy and closeness to the sea for bathing, combined with accessibility (a station was under construction just 2.4 kilometres/1½ miles away), were all thought ideal, as was the good state of repair of the estate's many buildings. But most appealing to the prince was that it had 'wild fowl and every description of game and . . . shooting of every kind in abundance'. Just a few weeks before the prince's twenty-first birthday the estate was purchased for £220,000.

After a difficult childhood in which he had struggled to live up to his parents' high educational expectations, Albert Edward had found freedom and his own interests when he attended Oxford, the first heir to the throne to go to university since the Middle Ages. There he had made friends and discovered restaurants, theatres and field sports. In 1860 he made an official tour of Canada, travelling through New York as he did so, and made a real success of the trip through his sociable, convivial personal style. A year after the purchase of Sandringham his entry into adulthood was completed by his marriage, at the age of twenty-two, to the Danish Princess Alexandra.

After Prince Albert's death the grief-stricken queen was reluctant to give her son a formal role in royal affairs, and so much of the prince and princess's time and energy went into travelling and entertaining in a lifestyle of enforced leisure. Though it was judged 'of no architectural pretensions', the stuccoed 1770s house at Sandringham, with its twenty-nine bedrooms, was at first to be retained. But within a few years the couple had decided to rebuild, demolishing everything but the conservatory in polychromatic brickwork by the Victorian architect Samuel Teulon. The architect for the new house, A.J. Humbert, was given the task of composing something in a 'Norfolk style' that could incorporate Teulon's retained building. Drawing on Blickling Hall in the east of the county, Humbert created a large neo-Jacobean brick house with Dutch gables and bay windows with stone quoins. At Sandringham, and their

London home, Marlborough House, the prince and princess became famous hosts. But while the form of the new house was ideal for parties, the prince's terrifying brush with typhoid, and another experienced by the couple's eldest son three years later, prompted an urgent review of the quality of the estate's water.

The task of assessing the Sandringham water and advising on improvements was given to the country's most distinguished public sanitation engineers. Taking the lead was Robert Rawlinson, a man who made his name devising ingenious sanitation arrangements for the British army during the Crimean War. The detail of the new system, which was also to include new drains and sewage works, was put in the hands of James Mansergh, another internationally renowned water engineer who was then overseeing a colossal project to bring fresh water from Wales to the city of Birmingham via a 117.5-kilometre/73-mile long aqueduct. Having confirmed the poor quality of the existing water, Rawlinson surveyed the streams and springs of the estate and opened a number of exploratory bore holes. Sandwiched between the silty waters of

the Wash to the east and a series of large estates to the west, Sandringham is extremely low-lying. On the western edge, however, in the old parish of Appleton, the land climbs upwards towards Anmer and Flitcham. Here, in Den Beck Wood, about 1.6 kilometres/1 mile from the house, Rawlinson identified a chalk spring that suited his purposes: not only did it produce excellent fresh water, it also lay close to an elevated ridge that would help generate the pressure he sought.

The scheme that Rawlinson and Mansergh devised was to carry water from the Den Beck spring in large earthenware pipes across flattish ground to a new pumping station at Appleton Farm. Here the water would first be softened and purified and then pumped up a steep incline into the elevated tank of a new water tower to be built on the ridge above. From there the water would, through gravity, be carried under pressure down a series of pipes, 10 and 15 cm/4 and 6 inches in diameter, to Sandringham house, its stables and gardens and the houses of West Newton village. The height of the tower ensured not only that the pressure was sufficient for domestic

Being octagonal, the interior rooms of the tower afford views in every direction.

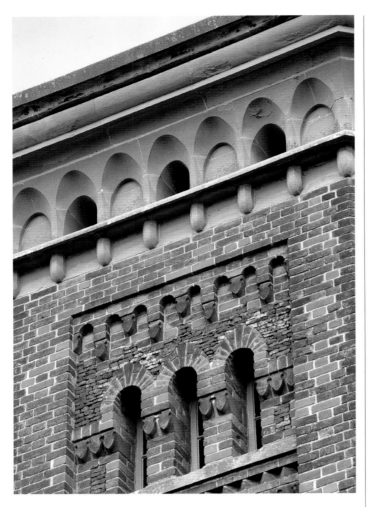

Appleton's decorative
brickwork belies the utilitarian
purpose of the water tower.

The stair turret attached to the tower gave
access to the upper storeys, bypassing the
lower two storeys where the keeper lived.

use, but also that a series of fire hydrants around the estate and village would be more than adequately supplied with water.

In East Anglia, the difficulties of providing running water in a flat landscape had long necessitated the pumping of water and the creation of raised tanks. A variety of creative approaches to incorporating the tanks into polite buildings had been found. One of the most elegant was not far distant from Sandringham, at Houghton, where, in the 1730s, Walpole had disguised his water tank as a Palladian garden building, used as the focus of one of his avenues. At Somerleyton Hall, a neo-Jacobean house of the 1840s near Great Yarmouth, an enormous domestic water tank had been incorporated into a 25.5-metre/84-foot Italianate tower. It was in this inventive spirit that a virtue was made of the need for a tall building on one of the highest parts of the Sandringham estate, and from the first a highly decorative structure was envisaged.

Rawlinson's original design provided for access onto the roof of the 18.25-metre/60-foot-high structure via an attached stair turret. This notion was further refined in the tower as built. The lower two floors contained lodgings for the keeper of the pumping station, while the stair turret gave exclusive access to a handsome prospect room in the middle of the tower and the roof, both of which commanded spectacular views.

In July 1877, the foundation stone of the new water tower was laid by Princess Alexandra, her brother Prince Waldermar of Denmark and her inseparable sons Prince Albert Victor and Prince George (later George V). The man who helped Rawlinson devise the building's exuberant design seems to have been Martin W. B. ffolkes, a member of the ffolkes family of Hillington Hall. A civil engineer by profession, he lived in London but worked in Norfolk, including for the Bond Cabbells of Cromer Hall. His design for the tower was dramatic, producing a

The tower's top storey comprises
the great steel tank. A gauge allowed
water levels to be read externally.

building that was both local and exotic in character. The tapering plinth of local carstone carried four storeys, three of carstone slips dressed with brick and the fourth the great steel tank itself, given architectural flourish with delicate iron cresting. The two-light arched windows, cornice and slender staircase tower are all Italianate in appearance but the materials are characteristic of houses all over this part of west Norfolk.

The practical results of the new water system were considered excellent: it provided 'pure and wholesome water free from contamination' and enough pressure to satisfy the Chief of the Metropolitan Fire Brigade who carried out a personal test. The system would provide the estate's water for a century, until, in 1973, it was finally rendered redundant. In April 1976, in John Smith's gentle euphemism, 'a public-spirited local landowner' leased Appleton Water Tower to the Landmark Trust. While the building was sound, the turret and tank both

needed new roofs, the decorative ironwork required repair and new doors and windows were necessary throughout. As there had never been any communication between the keeper's accommodation in the lower floors, accessed by an external door, and the prospect room and roof above, the building needed careful internal rearrangement. M. and S. Gooch architects of Norwich were employed to devise the scheme. Experienced in building new houses as well as undertaking conservation work, they were well placed to tackle the project. They created one dwelling with the insertion of an internal stair between the lower and upper sections, making an elegant bedroom cum sitting room in the first-floor prospect room.

The reordering of 1976–7 remains in place today, slightly refined by an additional refurbishment in the mid-1990s. The building had its first guests exactly a century after the foundation stone was laid. **AK**

GODDARDS
SURREY

1898

ARTS AND CRAFTS ALMSHOUSE

'Among the social changes in the London that I have known during my lifetime, none is more striking than the passing out of the picture of personal almsgiving,' wrote the social pioneer Beatrice Webb between the First and Second World Wars. The industrialization of Britain during the nineteenth century and the international empire that it helped create had brought about an explosion in wealth, making millionaires overnight. Population growth and urbanization brought their own problems, including destitution and discontent, and from these extremes of wealth and poverty was born the great age of philanthropy. Among the richest of the rich in the late Victorian age were the shipping magnates and the department store moguls, and it was the combination of fortunes from these two industries that brought into being a remarkable philanthropic endeavour: Lutyens' Arts and Crafts gem, Goddards.

In September 1898, Frederick Mirrielees and his wife Margaret were introduced to the young and irrepressible architect Edwin Lutyens by his friend and patroness, the 55-year-old Gertrude Jekyll. The Mirrieleeses had recently settled in the comfortable wooded landscape of Surrey after a restless early marriage. Frederick's father was the founder of Russia's largest department store, Mirrielees and Muir, where Countess Tolstoy bought her hats and after which Anton Chekov named his dogs. The store was at the forefront of contemporary technological and customer-service innovations: it was the first building in Moscow with lifts, and the first to offer a money-back policy to customers. Margaret was the daughter of the shipping magnate Donald Currie, whose Castle Line ran the main supply route from London to South Africa, and who was chairman of the London board of De Beers Mines. Despite their immense wealth, the couple, each the child of a hard-headed industrialist, lived comparatively modestly, and built a house for themselves near Abinger Common for which Jekyll was creating a rock garden. The idea Frederick discussed with Lutyens was for a small-scale charitable establishment, a building on a plot of land near their house that might serve as a place of rest and recuperation for those in need. It was unclear at this stage whether a commission would actually materialize, but Lutyens could see that the pair were valuable potential clients, writing to his wife, 'Mrs M. is a daughter of Sir. D. Currie and will eventually come into a £1,000,000 of money so they say, so it's, say I, worth business while to "cultivate."'

Mirrielees' scheme 'to build a little house or rather two cottages with a common room behind to lend poor people, sick children, etc.' was rather vague at first but quickly became more

Goddards was designed to face the west; visitors spent much time in the common room and formal garden, enjoying the afternoon light and warmth.

specific: a 'house of rest' for impoverished working women. Implicated in this change was the Mirrielees' daughter Margaret. It was her initials that would adorn the keystone above the entrance and, by 1904, Mirrielees had 'given' Goddards to her: 'It is hers and those who enjoy it are his little daughter's guests.' Margaret was looked after by a 28-year-old governess from Wolverhampton called Janet Smith, and it was perhaps concern for the difficulties of governesses, who were often unable to take holidays of any kind, that played a part in the focus for Goddards.

The nineteenth century had seen an increase in the numbers of working women, some doing so by choice but most out of necessity. With men travelling overseas to take up positions in the sprawling empire, the numbers of unmarried and unprovided-for women rapidly increased. By the mid-nineteenth century, there were some 25,000 governesses in England and Wales. A governess's life spent in an employer's house isolated from adult company – at home neither in the drawing room nor the servants' hall – was often an unhappy one. Charlotte Brontë's own experience as a governess, which inspired *Jane Eyre*,

had been miserable: 'A private governess,' she wrote, 'has no existence, is not considered as a living and rational being except as connected with the wearisome duties she has to fulfil.'

At Goddards, Lutyens created a comfortable house where a small community of single women could live for a week or two away from the cares and hardship of their professions. The house was run by a matron 'who undertakes the complete management so that the visitors need not "take thought" either for the day, or for the morrow and may enjoy in uninterrupted leisure their brief but welcome interval of quiet, comfort and repose'. The building was designed, as Mirrielees suggested, as two cottages linked by a large common room, forming an I-shape in plan, and was realized in the gentle, Surrey-inspired vernacular that Lutyens made so much his own. Rough-cast walls with brick-dressed casement windows and soaring brick chimneys all had a timeless rural character that also spoke of the almshouses to which it was related in function.

On the ground floor in the southern cottage were the kitchen, dining room and parlour; the common room made up the central range, and the northern cottage housed a studio

Goddards, with its almshouse-inspired design and garden laid out in collaboration with Gertrude Jekyll, provided a retreat for single working women in the early twentieth century.

and the building's most memorable feature – an indoor bowling alley, for which the 1890s saw a real vogue. On the first floor, a run of simple single bedrooms accommodated the guests. Visits to Goddards involved every pleasant diversion: 'They have a bright social life there, readings, games and music in the evening and . . . a lovely garden,' the last part of which Gertrude Jekyll almost certainly laid out.

The house was in full operation by 1900, and by the following spring, Edith Marriott, a 32-year-old unmarried woman from Seaford, East Sussex, was appointed as matron. Her charges were single women, predominantly nurses and governesses. On the night of 31 March 1901, she had four nurses staying, from London, Winchester and Staffordshire, each in her twenties. When Lutyens visited that August, there were three nurses and two governesses in residence, and 'we all played a game of skittles in my alley'. With a brief that requested none of the luxuries so often demanded by his Edwardian clients, Lutyens could give full expression to his taste for simple vernacular aesthetics inside and out. The plain oak floors, large brick fireplaces and occasional flourishes of craftsmanship were the antithesis of high Victorian fussiness. Without electric light and provided with simple country furniture, including 'old-fashioned ornaments contributed by country people out of their own houses', Goddards embodied the Arts and Crafts ideal of an honest, unpretentious home.

A decade after the completion of Goddards, family circumstances were changing. Margaret was now an adult and would soon marry Waldemar Craven, eldest son of Florence Lees, the founder of district nursing, and a godson of Florence Nightingale. So, in 1910, Lutyens was invited to return to remodel Goddards as a house that could be used by Margaret's brother, Donald, and his American wife, Mary Pangbourne – with the ladies accommodated elsewhere on the estate. Lutyens' solution was simple and elegant: a large room was added to the north and south, which extended each 'cottage' west. A library and drawing room were thereby created on the ground floors and a large bedroom on the floors above.

In January 1914, Frederick Mirrielees died in an unexplained shooting accident; after his wife's death, Goddards was left to Margaret, who sold it in 1927. In 1953, the house was bought by Bill and Noeline Hall, who, on the death of their son Lee, an architect, gave Goddards to the Lutyens Trust in his memory. The Landmark Trust was approached by the Lutyens Trust to assist with this remarkable house, by then listed Grade II*, and in 1996 Landmark took on a long lease.

Just as Lutyens was able to realize his vision of a sparse, vernacular way of life without the demands of a single

The life of a nineteenth-century governess was often one of isolation and hardship, in contrast to the company and repose offered at Goddards.

Despite his rather formal appearance, Edwin Lutyens was a man of humour and bonhomie. His love of the buildings and landscape of Surrey originated in his childhood.

Goddards was constructed
from materials reflecting the
simple rural vernacular
favoured by Lutyens.

Stained glass and Delft wall tiles
were among the few internal
decorative details.

permanent resident, so the Landmark Trust was for the same
reasons able, in 1996–7, to restore and furnish the building
largely to its form of 1910. Partitions added subsequent to this
date were removed to reinstate the original kitchen and parlour,
which had been moved in 1953, while repairs to the structure
were undertaken and the gardens restored, making Goddards
ready for its first Landmark Trust guests in 1997. A collection of
Lutyens' family paintings, including several portraits by Edwin's
father, now hang in the house, and the Lutyens Trust keeps the
library as its office. In taking on this extraordinary building, the
Landmark was, unusually, reviving something of the building's
original function, as the people who now stay for a few days at
a time enjoy the very simplicity, beauty and sense of escape
that were part of Lutyens and Mirrielees' original enterprise. **AK**

The southern side of Goddards was
given over to a long bowling alley,
where Lutyens recorded playing
skittles on a visit soon after the
house was complete.

The Common Room was the most
important room in the house, spacious
enough for visiting ladies to read,
paint and play music.

The interior of the Mackintosh house at Comrie contains a wealth of the architect's signature features, including dark panelled doors.

Mackintosh reached the height of his career at the turn of the twentieth century while still only in his thirties.

THE MACKINTOSH BUILDING
PERTHSHIRE

EXPRESSION OF THE GLASGOW SCHOOL

At about half past midnight on Friday, 29 May 1903, a resident of the Perthshire village of Comrie was returning home when he noticed smoke pouring from a window at the back of the town's largest shop. The premises was that of the draper and ironmonger Brough and Macpherson on the main street. He raised the alarm and John Maclaren and his fellow members of the Comrie fire brigade stumbled from their beds to douse the flames, while someone was sent by bicycle to Crieff. The shop itself was already beyond saving and efforts were concentrated on preventing the fire spreading. By the time the Crieff engine arrived at 2:30 AM, work was well advanced and the flames were finally extinguished as dawn broke. Though no one was hurt in the blaze, the stock was burnt or damaged beyond retrieval, and the building itself, 'a pretty old one', was gutted with nothing but the walls left standing. Luckily for all concerned, Brough and Macpherson was well insured, and so it was only four months before it was announced that it would be rebuilt. The architects chosen were Honeyman and Keppie of Glasgow, who had recently acquired a third partner, Charles Rennie Mackintosh, who, in 1903, was thirty-five.

A Glaswegian born and bred, one of a police clerk's eleven children, Mackintosh had risen, through hard work, originality and a genius for design, from modest working-class beginnings to become a designer of international reputation. Training on the job as an architect, and developing his strange, sophisticated design style at the Glasgow School of Art, which he would spectacularly rebuild, he was in demand. Three years before the Comrie fire he had married his friend and artistic collaborator, the watercolourist Margaret Macdonald, and with her help and inspiration was enjoying the most successful and creative decade of his career. In 1903, Mackintosh was, among much else, working as both architect and interior designer on the Willow Tea Rooms on Sauchiehall Street, for Glasgow businesswoman Kate Cranston. Mackintosh created an elegant and exotic house style for her tea rooms, an eclectic, art nouveau modernism that one observer called 'domestic novelties in buildings and decorations not otherwise easy to define'.

The client for the new premises at Comrie was the draper Peter MacPherson, a man of progressive political views and a respected local figure. In 1925, in a debate in the Comrie War Memorial Institute, he would be the proposer of the motion in favour of socialism, which the crowd voted overwhelmingly against. However, his politics were no barrier to his place in Comrie society, and he would be both chairman of the Comrie merchants' association and a magistrate.

The draper's shop in Comrie is
strikingly different from the brown
Victorian houses of the village,
drawing on Scottish vernacular
building style and materials.

Left: The simple but distinctive Mackintosh-designed fireplace in the first-floor flat of the Comrie building.

Above: In the 1890s, Mackintosh, a life-long sketcher, recorded traditional Scottish buildings, such as this one with its corner tower.

It seems likely that MacPherson's wider-than-usual horizons played their part in his decision to commission a distinguished Glasgow firm to rebuild his shop. By September 1903 MacPherson had purchased the site of the shop (which he had not until then owned), and the *Strathearn Herald* reported that 'plans are being prepared to have the shop and other parts rebuilt'. Surviving job books for Honeyman, Keppie and Mackintosh itemize the sums agreed with the various tradesmen, all from neighbouring villages. By the summer of 1904 the building was up and decorating was about to start.

While MacPherson was himself a draper, the town directory listed Brough and MacPherson as linen and wool drapers, tailors, boot and shoemakers, ironmongers and seed merchants. The new building was to occupy the same plot as the old, on the corner of Dunira Street, and a surviving lower range immediately to the west was incorporated into the plan.

The appearance of the building erected over the first six months of 1904 was both gently familiar and strikingly new. Comrie's prosperity in the closing decades of the nineteenth century had brought much rebuilding and the streets had become peppered with heavy Victorian villas, of sandstone ashlar with large, stone-framed windows. The building Mackintosh created for MacPherson rejected all of this. A corner building of two storeys with an attic, it drew on the traditional language of Scottish vernacular buildings: harled (rendered in lime and gravel) white walls, slate roofs and a broad corner turret. Blended into this was Mackintosh's distinctive styling: a steep-pitched roof of Ballachulish slate, high, tapering chimneys and tall windows with small panes. On the surviving adjacent building he added blind dormer windows to increase the appearance of verticality. His feel for traditional Scottish building forms and his ability to create something at once harmonious and exceptional are clear in every detail.

Mackintosh's design work extended beyond the shell of the building. Inside, in the ground-floor shop, he created a large U-shaped shop counter, shelves and other elements of joinery, all of which remain. In the two-bedroomed flat above, his

Hill House in Helensburgh, built by Mackintosh for the publisher Walter Blackie. John Smith helped to fund the repair of the whole of this building, where Landmark had an apartment from 1971 to 2014.

characteristic painted panelled doors survive, along with many other features. The sitting room, which extends into the turret, has a handsome decorative fireplace with classic Mackintosh detailing. Above, the attic storey contained small tailors' workrooms, accessed originally by a separate external stair.

Charles Rennie Mackintosh died of cancer of the tongue in 1928, his career never having regained the heady successes of the years before the First World War. While his work would soon be recognized as of immense importance in the history of twentieth-century architecture, the modest building at Comrie escaped attention entirely. Peter MacPherson lived until 1950, and in the late 1960s the flat was sold to Ray Smith, the retired owner of the local shoe shop, and its importance was little known until, in 1971, the building was listed Grade A.

In 1979, the Landmark Trust became involved with another Mackintosh building, the remarkable Hill House, built for the publisher Walter Blackie in Helensburgh in 1903. The building then belonged to the Royal Incorporation of Architects in Scotland (RIAS), which was struggling to cope with this large and complex building. John Smith wrote offering assistance, as a consequence of which the Manifold Trust made a substantial grant to the RIAS, and the Landmark Trust took a lease on the third-floor flat. It was hearing of this that prompted Ray Smith in Comrie to contact Smith in 1984 about the sale of his flat in the Mackintosh Building. Landmark acquired it in early 1985, and the following year the granddaughters of Peter Macpherson sold the ground-floor shop to Landmark, fulfilling John Smith's desire to bring the building back into single ownership again. The architects employed to prepare the flat for its new use were Stewart Tod & Partners of Edinburgh, who had also worked at Hill House. The fitting out was simply done; the linoleum in the kitchen, for instance, was brought from Saddell Lodge in Kintyre. Internally, the joinery was returned to its original dark-green finish, and the kitchen and rooms were furnished in sympathetic style.

The National Trust for Scotland became the owners of Hill House in 1982 and, with the future of that building consequently secured, the Landmark Trust lease came to an end by mutual agreement in 2014. At the Mackintosh Building in Comrie, the first-floor flat continues to be used by Landmark's visitors, and the charity acts as landlord for the shop on the ground floor, which remains, as it ever was, an emporium of goods. **AK**

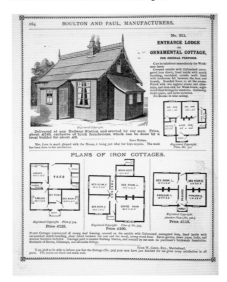 

CASTLE BUNGALOW
DEVON

C. 1920

PREFABRICATED HOUSING

'Cool in summer, Warm in winter. No possibility of damp. Can be inhabited the moment they are finished.' So claims an 1888 catalogue of a prefabricated bungalow. Far from being a modern idea, the principle of prefabrication goes back to the days when carpenters pre-erected timber-framed buildings in the woods and timber yards, numbering their parts for easy reassembly. Landmark has several true prefabs: one is Castle Bungalow in Peppercombe, a beautiful wooded valley leading down to the sea in North Devon, named after its river, the Pippa.

Castle Bungalow was made by an engineering firm, Boulton & Paul of Norwich. The company began in 1797 by making agricultural implements, but by the mid-nineteenth century it was also manufacturing all manner of 'portable structures' of timber and galvanized corrugated iron. By 1869, under the management of W.S. Boulton and John Dawson Paul (who had joined as an apprentice sixteen years earlier), the company was reborn as Boulton & Paul.

Their 1888 catalogue ('No. 43, revised edition, all previous catalogues withdrawn') included everything from cattle sheds, poultry houses and kennels to a school room, billiard room,

parochial hall, suburban residence, even a hospital, to be despatched not only across Britain but all over the British Empire. A five-roomed cottage could be bought for £180: 'Carriage paid to the nearest railway station. Erected by our men on purchaser's light brickwork foundation, he providing assistant labour.' Interiors were faced with lined matchboarding; outside woodwork had three coats of paint.

Castle Bungalow is not in this surviving catalogue, and began its life around 1900 as a boathouse at Portledge, in the next valley to the east. Today it stands in Peppercombe on the site of an earlier building, Peppercombe Castle, a large, castellated, seaside villa in a stunning position right above the beach. The Castle was built around 1810 by William Tardrew, a lime and coal merchant from Bideford. He had established his business on the beach below in 1807, when smallholders' cottages shared the valley with lime kilns and the huts used by stonebreakers who dragged pebbles up from the beach for road mending. By the end of the nineteenth century, the kilns had been pushed out of business by competitors at Bideford and Barnstaple.

Ownership of the valley and Peppercombe Castle had meanwhile passed to local gentry, the Pine-Coffins; their main seat was at Portledge, and the Castle became a secondary residence. Around the turn of the century, needing a boathouse for the lake at Portledge, they ordered one from Boulton & Paul, and no doubt it was delivered by railway from far-off Norwich.

The relocated Castle Bungalow stands
looking out to sea in a lovely valley
on the North Devon coast.

In 1909, the Castle suffered severe subsidence and developed dangerous cracks (the Pine-Coffins blamed the council, who had been quarrying for gravel below). With the removal of the roof, the building soon became derelict.

But the Pine-Coffins missed the view (and, it is said, the prawns) from Peppercombe and in 1926 they decided to move the boathouse there from Portledge, for use as a summer pavilion on the site of the former Castle. It cost £150 for estate workmen to move the bungalow, probably as much as it cost to buy in the first place. A horse dragged the cottage in sections along the coast on a specially made track to the old Castle site, where the boathouse was renamed, perhaps with irony, Castle Bungalow. Initially looking out over the ruins of formal gardens and tennis courts, it was used by the family for picnics, and for prawn-catching expeditions to the beach.

Castle Bungalow passed to Landmark, along with a smallholder's cottage in the valley, after the National Trust's acquisition of Peppercombe Valley in 1988. Holiday use would help to protect the magic of this secluded valley, and was the only option for this quirky and representative little building.

Sadly, Boulton & Paul went out of business around the time Landmark took on Castle Bungalow. They had been a force to be reckoned with, employing 3,000 workers in Norwich at their peak. They supplied huts for Scott's ill-fated Antarctic expedition in 1910, and, as the First World War broke out, were asked to add military aviation to their production line; they were soon producing twenty-eight Sopwith Camels a week. In the 1920s, the company produced the R101 airship for assembly in the mighty Cardington hangars in Bedfordshire, but the disaster of its maiden voyage in 1930 put an end to airship production (Boulton & Paul were formally cleared of any blame for the accident). When the Second World War came, Boulton & Paul took on the unglamorous job of supplying Nissan huts and other prefabs to the armed forces, making Norwich a target for German bombing raids.

Prefabs continued in demand after the war as they provided quick, inexpensive, functional housing to replace some of the many homes destroyed during the Blitz. The Housing (Temporary Accommodation) Act of 1944 led to a standard specification for development schemes led by local councils,

The former boathouse was dilapidated when Landmark took it on in 1989 after the National Trust acquired Peppercombe Valley.

Today, Castle Bungalow is once more neat and trim, with an added veranda from which to enjoy the sea views.

resulting in the construction of whole estates of prefabs. By 1948, almost 160,000 such homes had been built in Britain, many of them by Boulton & Paul. By the late 1960s, however, rising standards of living meant that people were no longer content to live in prefabricated housing, and, lacking orders, the company began its terminal decline.

Prefabs were designed with a lifespan of only five to ten years in mind, but many survived for much longer. Today, some are even listed, like those at the Excalibur Estate in Catford, south London, constructed by German and Italian prisoners of war. And many even earlier examples of prefabs, built for leisure, utilitarian and institutional uses, survive right across Britain. Castle Bungalow, quietly sitting out the wartime destruction in its Devon valley, is just one example.

When Landmark arrived, all the building needed was basic redecoration and repair The doors were stripped down and re-grained, as they always had been, in the universal Victorian and Edwardian fashion, and the cracks in the floorboards were caulked like the deck of a ship against drafts. To fit all the accommodation within the original walls again, a later lean-to with bathroom was taken down. The biggest job was to replace the leaking painted-iron roof. The original, ridged iron was no longer manufactured, so ordinary galvanized corrugated iron had to be used instead.

Landmark's project at Peppercombe was mirrored by a similar collaboration with the National Trust at Coombe, a nearby ancient hamlet just into Cornwall. Beginning in the 1970s, this, too, was primarily an exercise in landscape protection, but as part of protecting Coombe John Smith also acquired another prefab, this one lying between the hamlet and the sea. Coombe Corner, a large, sunny bungalow with wonderful views and generous rooms, is instantly redolent of the 1930s. It was typical of John Smith that he was always so affectionate towards such humble and potentially transient structures.

Prefabricated buildings were invaluable in a rugged island setting like Lundy, just visible on the horizon from Peppercombe. Bramble Cottage, Hanmers and the corrugated-iron Old School (also affectionately known as the Blue Bung) all provide snug, warm shelters from the island weather, and receive exactly the same maintenance as any other Landmark property, modest or grand.

As for the future, architects continue to return to the idea of the prefabricated housing unit as an energy- and cost-efficient solution to housing. In 2014, the acclaimed architect Richard Rogers crowned his retrospective at the Royal Academy with his latest design – a prefabricated house that was erected in just one day in the courtyard at Burlington House. **CS**

Prefabs on the Excalibur Estate in Catford in the 1960s, erected by prisoners of war after the war; several are now listed.

Architect Richard Rogers' design for a prefabricated house appeared in his 'Inside Out' retrospective at the Royal Academy in 2014.

The seventeenth-century houses in Cloth Fair, shown here in 1884, were survivors of the Great Fire of London.

In the early 1900s, many of the houses, like the Dick Whittington pub shown here, were demolished as unsound.

CLOTH FAIR
LONDON

C. 1950

CRUSADING FOR CONSERVATION

'Why cannot the City form a ... committee and grant it a roving commission to move whenever some ancient memorial is threatened, or action to preserve an interesting old building is needed? ... it would create public opinion and bestir the citizens in defence of the few architectural links that remain, to unite this prosaic and drab century with the more light hearted, if in many ways far less happy, times of the Tudor era.'

This indignant demand appeared in *The City Press* in 1914, protesting the proposed demolition of a portion of Cloth Fair, a lone survivor in the City of London of the Great Fire of 1666. Today, Nos. 41 and 43 of the street, owned by Landmark, present more of an eighteenth-century air, but the timber frames, hidden behind the later facades, date from around 1600. The row of houses stands almost in the shadow of St Bartholomew the Great, founded in 1123 as an Augustinian priory and London's oldest surviving church: it, too, withstood Fire and Blitz alike.

Even in the priory's heyday, this was an area of bustling commerce rather than cloistered seclusion. Nearby Smithfield was a noisy livestock and meat market from the twelfth century, and once a year the priory held a great cloth fair on its patron saint's day, 24 August. The present-day street of Cloth Fair stands on the site and is named after that historic annual event.

At the Dissolution, the priory, a highly desirable property, was bought by Sir Richard Rich, Chancellor of the Court of Augmentations and Thomas Cromwell's right-hand man. Rich moved into the prior's lodgings in 1540, but it was his grandson, Robert, the third Baron Rich, who began to build extensively on the priory grounds, throwing up speculative housing three and even four storeys high, on thirty-one-year leases.

Cloth Fair is included here, however, not for its Tudor origins, but as an emblem of the conservation battles of the twentieth century. Urban buildings, no less than the City itself, evolve to meet current purposes. In this case, Georgian re-facings and Victorian shopfronts came to mask the old jettied timber frames. The restoration of St Bartholomew's in the 1880s first focused attention on the area. The first Ancient Monuments Protection Act was passed in 1882, with the Ancient Monuments Consolidation and Amendment Act of 1913 recognizing for the first time that physical remains of the nation's history are so important that the state has a duty to ensure their continued survival. This Act is generally counted as the foundation of modern statutory protection, although it was many years before that was fully established.

By 1913, however, the crowded Elizabethan houses around Cloth Fair had become squalid, overcrowded tenements and

Only Nos. 39 to 43 Cloth Fair were
saved, bought and repaired in the
1930s and 1940s by architects
Paul Paget and John Seely.

were understandably vulnerable to the strictures of a more sanitary age. Cloth Fair, with its acquired eighteenth-century proportions, stood its ground rather better than the ramshackle alleys behind it, which the Sanitary Committee for the City Corporation condemned for demolition in 1914. Even the proposal to clear the hinterland area was not without controversy (the movement to conserve was gathering pace), but there was nothing in place to enable present need to coexist sympathetically with the resonance of the past, and the timber-framed tenements behind Cloth Fair were felled.

Cloth Fair itself might have gone the same way had not salvation arrived in February 1930 for Nos. 41 and 42, 'the last Jacobean houses in London', in the shape of architects Paul Paget and John Seely. The houses had been scheduled as dangerous structures but Messrs. Paget and Seely had the vision, and the professional skills, to see how they could be saved. The acquisition of others in the row followed.

In 1954, Paget came into contact with one of England's most effective architectural conservation campaigners, the poet John Betjeman, through 'a battle about a television mast in the Isle of Wight'. 'Of course I have to live here,' said Betjeman, and he took a lease on the upper floors of No. 43, which he used for the next twenty years as a convenient London bolthole from which to conduct his affairs and campaigns. Betjeman was 'a poetic visionary who spoke for England', a passionate yet accessible spokesman for architecture's soul as well as its aesthetic qualities. In 1958, Betjeman was a founding member of the Victorian Society, which today continues to champion what was then unfashionable and disregarded.

Like John Smith, John Betjeman represents a distinctively English aspect of the country's tradition of building conservation: the impact of passionately committed private individuals, often championing building preservation in direct opposition to state-sponsored development. The Society for the Protection for Ancient Buildings was founded by William Morris in 1877, several years before the first Ancient Monument Act was passed. The National Trust was founded as an independent charity in 1895 by Octavia Hill, Sir Robert Hunter and Hardwicke Rawnsley, all private individuals concerned both at creeping urbanization in the natural landscape and the

Despite protests, the Euston Arch was demolished in 1961; it was one of the most bruising defeats for building conservationists of the time.

A protracted conservation campaign has so far preserved London's Smithfield Market, designed by Sir Horace Jones in the 1860s.

destruction of historic buildings. John Betjeman gave a voice and a genial face to this gathering crusade for building conservation in the mid-twentieth century.

Through his poetry (he was appointed Poet Laureate in 1972), and eventually his radio and television programmes, Betjeman became 'the minstrel of middle class suburbia', chronicling with acute but affectionate insight his own time: the 'Metro-land' of the commuter belt, and life in the suburbs as the creep of ribbon development reached deep into the Home Counties. One poem, 'Middlesex' (1954), begins: 'Gaily into Ruislip Gardens/Runs the red electric train,/With a thousand Ta's and Pardon's/Daintily alights Elaine;/Hurries down the concrete station/With a frown of concentration,/Out into the outskirt's edges/Where a few surviving hedges/Keep alive our lost Elysium – rural Middlesex again.'

It was from Cloth Fair that Betjeman campaigned to save Euston Arch, an 1837 masterpiece of the Greek Revival designed by Philip Hardwick. It was demolished in 1961, one of the most bruising deliberate architectural losses London has suffered. Betjeman was more successful in lobbying for the late Gothic Revival glory of St Pancras Station, now triumphantly restored and redeveloped as the Eurostar Terminal, where he may be seen, captured posthumously in bronze as Everyman in a crumpled raincoat, gazing up in wonder at the mighty span of William Barlow's train shed roof.

Without people like John Betjeman, Paul Paget, John Smith and many other advocates, Londoners would live today under very different skylines. London in the twenty-first century is a vibrant city that celebrates both its past and its future, private initiative tested and refined by a framework of robust statutory protection. The debates, for example over the future of the great Victorian covered market at Smithfield, are as fierce as ever.

Landmark's involvement with the Cloth Fair houses began in 1970; it even briefly occupied the offices at No. 43. Seely and Paget moved out in 1976, tenants came and went, and Landmark took its chances to refurbish and restore the flats and offices when it could. In 1981, a flat at No. 45a became a Landmark, and this was followed in 1986 by John Betjeman's former apartment at No.43. The building was cleverly strengthened and extended to create a wine bar on the ground floor and three flats above – a demonstration of John Smith's acumen as a developer as well as a conservationist.

Betjeman's flat was redecorated, but still looks much as it did when he lived there. The wallpaper in the sitting room was, appropriately enough, a William Morris design called 'Acorn'. The colourway was no longer in production but happily, Sandersons agreed to reprint it specially. **CS**

A statue of poet John Betjeman at St Pancras International railway station commemorates his role in saving the station and his love of railways.

No. 43 Cloth Fair was furnished much as it was during Betjeman's long residency, complete with William Morris 'Acorn' wallpaper.

The roof appears to float above the
Anderton House, while the use of glass
merges inside and outside spaces.

ANDERTON HOUSE
DEVON

1972

DOMESTIC EXPRESSION OF MODERNISM

'In order to get on the road towards modernization, is it necessary to jettison the old cultural past?' (Paul Ricoeur, 1961). In 2000, Landmark took a bold decision for a historic buildings preservation charity: it acquired the Anderton House (formerly known as Riggside) in Goodleigh, near Barnstaple in Devon, its first house by a living architect. Its significance recognized by its Grade II* status, this modernist house, built in 1970–2, is one of the best-known designs of Peter Aldington and John Craig, who together formed a modernist architectural practice highly influential in British post-war domestic housing.

'Modern architecture' was an invention of the late nineteenth and twentieth centuries, conceived in reaction to the supposed chaos and eclecticism of the various revivals of historical forms during the nineteenth century. The task was to discover an architecture suitable for the needs and aspirations of modern industrial societies, a new set of symbolic forms that directly reflected contemporary realities rather than a derivative ragbag of historical styles. By the 1920s, an apparent consensus had been reached in the so-called International Style, but cracks began to appear almost immediately as practitioners realized

that the architect, no less than the artist, philosopher or scientist, is part of a specific tradition. There came a creeping realization that the modernist project called not for the rejection of history per se, but rather of its facile and superficial reuse.

Two giants of early to mid-twentieth-century architecture made this revision of pure modernism explicit in the domestic as well as the public sphere: Frank Lloyd Wright and Charles-Édouard Jeanneret-Gris, known as Le Corbusier. The Anderton House has echoes of both.

American Frank Lloyd Wright's work emerged from the American Arts and Crafts tradition. His first trademark design was the so-called Prairie House, named after the horizontal line of the prairie in the Mid-west: low and spreading; overhanging eaves; rooms running into each other; terraces merging with gardens. Equally important was the house's relationship to its environment; for Wright, a building had as much right to its place as a tree, and should be as much a part of the site. Horizontality, open plans, functional bedrooms and emphasis on the natural qualities of materials typified Wright's buildings, and all these aspects are apparent in the Anderton House.

Wright also appreciated the potential of light in modern architecture, a potential that had gradually increased through the centuries as technology first perfected glass as a means to admit light, and then as a barrier to the elements. In *Modern Architecture* (1931), he stated: 'Glass has now a perfect visibility,

thin sheets of air crystallized to keep air currents outside or inside . . . Shadows were the "brush work" of the ancient architect. Let the Modern now work with light, light diffused, light reflected, light for its own sake, shadows gratuitous.' At the Anderton House, glass has allowed the quality of light in the living area to be the equivalent of that outside.

Le Corbusier, more than Wright, was closely integrated with the International Style movement in Europe, and worked more in the public sector. Appreciation of the underlying structures of nature and the beauty of simple geometrical forms lay at the heart of his work. And while town planning and the mass-production of housing were his major preoccupations, Le Corbusier was also interested in a new type of private house, white and cubist, with rooms flowing into each other. Like Wright, Le Corbusier came to recognize that even modernist design did not exist in a vacuum. 'The composition is structured by the landscape,' he wrote of a holiday house he designed outside Toulon, France, in 1931. In the late 1920s, Le Corbusier's domestic architecture developed a stronger, more self-conscious link with the natural environment as he lost faith in the

workings of machine-age civilization. He came to accept the vernacular as a valid mode of expression, and used rough-hewn materials (what he called 'expressive bricolage') in a willing revisiting of vernacular structural modes. Equally, Peter Aldington's work looked expressly to local forms, the Anderton House being inspired in part by ancient Devon longhouses.

In Britain, the post-war period was a time of reconstruction, much of it necessarily utilitarian in a period of recovery. In the late 1950s and 1960s, the agenda was set by the need for new towns, power stations, factories and hospitals. The qualities of small-scale human habitation were often disregarded, as tower blocks and brutalism became the order of the day. Concern grew that a sense of community and scale, felt in small rural towns and villages, was in danger of disappearing.

In contrast to their large public works, a few architects began to build houses for themselves or their friends that were at once self-effacing and more intimate. Such small houses offered the perfect opportunity for architectural experimentation and free planning in a number of idioms as architects sought to reinstate a more humane element. The detached house is thus a revealing

The design of the Anderton House adapts the form of ancient Devon longhouses, like Landmark's Sanders at Lettaford.

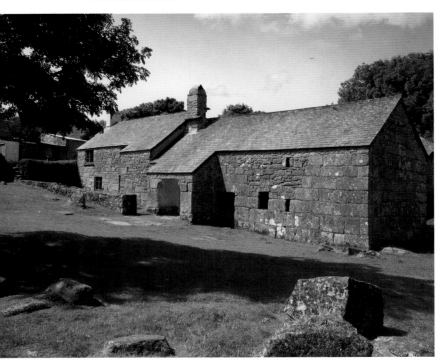

The horizontal lines and simple shapes of Le Corbusier's work (here Villa Savoye) find echoes in the Anderton House.

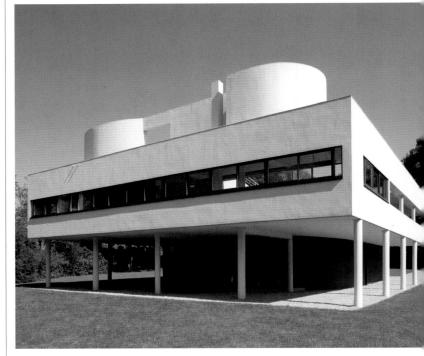

index of such post-war thinking about architecture. The Anderton House is also a thoughtful statement of English domestic architecture around 1970. With nods to both Frank Lloyd Wright and Le Corbusier in its willingness to blend the traditions of the local vernacular with the austerity of the modernist movement, it exemplifies Peter Aldington's approach of 'listening to the past to make a building of the present that would serve for the future'.

Aldington's commission came about in 1969, when his friends Ian and May Anderton asked him to design a small family home in Goodleigh for themselves and their daughter, Liz. Ian Anderton was a commercial pharmacist and wanted the new house to be suitable for his eventual retirement. Peter Aldington's partner, John Craig, first drew up a highly detailed brief with the clients. Their request was for a house that made the most of the views across the valley, that encouraged a main open-plan living area, and that had three private and acoustically insulated bedrooms. Finally, a study area was required for Ian Anderton, one that was not secluded from daily activity but rather right at the heart of it in the living area.

It was important that his inevitable clutter of papers and books could be concealed when preferred.

The almost barn-like form of the Anderton House represents one of the simplest structural forms of shelter. As Peter Aldington himself expressed it, 'By using a frame and a tent-like roof we were able to make a living room on a small footprint into an apparently endless space.' Explicit expression of structure gives the materials an aesthetic as well as a formal role: in the Anderton House, the texture of almost every brick and piece of timber is readily visible beneath a simple coat of paint or varnish.

Through the clever use of a narrow clerestory, which flows into the glazed gable ends, the simple, timber-framed roof appears to float above the walls, giving an effortless flow of space. The passage of light through glass is used to accentuate different zones and moods through the house. This is most clearly seen in the living space, where large sheets of toughened, laminated glass allow the long views to be appreciated both inside and out. This sense of involvement with the landscape is further heightened by the extension outside onto the terrace

Anderton House was 'perhaps the nearest we came to the integration of inside and outside spaces,' said Peter Aldington.

Anderton House is a remarkably
intact example, inside and out,
of carefully considered and
coherent 1970s architecture.

The bedrooms are functional spaces –
here also adapted as a study for Liz
Anderton, then a student.

The Anderton House needed urgent
refurbishment by the time Landmark
acquired it in 2000.

of the quarry tiles used for the floor of the living space, and by
the lack of a definable edge to the glass corner of the living
room. 'It was,' wrote Peter Aldington, 'perhaps the nearest we
came to an integration of inside and outside spaces.'

By contrast, darker, textured glass was used for the entrance
to the building on the north side and the bathroom windows, so
the visitor enters an almost burrow-like space before reaching
the bright openness of the open-plan living area. The Anderton
House is modern but far from minimalist, and at times is almost
playful, drawing warmth from varnished pine. An innovative
solution to the requirement for a central study area was found
in the high-sided box that dominates the open-plan living area,
dubbed the 'doghouse'.

The bedrooms are functional sleeping spaces, but here, too,
there is warmth and practicality, with roomy, built-in cupboards.
The Andertons were delighted with the end result, and it
remains instantly evocative of the early 1970s. Here is a
comfortable family home, almost like so many others built
across the countryside in the last decades, and yet lifted to
a different level of experience by an architect who is a master
of his chosen idiom.

The Andertons lived happily in the building for over
twenty-five years. After their deaths, the house came on the
market in 1998, a remarkably intact example of carefully
considered architecture from the early 1970s, for which it was
listed Grade II*. However, like the rest of Goodleigh, the house
had suffered flooding problems on its sloping site, its picture
windows twice bursting under the weight of water, and it did not
sell. Liz Anderton was keen that the architecture of her parents'
house should be preserved and offered Landmark a generous
reduction in its price to achieve this. The house met all of
Landmark's usual criteria of merit, including genuine
vulnerability, and the trust was able to raise the balance needed
to acquire the building.

Taking on the Anderton House was a gamble for Landmark
at the time, despite its significance. How would its supporters,
so passionate about the past, respond to such recent
architecture? There was no need for concern. The Anderton
House instantly became one of Landmark's most popular
buildings, proof of Landmark's continuing relevance as a
saviour of even the most recent of buildings. **CS**

Lady Jane Grey (1536–54) was one of Astley Castle's best-known owners.

Jane the Quene

Sunlight streams through ancient window frames across the open court at Astley, giving the sense of living within a ruin.

ASTLEY CASTLE
WARWICKSHIRE

2012

'A LANDMARK FOR THE TWENTY-FIRST CENTURY'

This last account is less about the past than about the present. When the Landmark Trust celebrated its fortieth birthday in 2005, it sought to set itself an appropriate challenge. Not all of its projects come to full fruition, and the failure of one was especially frustrating. This was Astley Castle, a moated, fortified manor dating back to the fourteenth century, located beside a beautiful collegiate church in the Warwickshire countryside. It was a site of deep historical resonance, occupied for longer than the seven-and-a-half centuries covered by this book.

The castle was crenellated and moated in 1266, and, in 1338, Sir Thomas Astley founded the adjacent parish church. By 1420, the manor had passed via marriage to the Grey family, through whom it earned association by ownership with three queens of England: Edward I's Elizabeth Woodville (her first marriage was to a Grey); her daughter, Elizabeth of York, queen to Henry VII; and the unfortunate Lady Jane Grey, queen for just nine days. Both Jane and later her father were beheaded for treason – her father, by now the Duke of Suffolk, was captured at Astley.

In 1600, the castle was bought by Sir Edward Chamberlain, whose family restored the church, and improved and extended

As at all Landmarks, visitors are inspired to leave their impressions of the building in its logbook.

Astley Castle was a shell in the landscape until Landmark found a way to save it in 2005.

the castle. In 1674, Astley Castle was bought by the Newdigates, who owned the neighbouring Arbury Estate, and the castle became a secondary dwelling, later inspiring writer George Eliot, born Mary Ann Evans, who grew up on the Arbury Estate.

In 1978, Astley Castle, by now a hotel, was gutted by fire and left a forlorn ruin, at the mercy of local vandals. Landmark spent several years on the project, but came to the reluctant conclusion that this ruin, still listed Grade II*, seemed intractable to conventional restoration. Its economics, too, were challenging even for Landmark's dogged fundraising model; the lease was reluctantly surrendered back to the Arbury Estate.

This rankled. Could Landmark not find a way to resurrect this once-fine building, now so remote from useful purpose, degraded to an object of dwindling archaeological interest in the landscape? In its fortieth year, Landmark initiated a more radical approach. Rather than trying to reconstruct the crumbling castle (by now far beyond 'restoration' through weather and pillaging), it invited twelve architectural practices to outline ideas for placing accommodation within this ancient shell. 'The Trust is not trying to build the "ideal" modern house,' the brief stated, 'rather it seeks to challenge contemporary architects to find a sympathetic and intelligent response to a beautiful but intractable structure, set in a fine historic landscape.'

Historic conservationists, no less than practitioners of any other discipline, are creatures of their time. Building conservation is a relatively new concept, fully expressed in Britain only from the late nineteenth century, when William Morris and John Ruskin established the first ground rules. But there is nothing absolute about building conservation: on individual projects the debate about the relative merits of conservation, preservation and restoration rages as fiercely as ever, and building conservation, no less than any other aspect of human behaviour, is subject to fashion.

There is also an inherent danger that Ruskinian respect for patina can encourage a timorous approach to building conservation. Statutory protection is certainly necessary, but it can inhibit innovation in reinvigorating and adapting historic buildings. If over-rigid, it can trap architects in constrained replication of earlier forms of treatment of historic buildings, and sap confidence to leave the stamp of their own time alongside those of their predecessors.

Twelve excellent competition entries were received for Astley Castle, ranging from mirrored pods on stilts to replica timber-framed cottages. But the winning entry, from a young practice, Stephen Witherford, Chris Watson and William Mann of Witherford Watson Mann Architects (WWM), immediately caught the imagination. Their scheme centred on the oldest, most significant part of the castle, integrating its historic walls into the new accommodation. Massive concrete beams provided an intelligent structural solution to the unstable historic walls, performing structurally as well as aesthetically, to tie the outer and spine walls together. The profile of the castle in the landscape was left largely unchanged, and the main living space was placed on the first floor in the old medieval hall area, maximizing views out to the surrounding landscape. Looking through ancient openings and huge glass windows, visitors were encouraged to read traces of the past eight centuries in the ruined courts, the church and the picturesque landscape.

In a sense, winning the competition was the easy bit. After this was announced in 2007, everyone on the team had to take a deep breath, knowing they now had to make it happen. It took all the tenacity and problem-solving capacity learned over nearly fifty years to bring the project to fruition. English Heritage were consulted at the earliest stage and proved supportive throughout. There was also the small matter of the £2.5 million required to carry out the project, a sum that could

not have been raised without support from the Heritage Lottery Fund (HLF), and similar demonstrations of faith from private donors – sums from the small to the enormous.

Before any work could begin, exhaustive archaeology was required, particularly challenging for this large and degraded site about which there was very little documentary evidence, in order to understand the significance of the various areas of the site. This, in turn, would inform the repair and conversion scheme. Refining their design, WWM always had to work within the heritage protection framework. Uniquely for a Landmark project, every step of the design development discussions was reflected by WWM's evolving model, an essential three-dimensional visualization of this complex project. The model was even submitted to detailed daylight-simulation modelling that tracked the passage of light through the proposed spaces at various times of the day and the year.

The work on site was approached in two broad phases. First came selective demolition, clearance of the debris and consolidation of the ruin through painstaking repointing, reconstruction and stabilization, just as the HLF application was

The large first-floor living room, looking out on the landscape and the open court, was once the medieval great hall.

Many volunteers participated in the project; some created this modern take on an ancient knot garden.

A modern staircase appears to float up to the main living area.

prepared and its outcome awaited. This, at least, was business as usual for Landmark. Once the appeal target had been met, the more adventurous phase began, as WWM's dramatic new spaces were created out of the massive concrete beams and meticulously specified new brickwork that meshed, tooth-like, with the jagged edges of consolidated masonry. Concern for the future environment required that the castle should be heated with renewable energy, working in tandem with a wood stove. Discussions were intense and often protracted throughout, as they usually are on Landmark's projects, and, also as usual, there were moments of despondency as well as exhilaration. Finally, months of attention to detail and rigour paid off. On a rainy day in July 2012, Astley Castle was officially opened, radically reborn and yet still a surprisingly familiar form in the landscape.

Astley Castle's new manifestation was immediately acclaimed, by both Landmarkers and the architectural press. '[A] brilliant restoration . . . which weaves walls of timber and

brick into the stone ruin to create a powerfully layered interior,' wrote the *Guardian*. In September 2013, Astley Castle was announced the overall winner of the Royal Institute of British Architects' Stirling Prize for Architecture, as the building that had made the biggest contribution to British architecture in the last year; it was the first time a conservation project had been awarded this ultimate architectural accolade. Here was incontrovertible proof that historic building conservation and modern architecture can have mutual, even complementary, relevance to the contemporary world.

In fact, WWM's work at Astley Castle falls squarely within William Morris's enduring strictures on adapting old buildings, set down so compellingly in his manifesto in 1877 for the founding of the Society for the Protection of Ancient Buildings. The manifesto argues above all for honesty of repair in historic buildings, not the fakery Morris saw around him. He wrote: 'In early times . . . forgery was impossible, because knowledge

failed the builders, or perhaps because instinct held them back. If repairs were needed, if ambition or piety pricked on to change, that change was of necessity wrought in the unmistakable fashion of the time . . . every change, whatever history it destroyed, left history in the gap, and was alive with the spirit of the deeds done 'midst its fashioning.'

Morris also argued for confidence to be placed in our own contemporary style in engaging with an old building: 'If it has become inconvenient for its present use . . . raise another building rather than alter or enlarge the old one.'

Perhaps the manner of Astley Castle's rescue will eventually come to seem another fashion, yet it stayed true to Morris's tenets, and makes the case convincingly that contemporary architectural design, informed by our own age and materials alongside the styles of past eras, has a compelling role to play in the palette of options available to those engaged in saving buildings. Morris's articulation of this cannot be bettered:

'Thus, and thus only, shall we escape the reproach of our learning being turned into a snare to us; thus, and thus only can we protect our ancient buildings, and hand them down instructive and venerable to those that come after us.'

This history of Britain told through fifty Landmarks opened with L.P. Hartley's observation that 'the past is a foreign country'. In many ways so it is, and yet the experience of staying in a Landmark confirms time and again the familiarity of our predecessors' habitations. We are not just children of our own age, we are also a part of the great continuum of time, even more responsible for shaping the future than for preserving the past. Better, of course, that a historic building should never fall into decay and disrepair. But if it should, then we may be grateful for the existence of an organization like the Landmark Trust, whose collective vision and refusal to give up over the past fifty years have saved so much that enriches Britain's landscape for the inspiration and pleasure of future generations. **CS**

FURTHER READING

PURTON GREEN

George and Sylvia Colman   'A Thirteenth Century Aisled House: Purton Green Farm, Stansfield, Suffolk',
    Proceedings of The Suffolk Institute of Archaeology, 1965, Vol. XXX, Part 2.

W. A. Copinger   *The Manors of Suffolk*, 1909.
W. G. Hoskins   *The Midland Peasant : The Economic & Social History of a Leicestershire Village*, 1957.
Sir Maurice Powicke   *The Thirteenth Century*, 1953.
J. L. Walker   'Purton Green, Stansfield, Some Later Observations On The Early Aisled Hall'
    Proceedings of The Suffolk Institute of Archaeology, Vol. XXXVIII, Part 2, 1994.

THE CASTLE

Calendar of Liberate Rolls, 1240–5, p. 170.
Calendar of State Papers Domestic, 1633–4, 30 July 1633.
Close Rolls of Henry III, IV, 1237–42, p. 451.
Howard Colvin, ed.   *History of the Kings Works*, 6 vols, II, 1964–82, pp. 732–3.
A. and M. Langham   *Lundy*, 1970.
Matthew Paris   *Chronica Majora*, 1242.
F. M. Powicke   *King Henry III and Lord Edward*, 2 vols, II, 1947, Appendix B.
Myrtle Ternstrom   *The Lords of Lundy*, 2010.

BATH TOWER

Jeffrey Gantz   *The Mabinogion*, 1976.
John Goodall   *English Castles 1066–1650*, 2011.
Sir Maurice Powicke   *The Thirteenth Century 1216–1307*, 1953.
Arnold Taylor   *The Welsh Castles of Edward I*, 1986.

WOODSFORD CASTLE

A. Emery   *Greater Medieval Houses of England & Wales*, Vol. 3, 2006.
William Langland   *The Vision of Piers Plowman*, c. 1370.
May McKisack   *The Fourteenth Century*, 1307–99, *Oxford History of England*, Vol 5, 1959.
Mark W. Ormrod   *Edward III*, 2012.

ROSSLYN CASTLE

Louis A. Barbe   *Margaret of Scotland and the Dauphin Louis: An historical study based mainly on original documents
    preserved in the Bibliothèque National*, 1917.
W. S. Douglas   *Cromwell's Scotch Campaigns 1650–1, 1898*
R. A. Hay   *Genealogie of the Sainteclaires of Rosslyn*, 1822.
Andrew Kerr   'Rosslyn Castle', *The Proceedings of the Society of Antiquaries of Scotland*, 1877.

ST WINIFRED'S WELL

Linda Clark, ed. — *Of Mice & Men: Image, Belief & Regulation in Late Medieval England*, 2005.
Eamon Duffy — *The Stripping of the Altars*, 2005.
Ellis Peters — *A Morbid Taste for Bones*, 1977.
Susan Powell, ed. — John Mirk's *Festial*, Vol. 1, 2009.
Keith Thomas — *Religion and the Decline of Magic*, 1985.

THE PRIEST'S HOUSE

Patrick Cowley — *The Church Houses: Their Religious and Social Significance*, 1970.
Eamon Duffy — *The Voices of Morebath*, 2001.
Ronald Hutton — *The Rise & Fall of Merry England*, 1994.
David Underdown — *Revel, Riot and Rebellion*, 1985.

KINGSWEAR CASTLE

Calendar of Patent Rolls, 1476–85, p. 251.
Letters and Papers of Henry VIII, III (2), p. 997.
B. H. St J. O'Neil — 'Dartmouth Castle and other defences of Dartmouth Haven', *Antiquaries Journal*, 1935.
Paul Pattison — *Dartmouth Castle*, English Heritage Guidebook, 2013.
P. Russell and G. Yorke — 'Kingswear and its neighbourhood', *Transactions of the Devonshire Associations*, LXXXV, 1953.
Andrew Saunders — *Fortress Britain: Artillery Fortifications in the British Isles and Ireland*, 1989.

SADDELL CASTLE

Calendar of State Papers relating to Ireland, 1509–1573, p. 149.
The Register of the Great Seal of Scotland, 1424–1513, p. 678.
William Camden — *Britain, or, a Chorographicall Description of the most flourishing Kingdomes, England, Scotland, and Ireland*, 1610.
David MacGibbon and Thomas Ross — *The Castellated and Domestic Architecture of Scotland*, 5 vols, III, 1887–92, pp. 197–200.
Andrew McKerral — *Kintyre in the Seventeenth Century*, 1948.
RCAHMS Argyll — *An Inventory of the Ancient Monuments: Kintyre*, I: no. 313, 1971.

CAWOOD CASTLE

Calendar of Patent Rolls, 1266–72, p. 632.
N. K. Blood and C. C. Taylor — 'Cawood: An Archepiscopal landscape', *Yorkshire Archaeological Journal*, 64, 1992, pp. 83–102.
George Cavendish — *The Life and Death of Cardinal Wolsey*, 1963.
Peter Gwyn — *The King's Cardinal: The Rise and Fall of Cardinal Wolsey*, 1990.
W. Wheater — *The History of Sherburn and Cawood* (2nd ed.), 1882.

LAUGHTON PLACE

The Letters and Papers of Henry VIII, IV, V, VI.
John Farrant, Maurice Howard, David Rudling, John Warren and Christopher Whittick — 'Laughton Place: a manorial and architectural history with an account of recent restoration and excavation', *Sussex Archaeological Collections*, 29, 1991, pp. 99–164.
Richard K. Morris — 'Architectural Terracotta Decorations in Tudor England', in Phillip Lindley and Thomas Frangenburg, eds., *Secular Sculpture* 1300–1550, 2000, pp. 179–208.
'John Pelham, d. 1429. of Pevensey and Laughton' — *The History of Parliament*, 1993.
Terence Paul Smith and Bruce Watson — 'Suffolk Place, Southwark, London: A Tudor palace and its terracotta architectural decoration', *Post-Medieval Archaeology*, 48/1, 2014, pp. 90–132.

WOODSPRING PRIORY

Margaret Aston — 'English Ruins & English History: the Dissolution & the Sense of the Past', *Journal of Warburg & Courtauld Institutes*, Vol. 36, 1973, pp. 213–55.
Christopher Crook and David Tomalin — *Woodspring Priory – History*, Landmark Trust, 2014.
G. R. Elton — *Reform and Reformation: England 1509–1558*, 1977.
H. F. M. Prescott — *The Man on a Donkey*, 1952.

DOLBELYDR

John Gwynfor Jones — *The Welsh Gentry 1536–1640*, 1998.
D. Huw Owen — *Settlement & Society*, 1989.
Henry Salusbury — *Grammatica Britannica*, facsimile reprint, 1969.
Glanmor Williams — *Recovery, Reorientation and Reformation: Wales c. 1415–1642*, 1987.

FRESTON TOWER

Nicholas R. Amor — *Late Medieval Ipswich: Trade and Industry*, 2011.
W. H. Richardson — *The Annals of Ipswich by Nathaniel Bacon*, 1884.
Mark Bailey — *Medieval Suffolk: An Economic and Social History 1200–1500*, 2007.
George Bishop and John Norton — *William Camden, Britain, or, a Chorographicall Description of the most flourishing Kingdomes, England, Scotland, and Ireland*, 1610.
Michael Reed, ed. — *The Ipswich Probate Inventories 1583–1631*, 22, 1981.
Tom Williamson — *England's Landscape: East Anglia*, 2009.

TIXALL GATEHOUSE

G. R. Elton — *England Under the Tudors*, 1961.
Antonia Fraser — *Mary Queen of Scots*, 1969.
L. S. Marcus, ed., et al — *Elizabeth I Collected Works*, 2000.
Charles Nicholl — *The Reckoning: the Murder of Christopher Marlowe*, 2002.
Alison Weir — *Elizabeth the Queen*, 1999.

CASTLE OF PARK

Ian B. Cowan, — *The Scottish Reformation*, 1982.
David Henry — 'Glenluce Abbey', *Archaeological and Historical Collections relating to Ayrshire and Galloway*, V, 1885.
David M. Robinson, ed. — *The Cisterian Abbeys of Britain*, 1998.
RCAHMS, Galloway — I: *Wigton*, 1912.

BEAMSLEY HOSPITAL

D. J. H. Clifford, ed. — *The Diaries of Lady Anne Clifford*, 1990.
Karen Hearn and Lynn Hulse, eds. — *Lady Anne Clifford: Culture, Patronage and Gender in 17th-century Britain*, 2009.
Nicholas Orme and Margaret Webster — *The English Hospital 1070–1570*, 1995.
George C. Williamson — *Lady Anne Clifford, Countess of Dorset, Pembroke and Montgomery 1590–1676*, 1922.

MANOR FARM

W. G. Hoskins — *Provincial England*, 1964.
Matthew Johnson — *Housing Culture: Traditional Architecture in an English Landscape*, 1993.
Vernacular Architecture Group — Ongoing contributions to the 'great rebuilding debate' in its journal, *Vernacular Architecture*.
Keith Wrightson — *English Society 1580–1680*, 1982.

OLD CAMPDEN HOUSE

Mrs. W. Hicks-Beach — *A Cotswold Family: Hicks & Hicks-Beach*, 1909.
Timothy Mowl — *Elizabethan & Jacobean Style*, 1993.
Stephen Porter — *Destruction in the English Civil War*, 1994.
Lawrence Stone — *The Crisis of the Aristocracy 1558–1641*, 1985 edition.

SWARKESTONE PAVILION

Malcolm Airs, ed. — *The Tudor & Jacobean Country House: A Building History*, 1995 ed.
Mark Girouard — *Robert Smythson & the Elizabethan Country House*, 1985.
Timothy Mowl — *Elizabethan & Jacobean Style*, 1993.
A. L. Rowse — *The Elizabethan Renaissance: The Cultural Achievement*, 1972.
John Summerson — *The Booke of Architecture of John Thorpe*, 1966.

COWSIDE

W. C. Braithwaite — *The Beginnings of Quakerism*, 1955.
Edmund Cooper — *The Quakers of Swaledale & Wensleydale*, 1979.
Ronald Hutton — *The Restoration: A Political & Religious History of England & Wales 1658–1667*, 1985.
J. L. Nicholls, — *Journal of George Fox*, 1952.
Harry Speight — *Upper Wharfedale*, 1900, reprinted 1988.

MAESYRONEN CHAPEL

D. B. Hague — 'Maesyronnen Independent Chapel', *Archaeologia Cambrensis*, 1956, pp. 144-7.
John Harvey — *The Art of Piety: the Visual Culture of Welsh Nonconformity*, 1995.
D. Huw Owen — *The Chapels of Wales*, 2012.

PRINCELET STREET

	The Survey of London.
Stephen Porter	The Great Fire of London, 1996.
John Summerson	Georgian London, 2003 ed.

THE GEORGIAN HOUSE

John M. Beattie	The English Court in the Reign of George I, 1967.
Ragnhild Hatton	George I: Elector and King, 1978.
Simon Thurley	Hampton Court Palace: A Social and Architectural History, 2004.

FOX HALL

Rosemary Baird	'Fox Hall, West Sussex', Country Life, 17 January 2002.
Rosemary Baird	Goodwood: Art and Architecture, Sport and Family, 2007.
Daniel Defoe	A Tour Thro' the Whole Island of Great Britain, 2nd ed., 1737.
The Earl of March	Records of the Old Charlton Hunt, 1910.
Anna Keay	The Last Royal Rebel: The Life and Death of James, Duke of Monmouth, 2016.

GOTHIC TEMPLE

Chris Brooks	The Gothic Revival, 1999.
George Clarke, et al	The Splendours of Stowe, 1973.
Michael Hall, ed.	Gothic Architecture & its Meanings 1550–1830, 2002.
Giles Worsley	Classical Architecture in Britain: The Heroic Age, 1995.

CULLODEN TOWER

Juliet Allan	'New Light on William Kent at Hampton Court Palace', Architectural History, 27.
Cedric Collyer	'Yorkshire and the "Forty-Five"', Yorkshire Archaeological Journal, 38, 1952, pp. 71–95.
Howard Colvin, ed.	'Design and Practice in British Architecture', Studies in Architectural History, 1984, pp. 50–58.
Peter Leach	'In the Gothick Vein: The Architecture of Daniel Garrett', Country Life, 12 September 1974, pp. 694–7.
Bruce Lenman	The Jacobite Risings in Britain 1689–1746, 1980.
Nicholas Pevsner	The Buildings of England. Yorkshire, The North Riding, 1966, p. 297.

AUCHINLECK HOUSE

James Boswell	The Journal of a Tour to the Hebrides, 1785.
Linda Collet	Britons: Forging the Union 1707–1837, 1992.
Adam Sisman	Boswell's Presumptuous Task: Writing the Life of Dr. Johnson, 2000.

THE RUIN

Malcolm Balen	A Very English Deceit, 2002.
John Carswell	The South Sea Bubble, 1993 ed.
Patrick Eyres	'Hackfall: A Sublime Landscape', New Arcadian Journal, 1985.

NORTH STREET, CROMFORD

Brian Cooper	Transformation of a Valley, 1991.
R. S. Fitton	The Arkwrights: Spinners of Fortune, 1989.
R. S. Fitton and R. P. Wadsworth	The Strutts & the Arkwrights 1758–1830, 1958.
Richard Guest	A Compendious History of the Cotton Manufacture, 1823.

THE PINEAPPLE

Lawrence James	The Rise and Fall of the British Empire, 1995.
Frances H. Kennedy, ed.	The American Revolution: A Historical Guidebook, 2014.
Simon Schama	Rough Crossings: Britain, the Slaves and the American Revolution, 2005.

LENGTHSMAN'S COTTAGE

Miles MacNair	The Man who Discovered George Stephenson, 2007.
Peter Mathias	The First Industrial Nation: An Economic History of Britain, 2001 ed.
E. Paget-Tomlinson	Illustrated History of Canal and River Navigations, 1993.

THE MARTELLO TOWER

| W. H. Clements | Towers of Strength: Martello Towers Worldwide, 1998. |
| Andrew Saunders | Fortress Britain: Artillery Fortification in the British Isles, 1989. |

SWISS COTTAGE, ENDSLEIGH

Andrew Ballantyne — *Architecture, Landscape and Liberty – Richard Payne Knight & the Picturesque*, 1997.
Humphry Repton — *The Landscape Gardening and Landscape Architecture of the Late Humphry Repton, Esq: Being His Entire Works On These Subjects*, 2010 ed.
R. Trethewey — *Mistress of the Arts*, 2002.
David Watkins — *The English Vision: The Picturesque in Architecture*, 1982.

DANESCOMBE MINE

D. B. Barton — *A History of Copper Mining in Cornwall*, 1961.
The National Trust — *Cotehele, Cornwall*, 1991.
John Stengelhofen — 'The Industrial Archaeology of Cornish Mining and Transport', in *Cornwall, The Buildings of England* by P. Beacham and N. Pevsner, 2004.
Mårten Triewald — *Short Description of the Atmospheric Engine, published at Stockholm, 1734*, 1928.

OLD LIGHT, LUNDY

J. R. Chanter, et al — *Lundy Island – A Monograph*, 1998.
A. Denton and Nicholas Leach — *Lighthouses of England and Wales: A Complete Guide*, 2007.
G. G. Harris — *Trinity House of Deptford 1515-1660*, 1969.
Myrtle Ternstrom — *Light Over Lundy: A History of the Old Light and Fog Signal Station*, 2007.

BECKFORD'S TOWER

William Beckford — *Vathek*, 2013 ed.
Lewis Saul Benjamin — *The Life and Letters of William Beckford of Fonthill*, 1910.
James Lees Milne — *William Beckford*, 1990 ed.

THE EGYPTIAN HOUSE

Chris Elliott — *Egypt in England*, 2012.
Lucy Inglis — *Georgian London*, 2009.
Paul Strathern — *Napoleon in Egypt*, 2008.
David Watkin — *Thomas Hope, Regency Designer*, 2008.

THE GRANGE

Paul Atterbury & Clive Wainwright — *Pugin: A Gothic Passion*, 1994.
Asa Briggs — *The Age of Improvement 1783-1867*, 1999 ed.
Rosemary Hill — *God's Architect: Pugin & the Building of Romantic Britain*, 2007.
E. Llwyellyn Woodward — *The Age of Reform 1815-1870*, 1990 ed.

ALTON STATION

Basil Jeuda — *The Churnet Valley Railway*, 1999.
James Mulvihill — 'Consuming Nature: Wordsworth and the Kendal and Windermere Railway Controversy', *Modern Language Quarterly*, 56, 3, 1995, pp. 305-26.
John Ruskin — 'The Extension of Railways 1876', *On the Old Road*, Volume 2, 1876.
Jack Simmons — *The Victorian Railway*, 1991.

FORT CLONQUE

Asa Briggs — *The Age of Improvement 1783-1867*, 2000 ed.
Timothy Crick — *Ramparts of Empire: The Fortifications of Sir William Jervois, Royal Engineer, 1821-1897*, 2012.
Raymond Jones — *The British Diplomatic Service, 1815-1914*, 1983.
E. L. Woodward — *The Age of Reform 1815-1870*, 1963.

CHURCH COTTAGE

G. Kitson Clarke — *The Making of Victorian England*, 1962.
J. L. Davies and D. P. Kirby — *Cardiganshire County History*, Vols. I and III, 1994 and 1998.
I. G. Jones — *Communities: Essays in the Social History of Victoria Wales*, 1987.

POULTRY COTTAGE & THE FOWL HOUSE

Helen Long — *Victorian Houses and Their Details: The Role of Publications in Their Building and Decoration*, 2002.
J. C. Loudon — *The Encyclopaedia of Cottage, Farm & Villa Architecture*, 1834.
J. L. Moubray — *Treatise on Domestic and Ornamental Poultry: A Practical Guide*, 1854.

APPLETON WATER TOWER

Nat Bocking
Sidney Lee
Helen Walch

A Guide to the Water Towers of East Anglia, undated.
King Edward VII: A Biography, 2 vols, 1925.
Sandringham: A Royal Estate for 150 Years, 2012.
Engineering, 31 January 1879, pp. 91–3.

GODDARDS

Kathryn Hughes
Lynn McDonald, ed.
Clare Percy and Jane Ridley, eds.
Andrew Porter
Donald Rayfield

'Goddards', *Country Life*, 30 January 1904.
The Victorian Governess, 1993.
Extending Nursing: Collected Works of Florence Nightingale, 2009 ed.
The Letters of Edwin Lutyens to his wife Lady Emily, 1985.
Victorian Shipping, Business and Imperial Policy: Donald Currie, the Castle Line and Southern Africa, 1986.
Anton Chekhov: A Life, 2000.

THE MACKINTOSH BUILDING

John Gifford
T. Howarth
James Macaulay
David Walker

The Buildings of Scotland: Perth and Kinross, 2007.
Charles Rennie Mackintosh and the Modern Movement, 1952.
Charles Rennie Mackintosh, 2010.
'Charles Rennie Mackintosh', *The Architectural Review*, 144, November 1968.

CASTLE BUNGALOW

Colin Davies
Nick Thomson

The Prefabricated Home, 2005.
Corrugated Iron Buildings: Churches, Houses, Sheds and Huts, 2011.

CLOTH FAIR

John Betjeman

E. A. Webb
A. N. Wilson

Architectural essays: *First & Last Loves*, 2008.
Poems: 'A Few Late Chrysanthemums', 1954; 'Summoned by Bells', 1960.
The Records of St. Bartholomew's Priory and of the Church Parish of St. Bartholomew the Great, 1921.
Betjeman, 2007.

ANDERTON HOUSE

Peter Aldington, et al
Jane Brown
Elain Harwood
Thomas A. Heinz

Post War Houses (Twentieth Century Architecture), 2006.
A Garden and Three Houses: The Story of Architect Peter Aldington's Garden and Three Village Houses, 2010.
England: A Guide to Post-War Listed Buildings, 2003.
Frank Lloyd Wright's Houses, 2002.

ASTLEY CASTLE

William Morris

The Manifesto of the SPAB (Society for the Protection of Ancient Buildings), 1877.

A *History Album* containing a detailed account of the building is to be found on the bookshelves of each Landmark Trust property.

ACKNOWLEDGEMENTS

The authors would like to thank all those who have contributed to the Trust's historical research in ways large and small over its 50 years. Particular acknowledgement is due to the late Charlotte Haslam and the late Clayre Percy, Charlotte Mitchell (née Lennox Boyd) and Julia Abel Smith, on whose *History Albums* for Landmark this book draws. Thanks are also due to Martin Drury and Malcolm Airs for commenting on the text and to Donald Amlot for assisting with research.

INDEX

PICTURE CREDITS

Principal Photographers

Paul Grundy, John Miller, Jill Tate

Photographers

David Kirkham, Ian Sumner, Keith Hunter, John Miller, Warwick Sweeney, Paul Barker, Kelvin Barber, Mike Foxley, Lee Pengelly, Andy Tucker, Pauline Salt, Guy Henstock, Clive Boursnell, Harry Horton, Brian and Nina Chapple, Martin Charles, Angus Bremner, Ruth Patrick, Ian Christie, Ned Taylor, Anna Clayton, Tim Key, Peter Jeffree and Tom Jackson.

Any other images not specifically credited below are © The Landmark Trust.
Every effort has been made to credit the copyright holders of the images used in this book. We apologise for any unintentional omissions or errors and will insert the appropriate acknowledgement in subsequent editions of the book.

9 tr Courtesy of The Canal and River Trust **11** Lady Smith **17 br** Lady Smith **28 br** Simon de Montfort and the Barons demanding reforms from Henry III, 1258, engraved by Thomas Bolton, coloured engraving., Gilbert, Sir John, 1817–97. / Private Collection / The Stapleton Collection / Bridgeman Images **29t** © The Print Collector / Alamy **32tl** The drawing of William de Marisco, © GL Archive / Alamy **32tr** © Lebrecht Music and Arts Photo Library / Alamy **35t** © Angelo Hornak / Alamy **35b** © Paul Glendell / Alamy **36tl** akg-images / Osprey Publishing / Adam Hook **36tr** © Stapleton Collection/Corbis **37** © David Wall / Alamy **38** Caernarfon Castle and Town, © The Photolibrary Wales / Alamy **40tl** akg-images / British Library **40tr** © FALKENSTEINFOTO / Alamy **42bl** © Corbis **46tl** © Corson Collection, Edinburgh University Library **46tr** © Max Milligan/JAI/Corbis **48bl** Rosslyn Castle, Midlothian, Williams, Hugh William, 1773–1829. / Private Collection / © Mallett Gallery, London, UK / Bridgeman Images **49b** © GL Archive / Alamy **50tl** Universal History Archive/UIG via Getty Images **54tl** De Agostini Picture Library via Getty Images **57t** © travelib prime / Alamy **58tl** © INTERFOTO / Alamy **58tr** Universal History Archive/UIG via Getty Images **60t** © The British Library Board, Cotton Augustus I.i.35,36,38,39 **62tl** © Hazel Cunningham / Alamy **62tr** © GL Archive / Alamy **64t** © Marc Tielemans / Alamy **66tl** J. Haines, Isaac Basire, The outside and inside views of the Gatehouse to the archiepiscopal palace at Cawood, n.d., etching The Gott Collection, Wakefield Council Permanent Art Collection. Courtesy of The Hepworth Wakefield **66tr** Sampson Strong, circa 1550–1611. [Public domain], via Wikimedia Commons **71t** Universal History Archive/UIG via Getty Images **76bl** © V&A Images / Alamy **78tl** The National Archives, ref.E344/22 f.2 **81t** Illustration, from a late 12th century psalter, of the murder of St Thomas-a-Becket on the 29th of December 1170. Photo by CM Dixon/Print Collector/Getty Images **81b** Portrait of Thomas Cromwell by Hans Holbein the Younger, © Corbis **88** © Colchester and Ipswich Museums **89** © Justin Minns Travel / Alamy **90bl** © Colchester and Ipswich Museums **92** By R. Plot [Public domain], via Wikimedia Commons **94bl** Hulton Archive/Getty Images **95b** SuperStock/Getty Images **98t** © RCAHMS **98b** akg-images **104** © Abbot Hall Art Gallery **106t** © Georgios Kollidas / Alamy **106b** © Paul Barker/Arcaid/Corbis **110t** Jan van de Velde, III. [Public domain], via Wikimedia Commons **112tl** akg-images / Erich Lessing **117t** © David Reed / Alamy **117b** © Heritage Image Partnership Ltd / Alamy **120** © National Trust Images **123b** RIBA Library Drawings & Archives Collections **127b** © The Art Archive / Alamy **128** © Beryl Peters Collection / Alamy **130** © paul weston / Alamy **136l** © Heritage Image Partnership Ltd / Alamy **139** By John Rocque, File:Roque 1746 London a1.jpg, etc. [Public domain], via Wikimedia Commons **141** Workshop of Sir Godfrey Kneller [Public domain], via Wikimedia Commons **142t** © Old Royal Naval College **142b** © Skyscan Photolibrary / Alamy **143** © Heritage Image Partnership Ltd / Alamy **144** © Sotheby's / akg-images **146br** Charles, 2nd Duke of Richmond, Lennox and Aubigny, c.1730, oil on canvas., Philips, Charles, 1708-47. / Society of Antiquaries of London, UK / Bridgeman Images **148** © SOTK2011 / Alamy **149** © Ronnie McMillan / Alamy **151t** © Chronicle / Alamy **151b** akg-images / Bildarchiv Monheim **152** © Dave Pattison / Alamy **154** © UK Government Art Collection **156** © GL Archive / Alamy **160tl** © Lebrecht Authors/Lebrecht Music & Arts/Corbis **160tr** © PAINTING / Alamy **167** © Victoria and Albert Museum, London **168tl** The South Sea Bubble, print made by Thomas Boys, 1825, English School,, 19th century. / Private Collection / Bridgeman Images **168bl** akg-images **169bl** Wedgwood Collection. Presented by the Art Fund with major support from the Heritage Lottery Fund, private donations and a public appeal. Image © WWRD **169br** © Ripon City Council **172** © Bildarchiv Monheim GmbH / Alamy **173bl** © Pictorial Press Ltd / Alamy **174tl** © PRISMA ARCHIVO / Alamy **174bl** © Hulton Archive/Getty Images **175bl** akg-images **175br** © Martyn Williams / Alamy **176tl** © North Wind Picture Archives / Alamy **176br** © National Galleries Of Scotland/Getty Images **178** © Niday Picture Library / Alamy **179** StacieStauffSmith Photos / Shutterstock.com **182tl** © Science Museum / Science & Society Picture Library -- All rights reserved. **182tr** Courtesy of the Institution of Civil Engineers **184** © ImagesEurope / Alamy **185tr** © paul weston / Alamy **187** © GL Archive / Alamy **188** © Peter Bowater / Alamy **190tr** Hulton Archive/Getty Images **194bl** © Heritage Image Partnership Ltd / Alamy **196tl** © World History Archive / Alamy **200** © Trinity House **202tl** The Print Collector/ Print Collector/Getty Images **203bl** Time Life Pictures/Mansell/The LIFE Picture Collection/Getty Images **206tl** © The National Trust Photolibrary / Alamy **206tr** © Pictorial Press Ltd / Alamy **207** © David Hunter / Alamy **209bl** The Scarlet Drawing Room 1844 © Bath in Time – Bath Central Library Collection **211bl** The Art Archive / Bibliothèque Municipale Valenciennes / Gianni Dagli Orti **212tl** akg-images **212bl** © Hulton-Deutsch/Hulton-Deutsch Collection/Corbis **216tr** © Chronicle / Alamy **218br** © Arcaid Images / Alamy **221tr** Courtesy of the William Salt Library, Stafford **222tl** © Classic Image / Alamy **222bl** Joseph Mallord William Turner, Rain, Steam, and Speed – The Great Western Railway © The National Gallery, London. Turner Bequest, 1856 **223bl** Courtesy of the North Staffordshire Railway Company **223br** Courtesy of the North Staffordshire Railway Company **226tr** The Art Archive / Culver Pictures **229tr** DeAgostini/Getty Images **229br** The Art Archive / DeA Picture Library **232tr** © Chronicle / Alamy **235tr** © Pictorial Press Ltd / Alamy **236tl** Courtesy National Museums Liverpool, Walker Art Gallery. **238tl** Courtesy of Hordern House Rare Books, Sydney **238b** Crown copyright: Royal Commission on the Ancient and Historical Monuments of Wales **239** © Old Paper Studios / Alamy **243tr** © Heritage Image Partnership Ltd / Alamy **243bl** © Mary Evans Picture Library / Alamy **248tr** Gertrude Jekyll, 1843–1932. The Queen of Spades, 1996, oil & tempera on panel., Broomfield, Frances, Contemporary Artist. / Private Collection / © Frances Broomfield / Portal Gallery, London / Bridgeman Images **251tr** The Governess, 1861, w/c with pen & ink over pencil on paper., Squire, Alice, 1840-1936. / © Geffrye Museum, London, UK / Bridgeman Images **251br** Portrait of Sir Edwin Lutyens, 1869–1944. as Master of the Art Workers Guild, 1933, Frampton, Meredith, 1894-1984. / © The Art Workers' Guild Trustees Limited, London, UK / Bridgeman Images **254tr** © GL Archive / Alamy **256tr** © The Hunterian, University of Glasgow 2015 **257** akg-images / Schütze / Rodemann **258** Boulton & Paul, manufacturers, Rose Lane Works, Norwich : [catalogue no. 43]. [Public Domain.] **261t** © Jeff Gilbert / Alamy **261b** © epa european pressphoto agency b.v. / Alamy **262tl** © Heritage Image Partnership Ltd / Alamy **262tr** © Heritage Image Partnership Ltd / Alamy **264bl** © Allan Cash Picture Library / Alamy **264br** © brentonwest / Alamy **265tr** Steve Heap / Shutterstock.com **266tl** © Arcaid Images / Alamy **266tr** © Arcaid 2015 **268bl** © Paul Glendell / Alamy **268br** akg-images / Schütze / Rodemann **272tl** © Cameni Images / Alamy